BINDING THEIR WOUNDS

America's Assault on Its Veterans

Robert J. Topmiller and T. Kerby Neill

With a foreword by George C. Herring

Paradigm Publishers
Boulder • London

Copyright © 2011 by Paradigm Publishers

Published in the United States by Paradigm Publishers, 2845 Wilderness Place, Boulder, Colorado 80301 USA.
Paradigm Publishers is the trade name of Birkenkamp & Company, LLC, Dean Birkenkamp, President and Publisher.

Library of Congress Cataloging-in-Publication Data

Topmiller, Robert J., 1948-2008
  Binding their wounds : America's assault on its veterans / Robert J. Topmiller and T. Kerby Neill ; with a foreword by George C. Herring.
       p. cm.
  Includes bibliographical references and index.
  ISBN 978-1-59451-571-2 (hardcover : alk. paper) — ISBN 978-1-59451-572-9 (pbk. : alk. paper)
  1. Veterans—Medical care—United States—History. 2. Disabled veterans—Medical care—United States—History. 3. United States. Dept. of Veterans Affairs—History. I. Neill, T. Kerby. II. Title.

  UB369.T67 2011
  362.1086'970973—dc22

                                                                      2011004298

Printed and bound in the United States of America on acid-free paper that meets the standards of the American National Standard for Permanence of Paper for Printed Library Materials.

Designed and Typeset by Straight Creek Bookmakers.

15 14 13 12 11   5 4 3 2 1

Contents

CONTENTS

Foreword

I FIRST MET BOB "DOC" TOPMILLER in August 1994. He had just arrived at the University of Kentucky for graduate school; I had just returned from a year as a visiting professor at West Point. He was part of a very talented group of new graduate students coming to UK from all over the country. I had seen his application materials when I was at West Point. I knew of his military service at the epic 1968 battle of Khe Sanh, where he was a medic and known as "Doc." I was also aware of the excellent work he had done as an M.A. student at Central Washington University. I was especially impressed with his thesis on the Buddhist movement in South Vietnam, a phenomenon that was both crucial to the history of the Vietnam War and also, surprisingly, understudied. I was very excited at the prospect of working with him on his doctoral studies.

My anticipation was more than rewarded. As a student, Bob proved to be hard working and dedicated, a person who set high standards for himself and those he worked with. He quickly became the leader of his cohort of students. In seminars, he was an excellent presenter, a tough questioner of other student presenters, and a searching critic, always bringing a skeptical eye to the books he read. He helped to make the seminars of those years some of the best I ever taught. He proceeded smoothly and expeditiously toward the doctoral degree. Outside the classroom, he was an active runner and was legendary for his aggressiveness on the basketball court. During one of his summers in the doctoral program, he studied the Vietnamese language at the University of Wisconsin, an event, I believe, that changed his life in important ways.

For the dissertation, Bob expanded his work on the Buddhist movement in South Vietnam. He focused on the Buddhist-led revolt in northern South Vietnam in early 1966 that nearly brought the South Vietnamese government to its knees and that—more than either of us had previously realized—*nearly* produced in Washington a fundamental reassessment of the U.S. role in South Vietnam. New documentation he unearthed from the Lyndon Baines Johnson Presidential Library in Austin, Texas, made it very clear to us that, in the wake of the Buddhist upheaval and the Saigon government's resort to force to suppress it, some top U.S. officials came to doubt both the morality and the viability of the U.S. commitment to South Vietnam. Bob's dissertation was published in 2002 by the University Press of Kentucky under the title *The Lotus Unleashed: The Buddhist Peace Movement in South Vietnam, 1964–1966.* He also published an important article, "Confrontation in Danang: III MAF and the Buddhist Struggle Movement in South Vietnam, 1966," detailing the crisis of early 1966 involving a conflict between the Buddhists and the South Vietnamese government and its U.S. backers in the volatile area around Da Nang.

Bob never attempted to compartmentalize his scholarship and his powerful emotions about the war. During his first trips back to Vietnam, he made contact with Buddhists. He studied their beliefs, and became more and more convinced that their movement had offered a peaceful alternative to the war that wracked Vietnam through the sixties and into the seventies. He saw Lyndon Johnson and especially his secretary of defense, Robert McNamara, as prolonging the bloodshed in Vietnam for such abstract reasons as their own and their nation's credibility. On such subjects, he could become passionate, indeed outraged. I can vividly recall during the defense of his dissertation a spirited argument in which Bob, although outnumbered, held his ground on questions of scholarly objectivity against moral engagement, specifically, in this case, his firmly held contention that had the Buddhists been heeded in 1966 Vietnam might have been spared nine more years of war.

Doc's deepening reengagement with Vietnam during and after he completed work on his dissertation eventually took its toll. His experience as a young medic at Khe Sanh, he later wrote in his compelling memoir *Red Clay on My Boots,* "sparked a lifetime of profound alienation from the society around me." He may have sought by going back to Vietnam to exorcise the demons that still haunted him. Following completion of his degree, he returned as often as he could, in all fourteen times. He revisited Khe Sanh. But over time, his trips encompassed a much broader effort to learn more about the country and its people and thereby, perhaps, come to terms with the war. He traveled all over Vietnam and also into Laos and Cambodia. He talked to people in many walks of life. He discussed with monks in various pagodas in Ho Chi Minh City not only the events of 1966 about which he had written but also their own beliefs and especially their commitment to peace. He discovered much common ground with Vietnamese war veterans, from both the Army of the Republic of (South) Vietnam and the Peoples Army of (North) Vietnam. He also talked to hill people in the Central Highlands of Vietnam and in Laos. He listened to victims of the My Lai massacre of 1968 tell their horrific story. He especially connected with those Vietnamese children who were victims of Agent Orange, and he established close ties with a treatment center, the School of the Beloved, near Hue. He was outraged by the Vietnamese government's oppression of Buddhists and minority groups. He recalled that, at the end of his military service, he had hated the Vietnamese. But as a result of his travels and his conversations he developed greater understanding, empathy, and compassion. He grew in his appreciation of Vietnamese sacrifices during thirty years of war. Indeed, he claimed to have found more in common with the people of Vietnam than with many Americans. But he did not find peace of mind. Rather, he compared himself to Kien, the protagonist of Bao Ninh's powerful novel *The Sorrow of War,* who wandered for years seeking to make sense of the war but found only "shattered lives, broken hearts, ruined minds, and wrecked families."

After the attacks of September 11, 2001, Bob became an even more passionate advocate of peace and nonviolence. As war with Iraq began to appear inevitable, he created at Eastern Kentucky University a lecture series dealing with issues of war and peace, inviting such luminaries as Daniel Ellsberg to participate. He gave talks himself, and he took part in antiwar rallies. In a nation traumatized by the 9/11 attack and cowed by a Bush administration that sought to exploit the national fear to its own ends, he stood forth as a voice of courage and sanity. The beginning of the U.S. war with Iraq in early 2003 angered him deeply.

Doc's efforts to come to terms with Vietnam represented a journey that never ended. In part because of his tortured mental state, he resigned his teaching position at Eastern Kentucky University. From the time he left the service, Bob, like many other veterans, encountered frustrations in dealing with government agencies responsible for veterans' affairs. He decided to write a book about what he saw as the failure of American society to respond compassionately and effectively to the needs of those people it had sent to war. In the fall of 2008, he was scheduled to teach a course on the Vietnam War at the University of Kentucky. He seemed genuinely excited about the undertaking. He moved into an office at the university and put together a syllabus. Shortly before the course was to begin, he departed his house with the manuscript of his book and an ample supply of beer. He would never return, and was found several days later in a motel in nearby Georgetown, Kentucky.

The book that follows, lovingly completed by Bob's friends and compatriots Kerby Neill and Peter Berres, represents his last testament. His hope, I am sure, is that through it readers might come to a fuller understanding of the travails that face veterans of all wars and the urgent need for society to respond generously and humanely to their needs.

George C. Herring,
Emeritus Professor of History, University of Kentucky
Author of
America's Longest War: The United States and Vietnam, 1950–1975
From Colony to Superpower: U.S. Foreign Relations Since 1776
Lexington, Kentucky
July 14, 2010

Preface and Acknowledgments

I KNEW ROBERT "DOC" TOPMILLER for only four years. We met over our shared opposition to the Iraq War. Bob was personable and candid and we became friends easily. A veteran deeply committed to peace, Bob started this book but couldn't finish it. Persons committed to peace, even those who despair, can inspire others to pick up the cause. Less than two weeks before his death, Bob and I enjoyed lunch on the sunny patio of Bob's favorite haunt, Billy's Barbecue. We talked about this book, but I had no inkling of his level of distress over it. This book is the work of Bob and those who picked up his cause.

After Bob's memorial service, friends and family gathered for a reception at Billy's Barbecue. I offered to guide Bob's fellow Khe Sanh vets, Mike Archer and Steve Orr, from the graveside service to Billy's. Bob was special to both men and I think my first fantasy about finishing Bob's work occurred on that ride. When I asked Bob's wife, Terri, if I could see what Bob had written, she shared the disc Bob had sent to Paradigm Publishers. It contained two chapters on atomic vets, one on posttraumatic stress disorder (PTSD), one on Gulf War Syndrome, and a few pages on Agent Orange. Bob also wrote a brief introduction (material from which is worked into Chapter 1) and a few marginal notes on the history of the VA. Finishing Bob's work involved more than I anticipated but his family and friends stood ready to offer more help than I imagined.

Terri Topmiller was encouraging and provided an overview of Bob's career and family life. Bob's daughter, Jamie Topmiller Sadler, made available the moving tribute she wrote for his memorial service. Bob's older brother, Tom, supplied accounts of Bob growing up and found the tapes made by Doc at Khe Sanh.

Fellow Vietnam vets were extremely helpful. Peter Berres, who has taught university courses on Vietnam, completed the chapter on Agent Orange. Peter, an army Vietnam vet, joined Doc on some return visits to Vietnam, and visited the School of the Beloved in Vietnam with Doc and after Doc's death. Mike Archer, who wrote a compelling account of his Khe Sanh experience in *A Patch of Ground*, contributed powerful stories of Bob, offered unflagging support for this project, and reviewed each chapter meticulously—a clear expression of his affection for Doc. Rick Noyes, whom Bob treated twice at Khe Sanh, shared his memories. Journalist and vet Terry Anderson suggested I read Lewis Puller, Jr.'s *Fortunate Son* and read the chapters into which I incorporated Puller's experiences.

Dr. George Herring read everything and contributed historical corrections, references, and perspective to this work. He also wrote a fine Foreword. Both he and Dr. Eric Christianson shared rich observations of their student, and later friend and colleague, over drinks at Billy's. I received crucial help from members of the VA. Dr. Alan Fontana, a seminal researcher on veterans suffering from PTSD, offered excellent suggestions for the chapter on posttraumatic stress (though he expressed reservations about my objections to the term *posttraumatic stress disorder*). Dr. Cynthia Dunn, Bob's therapist at the VA, was gracious in discussing memories of Bob consistent with her duty to preserve confidentiality. Physician Nadia Rashid recounted her professional journey and the satisfactions she enjoyed working for the VA.

On a trip to Washington, I received guidance and resources from Joseph Wilson, deputy director for health care for the American Legion; Doug Vollmer of the Paralyzed Veterans of America (Doug also provided a copy of the *Life* exposé of the Bronx VA); and Margaret Adams of the National Archives.

Randy Mills, who chronicled the tragedy of Kenneth Kays, helped explore Kays's possible use of mental health treatment at the VA. Barbara and Jimmy Whitlock educated me on the mutual experience of a mother and son persevering with grace for over thirty years after Jimmy became a quadriplegic. Keith Whittle and Bridget Smith of the Atomic Veterans History Project were generous in sharing material from stories they have collected from Atomic Veterans over a number of years.

I want to thank my wife, Mary Ellen, to whom I entrusted the most rudimentary versions of my writing and whose suggestions were invaluable. Three of our sons, Brendan, Sean, and J. Kerby, helped polish my writing. Finally, at Paradigm Publishers, Leslie Lomas launched this project and Jennifer Knerr suggested helpful updates and clarifications. One always sends material to editors with considerable trepidation. Jennifer and Leslie responded with wonderful encouragement. Laura Esterman was most helpful with the fine details involved with overseeing the book's production.

Chapter One

"Help Me, Doc"

Navy corpsmen are called "Doc" by the Marines they fight to save.... To be called "Doc" is one of the highest accolades in the Corps.
    From the eulogy for Bob Topmiller by Khe Sanh veteran Mike Archer

IN HIS JANUARY 2009 INAUGURAL ADDRESS, President Barack Obama paid tribute to American servicemen who "fought and died, in places like Concord and Gettysburg, Normandy and Khe Sanh." The mention of Khe Sanh among those mythic battles in American history both honored and redeemed the U.S. troops that fought in Vietnam, a war that remains a source of controversy. Estimates of American wounded at Khe Sanh range as high as 3,000, and the number of American deaths is estimated at over 350.[1] At the northern edge of South Vietnam, the base at Khe Sanh was designed to lure the North Vietnamese into concentrating their troops, making them vulnerable to artillery and air power. It was a risky strategy. French colonial forces established a large forward base in Vietnam in the 1950s at Dien Bien Phu. Vietminh forces overwhelmed it, forcing the French to withdraw from Vietnam. At Khe Sanh, defenders could only hunker down in trenches and bunkers, occasionally snipe at the enemy, and call on artillery and air strikes to protect them. "I felt like bait in a rat trap," said one marine.[2] Fear that the base might be overrun was not confined to the beleaguered troops. The fear was shared by an American public who followed daily reports of the siege, by the Joint Chiefs of Staff, and by President Lyndon Johnson, who agonized over a terrain map of Khe Sanh in the War Room of the White House.

During the siege, North Vietnamese troops tunneled toward the base perimeter, hoping to strike from positions too close for American forces to use artillery and air cover. The defenders were aware the North Vietnamese had overrun the nearby Army Special Forces base at Lang Vei. Sound sensors around Khe Sanh alerted the troops when North Vietnamese gathered for assaults near their perimeter. Ground attacks at Khe Sanh were sporadic, but the incoming bombardment was unrelenting. Leaving one's bunker to traverse the base was a form of roulette; staying in one's bunker was no guarantee against a direct hit.

Bob Topmiller was a nineteen-year-old navy medic at Khe Sanh. "Help me, Doc!" were words he heard far too often during the siege. In caring for horribly wounded comrades while under fire, Bob forged an enduring commitment to his fellow soldiers. Sustaining that commitment forty years later, Bob was writing this book when he died. It is a book by a wounded veteran that is written for wounded veterans and those who care about them. It is critical of the recognition and care we offer our veterans and particularly critical of the Department of Veterans Affairs (VA). Bob's story gives this book its fire and legitimacy. Therefore, we begin with his story.

Doc at Khe Sanh

At Khe Sanh, Bob responded to the call of "Help me, Doc!" in "protected" bunkers and in open fields of fire. For many men he provided life-saving aid and patched them for further care; others were beyond help. In his fifties Bob wrote *Red Clay on My Boots,* offering his account of the siege and the memories that still haunted him. During the preparation of this chapter, Bob's brother Tom discovered three audio tapes that Bob sent to his father from Vietnam.[3] It was startling to hear Doc at only nineteen when he was so responsible for tending desperate comrades. On a tape made four days after his arrival at Khe Sanh, Bob reassured his dad, "I'm better off here than probably anyplace else in Vietnam; it's a real nice place, surrounded by mountains with extraordinary scenery." Bob continued, asking for canned peanuts, instant coffee, a subscription to *Sports Illustrated*, and his dad's help with his unfinished 1967 tax return. He reports treating his first marine, Rick Noyes, surprisingly an acquaintance of Doc's from Cincinnati. Rick, the source of the earlier "rat trap" observation, suffered shrapnel wounds during a probe outside the base perimeter. On tape, Bob also spoke with pride of his impending promotion to hospitalman third class. Later, in *Red Clay on My Boots*, his evaluation of his skills was less sanguine: "To think that my brief training had prepared me for what followed represented an absurd proposition worthy of a sadist and not the men who would come to depend on me."[4]

Two hours into the barrage that began the siege of Khe Sanh in earnest, Bob was working in the regimental aid station when a North Vietnamese rocket scored a direct hit on a nearby ammunition dump. Massive explosions tore into exposed troops and collapsed the roof of the aid station. Bob and his fellow medical staff frantically pulled wounded men, many with IVs running, across open ground to an alternate bunker. He then turned to the newly wounded. Mike Archer, a fellow Khe Sanh vet, chronicled the scene in *A Patch of Ground*: "The exploding ammo dump had sent a white phosphorous round into a group of marine artillerymen. One marine struck by the searing phosphorous was in excruciating pain. Doc [Topmiller] went to his aid, despite the extreme danger, and saved his life."[5] Bob relived that first day the rest of his life, though there would be other chilling images to invade his dreams and make even the promised relief of sleep fraught with risks. The siege, the stream of dying and wounded, lasted seventy-seven days. Although Bob suffered minor wounds himself, his deepest wounds were seared into his psyche.

Some vets demean those traumatized in combat as vulnerable soldiers. Certainly some men are more vulnerable than others, but many battle-decorated veterans make it clear that everyone is vulnerable and "heroism" waxes and wanes.[6] In *Red Clay on My Boots*, Bob wrote,

"Sometimes at Khe Sanh, I performed my duties and took risks that today seem extraordinary. Yet, on other days, I experienced a paralyzing trepidation that rendered me unable to move. I cannot really explain the difference but I believe that every human has a limit and many understand when they begin to approach it. This came home to me with dramatic clarity over the next few weeks as the constant shelling exacted a horrible psychological toll on many Marines."[7]

It was beyond the middle of the siege when Bob made a second tape for his dad. His voice is subdued and sometimes masked by background noise. Still reassuring, he reports that he is in one of the safest bunkers on the base and rarely leaves it. He does report North Vietnamese success in shooting down some aircraft. He also relates an instance when North Vietnamese troops gathered for a ground assault, but the fog cleared, "and we caught 'em with their pants down." He tells his dad about treating Rick Noyes for a "second Purple Heart" when Rick's bunker took a direct hit. "Rick was lucky," Bob reports, "he just got a burn on his hand." Bob knew the U.S. press was covering the siege closely. He told his dad that he himself had seen the dramatic photos of Khe Sanh in *Life* magazine. "I don't recognize the place," he comforted his dad, "doesn't pay to go walking around.... Nothing to worry about."

In contrast to Bob's sanitized report, four men died when Noyes's bunker was hit. The concussion ruptured Rick's eardrum and peppered him with shrapnel. A large man in the bunker whom Rick knew from training, a former golden gloves boxer, "lost it." Three men had to hold him down so he could be sedated and evacuated. Although Bob patched Rick up and sent him back to duty, his wounds became so infected that he continually returned to the aid station. "Everything was filthy," Rick later related, "even the aid station was dug into the dirt." Finally, Rick spiked a high fever. He was in a delirium when Bob helped carry him to a helicopter for evacuation.[8]

Khe Sanh could be grim without enemy assaults. Rats were everywhere and undaunted by the siege. Rick Noyes remembered some fed-up marines pouring kerosene into their trench and setting it afire to fry the rats holed up at the bottom. A man slipped into the flaming trench and, before his comrades could jerk him out, he was red all over. Rick walked the man to the aid station. Probably in shock, the man told Rick he felt no pain. Rick left him with Doc and said he would be back to check on him. Bob took one look and told Rick the man wouldn't make it. Rick felt that medics and the chaplain had the worst jobs on the base. "We would take the wounded and dying to the aid station, then it was all up to the staff."[9] Khe Sanh rats scrambled starkly through Bob's nightmares.

Khe Sanh had an airstrip to receive supplies and evacuate wounded. As the siege progressed several large C-130 aircraft fell to enemy fire and the base became dependent on parachute drops and more maneuverable helicopters. The loss of the larger planes cast a pall of vulnerability over the base. The stress of the siege rarely wavered. Near the end of the siege, Doc rushed to a cluster of men blasted by incoming artillery. "The first man I encountered had both of his legs blown off.... Unfortunately, I looked about me and saw wounded men sprawled around and realized that I had to abandon the seriously wounded man to go to guys who had a better chance of surviving. The look on his face when he realized I intended to leave him has haunted me ever since."[10]

In April of 1968, army, marine, and South Vietnamese units with heavy air support began the relief of Khe Sanh. Had the "trap" for the North Vietnamese worked? North Vietnamese losses have been estimated as high as fifty times U.S. losses, yet a 1981 U.S. Army post-mortem provides a tempered assessment: "while generally on the *tactical defensive*, the North Vietnamese assumed the *tactical offensive* when it suited their purpose. The most striking examples were the siege at Khe Sanh and the Tet Offensive. Both the North Vietnamese and the Viet Cong suffered heavy losses in these offensives, but, while they may have been tactical failures, they were strategic successes since, by eroding our will, they were able to capture the political initiative."[11] This assessment, especially of the Tet Offensive (for which some think Khe Sanh provided a critical diversion), goes on to suggest, "With their disastrous tactical defeat North Vietnam struck what was to prove a fatal blow against our center of gravity—the alliance between the United States and South Vietnam."[12]

Doc Prior to Khe Sanh

Who was this youth dropped into the horrors of Khe Sanh? Born in Cincinnati in 1948, Bob was the third son of Norbert and Rita Meyer Topmiller. Richard was the oldest and Tom was two years older than Bob. Their parents divorced when Bob was six. Norbert moved fifteen miles away, but visited most Sundays, taking his sons on outings or joining camping trips planned by Bob's mother. The boys were close to their mother, Tom remembers. "She did a good job of letting us be boys." Maybe the divorce hit Richard hardest. He was in trouble as a teen and more serious trouble as an adult. Bob attended Catholic grade school. He must have enjoyed it. Tom recalls that Bob regularly beat him out the door in the morning, even when it exposed Bob to the bully next door. A reluctance to back down was a prominent trait in Bob as an adult. Tom finally "whaled on the neighbor boy" and put an end to the bullying.

When Bob was eleven, his mother was diagnosed with a brain tumor. She called the boys' father and told him she was dying. Norbert Topmiller came home, moved the family into a new house, remarried his wife, and cared for her until she died three years later. During these years Bob and Tom hurried home after school to relieve the woman hired to care for their mother during the week. The boys shared the duty until their dad came home. Although their father's commitment to their mother earned tremendous respect from Tom and Bob, Bob still experienced his father as emotionally distant. In response to Richard's delinquency as a teen, Norbert Topmiller became a stern disciplinarian and the younger boys chafed under the repercussions from their oldest brother's behavior. Bob was never permitted to get a driver's license and obtained one only after leaving the service.

Bob was intensely competitive. He attended Archbishop Moeller High School, an athletic powerhouse in the state of Ohio. There he set the school record for the hundred-yard dash and was proud that the record lasted several decades. Though Tom was bigger, Bob held his own with him on the basketball court. Basketball remained a passion of Bob's throughout his life. Even friends who knew Bob in his fifties cite basketball in describing him. Two friends used the same phrase—"He took no prisoners!" The week Doc arrived at Khe Sanh, he noticed a basketball hoop nailed to a post and organized a pick-up game among the corpsmen. The game provoked the ire of the base commander, who quickly set the men to filling sandbags to reinforce the base's defenses.[13]

Bob carried a strong sense of responsibility. He had ample experiences to bolster it—twelve years of Catholic schools, his father's example and strict discipline, and his own experience of caring for his mother. Shaped in his youth by the values of duty and the threat of communism, Bob was ready to enlist in the marines on graduation from high school. Still seventeen, he needed his father's permission to enlist. The specter of Vietnam and the horrified reactions of Bob's aunts gave his father pause. He finally agreed to support Bob's second choice—the navy. Bob felt the experience of helping his mother guided his decision to become a medic on joining the navy. Neither Bob nor his family knew that the navy supplied medics for the Marine Corps. By the time he completed boot camp, Hospital Corps School, and field medical training, Bob's attitude toward the war had soured; yet curiosity and a wish to "prove" himself drew him on.[14] After toughening up at the hands of marines in Okinawa, Bob flew to Vietnam, arriving in Da Nang on January 12, 1968. He flew on to Khe Sanh the same day, nine days before the beginning of the siege.

Doc in Vietnam After Khe Sanh

The youth that arrived at Khe Sanh may have been vulnerable from rough times in his early years, though it is more likely he was toughened by them. He was certainly tough and savvy after Khe Sanh. His friend Mike Archer relates a story from Bob's stay at Phu Bai, Vietnam, while they awaited return to the States. Also awaiting return was Corporal Evans, a respected young marine from Seattle. Evans was placed in charge of the Communications Company wire platoon after his predecessor was evacuated from Khe Sanh. Instead of promoting Evans to sergeant, the marines flew a man named George (described by Archer as a "pompous ass") into Phu Bai to take the job. Archer felt that Sergeant George tried to compensate for his lack of combat experience by persistently aggravating Evans. After a night of drinking and poker, when George lost heavily but refused to pay up, Evans had enough. He went to his hut, grabbed his rifle and marched to George's hut yelling, "I'm coming to kill you George. Get ready to meet your maker!"

Evans started shooting through the screen door; George dropped to the floor and rolled out the back unharmed. Most of the platoon ran outside, where Evans was standing with a hot M-16 in his hands. They were sure he was going to prison for life. Only Bob Topmiller had the presence of mind to do anything. Doc snatched the hot rifle, ran to his hut, and returned with his own. He shoved it into Evans's hands just before the gunnery sergeant arrived with George hovering behind him. George accused Evans of trying to kill him and the gunny pulled the rifle from Evans. He smelled the barrel and checked the magazine. It was still full of bullets. Evans remained silent. The rest of the platoon began chanting—"Evans was with us all night; he never shot at anyone, not that this lying George didn't deserve to be shot," and so on. The gunny didn't believe any of it. He mustered the platoon and checked their rifles to see if any had just been fired. Doc, not technically part of the company, wasn't included in the inspection. The gunny also grasped George's status with his comrades. The matter was dropped, and a few days later George was shipped back to Okinawa. Though he didn't recoup his gambling winnings, Evans was back in charge of the wire platoon, not destined for decades in a naval brig.[15]

As news of the incident spread, respect for Doc grew. Three weeks later Doc was ready to "rotate stateside." Many of his company gathered at the enlisted men's club. At a long table with Doc as guest of honor, his comrades hoisted unrelenting toasts of warm beer. Keeping pace, Doc was soon drunk, while thirty comrades sang *Anchors Away*—blasphemous stuff for marines. "La, la, la," they substituted for the mysterious lyrics beyond the chorus. Tears filled Doc's eyes.

Doc Returns to Civilian Life

Back stateside, Bob served at the Great Lakes Naval Hospital in Chicago. There he met Terri Nicks, a navy corps WAVE, working with military dependents at the hospital. Terri saw lots of shattered vets at the hospital, and she knew Bob had seen worse. They dated for three months before getting married and settling in Terri's home state of Idaho. Bob suffered from nightmares; vivid images of Khe Sanh invaded his sleep throughout their marriage. He found a job with King's, a regional department store chain, and, in spite of frequently disrupted sleep, he proved a strong employee. He advanced to store manager at twenty-four and stayed with King's for fifteen years, winning more responsible assignments about every two years. Over those years Doc and Terri had three sons and a daughter. Maybe because his father was so distant, Bob made a point of hugging the children and telling them he loved them. He teased them with outrageous stories and took the family camping and fishing. Bob was also demanding. His daughter, Jamie, remembers begging him to lower the basketball hoop when she was little and Bob was teaching her free throws. He countered, "What's the point of shooting on a short goal? Learn to do it the right way, the first time, and then you'll always be good at it."[16]

When King's assigned Bob to start a new store in Bountiful, Utah, their children did not feel welcome in their new subdivision and the combined stresses of store construction, hiring, training, and managing began to get to Bob. His nightmares increased and he grew irritable and sometimes withdrawn. "Symptoms of posttraumatic stress disorder," Terri recalls, "though we didn't know it at the time." Bob quit King's and opened his own clothing store in Jerome, Montana, but the farm economy was weak and in a year the store went belly up. Having lost just about everything, Bob returned to store management with a firm in Oregon. He was soon promoted to corporate headquarters in the state of Washington, but couldn't abide the office politics. His PTSD symptoms were asserting themselves again. Bob was seeing a psychiatrist and told Terri the doctor encouraged him to leave his job.

With several of the kids in high school, Bob surprised Terri by initiating a move to Ellensburg, Washington, where Central Washington University had attractive tuition for veterans. In the fall of 1991, at age forty-two, he was a college freshman. Terri remembers the Ellensburg years happily. Bob enjoyed his studies and saw a private therapist, Karen Kitterman, for his PTSD. Karen wisely developed a wives' group for the vets she was treating and Terri found support there. Karen facilitated Bob's getting VA disability benefits after years of tortured sleep and recurring bouts of irritability and depression. Bob graduated in four years with both bachelor's and master's degrees in history, writing his masters thesis on Vietnam. Bob's return to Vietnam became an obsession, first in his studies and later in his travels. Pursuing this focus, Bob was accepted into the doctoral program in history at the University of Kentucky. He hoped to study with Professor George Herring, who authored the Vietnam classic *America's Longest War.* In the introduction to the book's fourth edition, Herring wrote, "I think, U.S. involvement in Vietnam was a logical, if not inevitable, outgrowth of a policy—the policy of containment—that Americans in and out of government accepted without serious question for more than two decades.... I believe now, as I did [when preparing the first edition], that U.S. intervention in Vietnam was misguided."[17] Many Vietnam veterans carry a bitterness about their involvement in a "misguided," and ultimately tumultuously unpopular, war. As a historian, Bob later found ample bases to question U.S. decisions in Vietnam from policy to strategy and tactics—decisions that contributed to his trauma and the loss and maiming of so many comrades.

Dr. Herring not only mentored Bob in his study of history but pressed him to enlarge his research potential by learning Vietnamese. He found Bob a huge asset in class discussions. His breadth of experience and provocative questions were powerful additions to the graduate program. Bob developed strong friendships in the History Department. He became a teaching assistant for Eric Christianson, the director of graduate studies in the department and a straight shooter like Bob. They became fast friends and late-afternoon regulars for beer at Billy's

Barbecue, the restaurant across the street from Bob's home in Lexington. Bob was passionate about his studies and also stubborn and demanding of others. The university library was notorious for losing books, and staff would feel his wrath if they couldn't find what Bob needed.[18] The library was a great resource for the second author (Kerby Neill) in preparing this book; ironically, when he sought to withdraw *The Lotus Unleashed,* Bob's book based on his dissertation, it was missing. A friend of Bob's supplied it.

In *The Lotus Unleashed,* Bob traced the history of the Buddhist peace movement in South Vietnam between 1964 and 1966. In those years leaders of the Buddhist majority rose to protest the appalling destructiveness of the war and South Vietnam's succession of unrepresentative governments propped up by the United States. Buddhists marched in massive protests and some, doused in gasoline, set themselves ablaze. But the Buddhist movement suffered divisions over the role of Communist insurgents in South Vietnam. One Buddhist camp saw the insurgents as more nationalist than communist and open to negotiations; the other camp was less hopeful. Still, the Buddhist movement for a negotiated peace held powerful sway in the northern areas of South Vietnam around Hue. In 1966, the movement nearly split the South Vietnamese Army and created grave doubts among American policy makers about the prospects for military success in a climate of eroding South Vietnamese support. Significant South Vietnamese groups differed as to whether the war was more of an American or a South Vietnamese cause. Bob's dissertation continued to expose him to the sad underbelly of U.S. decision making in Vietnam—the political calculations and miscalculations, the manipulations, the strategic disputes between army and marine commanders. As he wrote at the end of *The Lotus Unleashed:*

> For the United States, the 1966 decision to stay the course put it on the road to a humiliating defeat in Vietnam. While the war represented a monumental social catastrophe for the Vietnamese, the United States also paid a heavy price with the emergence of severe political dissension and polarization at home, a general loss

of faith in government, the breakdown of the Cold War foreign policy consensus, a damaged economy, the extreme disillusionment of the soldiers who fought in the war, and close to 58,000 Americans killed.... In the end the United States negotiated an exit from Vietnam in 1973 under conditions that were remarkably similar to the Buddhist position in 1966.[19]

Bob could count himself among the disillusioned veterans. He told his fellow Khe Sanh vets at their 2008 reunion that he wrote *Red Clay on My Boots* to show young people the horrors of war after he realized many of his students were in support of the Iraq War.[20] Still, Bob had a strong allegiance to the U.S. military and was proud that his three sons all served in the armed forces. In her eulogy for her father, Jamie Topmiller Sadler declared, "we will forever be a military family."[21]

Bob plied his teaching skills in the History Department at Eastern Kentucky University (EKU), where his colleagues remember his dedication, sense of humor, and strong opinions. Most importantly, Bob earned the respect of his students. After hearing of Bob's death, one student wrote, "his impact on my life was lasting. If it weren't for Dr. Topmiller's believing in a tobacco farmer's son who only really cared about music and never seemed to fit in, then I don't know if I would have graduated from college."[22] In *Red Clay on My Boots*, Bob recounts how he helped organize a movement at EKU to halt the American plunge into Iraq. He saw Iraq, like Vietnam, as a war of choice not necessity. Bob was incensed that the war was championed by what he called "chicken hawk neo-cons," who had carefully avoided America's previous war of choice. Bob's protests offended a "patriotic" staff member. Probably unaware of Bob's background, she fired a missive from her computer declaring, "There's no place in this country for people like you." Bob knew what made him different. "I have pushed the intestines back inside a horribly wounded man, I have tried to ease the pain of men burned so badly that their skin peeled off like a pair of gloves, I have witnessed men become comatose from the constant deluge of shelling...."[23]

Returning to Vietnam

One symptom of PTSD is "persistent avoidance of stimuli associated with the trauma."[24] Bob possessed many other symptoms of PTSD, but rather than avoid Vietnam, he grew more intrigued with it. In 1996 he renewed his Vietnam odyssey as part of his doctoral research. Although he had reassured Terri that he would not visit Khe Sanh while in Vietnam, he did. In 2002 he wrote:

> I could not say for sure in 1996, or now really why I had such a strong attraction to the hideousness I recalled as Khe Sanh. Certainly I felt curiosity about the spot where so much killing and devastation had occurred, but on a deeper, more visceral level, the country had compellingly called me back to settle the unfinished business of war. Somehow, I sensed a deep internal desire to finally confront the fighting where it had occurred so that I might shake loose from the emotional straightjacket of the conflict.[25]

Rather than resolve issues Bob had about Vietnam, his trips opened a Pandora's box of emotions. He returned to Vietnam fourteen more times, exploring the impact of the war on civilians and soldiers on both sides of the conflict. He visited sites of unspeakable horror in Vietnam and Cambodia. He brought a chilling array of new issues into the tent of his frayed emotions and personal responsibilities. Already burdened with survivor's guilt when so many of his comrades did not make it out of Khe Sanh, Bob also wrestled with the devastation America had wrought in Vietnam—the massive loss of life on both sides, the grief of the South Vietnamese after the United States abandoned Saigon in 1975, the ecological and human devastation of the defoliant Agent Orange. Bob visited and supported a medical orphanage run by a Buddhist nun for children suffering from birth defects likely caused by Agent Orange. He dedicated *Red Clay on My Boots* "to the sick children of Vietnam." After his death a memorial was erected to Bob at the Buddhist medical orphanage.

Bob developed a great respect for America's Vietnamese adversaries, at least the regular officers and soldiers. He developed a matching disdain for the Communist government of Vietnam and its oppressive policies, especially toward their former South Vietnamese opposition and Buddhist religious groups. Bob was personally religious, though he left the Catholicism of his youth. He was active in the Presbyterian Church and saw to the religious education of his children. The importance of his personal religious life, his respect for the sacrifice and fervor of the Buddhist peace movement, and his typical rage at injustice may all have contributed to the personal risks Bob took in visiting (or trying to visit) known Buddhists dissidents in Vietnam. He wrote an article published in a Vietnamese journal in France that was highly critical of religious persecution by the Communists in Vietnam and he continued to return to Vietnam even after he knew Vietnamese security forces were aware of his writings.

Doc and the VA

Having rescued maimed and trembling comrades, "Doc" had deep concern for the medical care received by veterans. After receiving a 30 percent disability rating for his PTSD while in college, he became a VA patient himself. Bob was pleased with the services he received at the Seattle VA hospital and assumed he would receive similar care when he moved to Lexington. For years Bob took antidepressants and a narcotic to take the edge off his recurring nightmares. In his first visit to the Lexington VA, he spent seven hours getting his VA prescribed medications refilled. At one point, he asked a VA employee why he received fine assistance in Seattle and such poor service in Lexington. She replied that the Clinton administration had tightened access while pressing Congress to adopt national health care. Worse, in an office full of employees, a social worker interviewing Bob broadcast, "I was in Vietnam too. I should probably be able to get compensation for PTSD like you."[26] Clinton's health care reform campaign crashed early in his first term. In 1996 he signed legislation allowing veterans to receive less-fragmented care by increasing access to many VA medical services previously denied those veterans whose illness was not connected to their military service. The income range of veterans eligible for service was also increased.[27]

With the advent of President George W. Bush, Bob found more to enrage him than "wars of choice." In his draft introduction for this book, Bob wrote, "Almost immediately after Bush took control of the U.S. government, co-pays on my medications increased, staff reductions took place, and access to medical care became increasingly limited, particularly as the VA moved toward a more privatized system of outside contractors."[28] Higher-income veterans who did not have a service-connected disability (priority-8 veterans) were no longer allowed to enroll for services after January 17, 2003. This narrowing occurred even though a number of troops already signed up for the "War on Terror" had been promised "health care for life" by zealous recruiters.

Convinced that VA policies were overly politicized, ideological, and, at times, deceptive, Doc was ready to turn his sense of injustice, his sharp pen, and his considerable research skills on the VA. Clearly he saw the VA as a valuable resource. In the summer of 2008, when he attended the reunion of his fellow Khe Sanh vets, he urged several to seek help for their PTSD symptoms at the VA. In his preface to *Red Clay on My Boots*, Bob credited Terri, his therapist in Ellensburg, and his therapist at the Lexington VA as the "three women who kept me from going over the edge."[29] Though he had discontinued therapy, Bob maintained his relationship with Dr. Dunn, his VA therapist. He dropped in to chat and invited her to attend classes he taught. Still, Bob bristled at national or VA policies that negatively impacted veterans and their care. He had risked his life and suffered his wounds to help his comrades in arms. For Bob, too many such men and women came home unappreciated or worse—to care and justice deferred or denied.

In September of 2007, Bob secured a contract for this book on the VA. It was to be a critical book, but not spiteful. Doc wanted the VA to be the best it could be. If the past runs the danger of becoming prologue, maybe these stories could be lessons, lessons to encourage vets to stay the course in struggles with the VA, lessons to the VA to avoid past errors, lessons to all of us to advocate for the support our veterans. The stories that Bob wished to document in the chapters on atomic veterans, Gulf War Syndrome, and Agent Orange are about policies that have denied or weakened care for veterans. Bob also wrote a chapter on his personal nemesis—posttraumatic stress disorder. He knew more was asked of others in Vietnam—their lives, their limbs, their dearest hopes. That can make it harder for both victims and the public to give the toll of PTSD its due. Bob wrestled with his trauma and survivor's guilt for years. At times, he imposed its burden on his loved ones. Flying in the face of the tendency to avoid reminders of the trauma, he confronted it on repeated trips to Vietnam. His agony was compounded by awareness that so much intense suffering was the result of misguided political and military egos. He was distressed when similar folly led to the hell of another war in Iraq. For Bob, the hell of war was no abstraction!

This book was a struggle for Doc. As he worked on it he became irritable and more withdrawn from Terri. In the summer of 2008, he sent the better part of four and a half chapters (the half-chapter addressed Agent Orange) and a rough introduction to his editor. He also told Terri the book was stirring up too many emotions in him and he doubted his ability to finish it. He attended the reunion of Khe Sanh veterans in Reno, Nevada, from the end of July until the third of August. At the reunion, Doc made a recording that a fellow vet preserved on his website.[30] He speaks of his previous books and describes the reunion as helpful and healthy, relishing the opportunities to renew acquaintances, share, and joke with those who shared the siege experience. Bob closed by saying he was working on a new book about "how poorly the VA has responded to our wounded warriors." Shortly after his return, the second author joined Bob at Billy's Barbecue, for lunch. Bob talked about this book and how the VA needed to do more in addressing PTSD. His spirits seemed good, but few people could really read him like Terri. She was worried.

Two weeks later, Doc took his draft manuscript for this book with him when he left home. It was with him in the motel room where he was later found dead of a self-inflicted gunshot. No one who knew Bob doubted that his PTSD figured heavily in his death. Neither did they doubt that all his family and friends loved him dearly. If this book was a burden, it is also clear from all those who have come forward to help with its completion that Bob had access to great support for this project. Sadly, among the list of PTSD symptoms is a "feeling of detachment or estrangement from others."[31] As a recent writer has said:

> It's not easy to come home from war. Even if you're lucky enough to have survived mentally and physically, you still have to get used to the fact that most Americans can't relate to where you've been, what you think, what you've seen, how you feel, and what you've done.[32]

The high rate of suicide in veterans gives profound emphasis to such estrangement and the need to reach out and treat those who suffer from PTSD. For them, the transition from war to home never fully ends, the pain can recur, and the alienation can sometimes be extreme. Sadly, vets can even turn on themselves and slip beyond the reach of those who love them.

The VA's Story

*With malice toward none, with charity for all, with firmness in the right as God gives us to see the right, let us strive on to finish the work we are in, to bind up the nation's wounds, **to care for him who shall have borne the battle and for his widow, and his orphan,** to do all which may achieve and cherish a just and lasting peace among ourselves and with all nations.*
                            Abraham Lincoln's Second Inaugural Address

THOUGH THE BOLDFACED PART of Lincoln's exhortation became the motto of the Department of Veterans Affairs, the national response to our veterans and their families has not always echoed Lincoln's hopes. Somewhere between malice and charity lie other factors—how we respect soldiers and the conflicts in which they serve, how we assess their wounds and complaints, what priorities we establish in our national budget,[1] and the political strength of veterans' groups. Our attitudes toward race and gender have also determined which veterans we embraced and which we shunned.

Early Pensions

Financial assistance to disabled soldiers has a long tradition in America. British law established precedents in 1593 when a weekly tax was levied on parishes to care for soldiers and sailors disabled in defeating the Spanish Armada[2] and that tradition was carried to the American colonies. The Colony of Virginia recognized an obligation to wounded veterans in 1624 and in 1636 Plymouth Colony decreed that the colony should maintain for life those "maimed" in its defense. The wounded were not the only ones compensated. George Washington, for example, enjoyed lands awarded for his service in the French and Indian War. To encourage recruiting during the American Revolution, the Continental Congress authorized future pensions and land grants (issued as promissory warrants) for members of the Continental Army. They also offered pensions of half-pay for life to seriously disabled veterans. These were hopeful promises since the Continental Congress controlled no land and lacked both funds for pensions and authority to assign such responsibility to the states. Indeed, the Continental Congress struggled to provide back pay to the Continental Army when it was disbanded in 1783. Only the army's threats not to demobilize, their intimidating march on Congress in Philadelphia, and the intercession of George Washington won the army's back pay.

The Continental Army helped create a new nation, but that nation bore a profound distrust of standing armies. The U.S. Constitution reflected this caution, authorizing Congress "To raise and support armies, but no appropriation of money to that use shall be for a longer term than two years." Armies were too often the instrument of tyrants. Compensation for those disabled fighting in the American Revolution was not on a reliable footing until 1793, ten years after the war ended. Some states awarded land or their own small pensions to veterans after the war,[3] but the new U.S. Congress did not manage to fulfill its predecessor's promise of land until 1796. Veterans who had the means or trust to hold on to their land warrants profited from them, but by 1796 many had despaired of ever gaining land and sold their warrants cheaply to speculators.[4] In the spirit of the people's revolution, soldiers of the Continental Army were considered but one part of a broad popular effort that achieved the nation's birth. "At the turn of the nineteenth century, Fourth of July orators reinforced this concept of a people's war with rhetorical images of the sacrifice, suffering, and patriotism of heroic mothers, sisters and ... 'citizen soldiers' alike."[5] Consideration of pensions for Continental Army veterans who were not disabled only followed the War of 1812.

By 1818, a number of changes, including "partisan conflict over defense policy, sentimental and revisionist histories of the Revolutionary War, humiliating defeats in the War of 1812, a surge of nationalism during and following that war, and appeals from poor and disabled Revolutionary War veterans" rehabilitated the image of Continental Army veterans.[6] The Revolutionary War Pension Act of 1818 aimed to help Continental Army veterans "in reduced circumstances," but bogus or affluent veterans soon scrambled to claim pensions designated for the destitute. Fortunately the scandal did not reverse the new gratitude toward Continental Army veterans and in 1820 Congress revised the pension program to prevent abuses. The program was administered by the War Department with special courts to determine who was eligible—who was to be included and who excluded. Legislation in 1832 offered more generous pensions to Continental Army veterans and, for the first time, included militia veterans, but by that time there were few surviving veterans.

Although Congress was late to resolve land grants and slower to award pensions, benefits for veterans became an American expectation. Land would remain in the benefit mix through the nineteenth century. Land on the frontier avoided demands on a slender treasury and helped expand national boundaries. Embracing such a land grant meant uprooting self and family and accepting risks and hardship on the frontier.

The War of 1812

On disbanding the Continental Army, Congress established a small regular army to guard military arsenals and protect areas where the British maintained bases and Indian alliances on the western frontier. State militias were considered the bulwark of national defense. At the start of the War of 1812, in spite of some mobilization to confront British provocations, the regular army of the United States numbered less than twelve thousand officers and men[7] and was woefully unprepared to resist British regulars. The time required for news to cross the Atlantic played a pivotal role in the War of 1812. Offensive British legislation that helped provoke the war was repealed two days *before* America's declaration of war and the major American victory at the Battle of New Orleans occurred *after* the peace treaty was signed in December of 1814. In between, hopes of some politicians to conquer Canada were dashed; opposition to the war in New England was so strong some threatened to secede from the Union; U.S. forces blunted British thrusts from Canada; British forces swept through Washington, D.C., burning the Capitol; and the defense of Baltimore's Fort McHenry inspired the *Star Spangled Banner.* Still, the veterans of 1812 did not enjoy the acclaim of the Continental Army.

The 1812 veterans argued for recognition comparable to Revolutionary War veterans but their land grants were typically less desirable and land warrants could not be sold to speculators.[8] Men who fought while in state militias were not included in land grants. Grumbles reached a new pitch when Congress sweetened incentives for recruits in the Mexican-American War with better land grants than were offered the vets of 1812. Final pensions and land grants for veterans of 1812 were comparable to those of the Continental Army but these adjustments came late in their lives. Critically, the pensions "fell due when the federal treasury was stretched to the limit by the Civil War,"[9] severely delaying their implementation.

The Mexican-American War

Seeds of the Mexican-American War were sown when Texas entered the union, dragging along its border dispute with Mexico. President James K. Polk seized the dispute as an opportunity for American expansion. He posted U.S. troops to the area claimed by Mexico. When Mexican forces predictably attacked, Polk gained a U.S. declaration of war. Opponents of the war were as diverse as Ulysses S. Grant and Henry

David Thoreau, whose essay on *Civil Disobedience* was prompted by the war. Confident of easy victory, Congress approved benefits for the wounded and disabled from the beginning. Military success, however, came at a high cost. More men fell in battle than expected and disease killed thousands more. Death benefits were granted for veterans who died in Mexico, but not for those whose illnesses claimed them after their homecoming. In the 1870s Mexican-American War veterans pressed hard for pensions,[10] but pension legislation did not pass until 1887, thirty-nine years after the formal end of the war. The unpopularity of the war may have contributed to the delay. As one distinguished historian wrote, "The undeniable fact is that it was an offensive war so completely stripped of moral pretensions that no politician of that era ever succeeded in elevating it to the lofty level of a "crusade."[11] Two other factors subverted the cause for pensions—expansion of slavery was a subtext of the Mexican-American War and many veterans of that war later fought for the Confederacy.

The Civil War

The incredible carnage of the Civil War evoked Lincoln's sentiment to "bind up the nation's wounds," but the challenge was enormous. Even during the war, care of most wounded Union soldiers beyond the battlefield fell to private initiatives, especially the philanthropically funded U.S. Sanitary Commission. Some veterans endured conditions for which their medical providers had little understanding—morphine addiction or the malaise called "soldier's heart." Others suffered profoundly disabling wounds requiring long-term care. Six weeks before his assassination, Lincoln initiated steps to address such long-term needs when he signed legislation that created a National Home for Disabled Veterans, an important precedent for today's system of veterans' care.[12]

Veterans first organized to influence legislation after the Revolutionary War, but early veterans' organizations were of minor influence compared to the Grand Army of the Republic (GAR), founded by

Union veterans in Illinois in 1866. The GAR adopted a hybrid military/Masonic model[13] and grew to include departments in every state and posts in towns of any size throughout the North. The GAR helped veterans preserve the camaraderie and shared experience of their military service and firmly established the place of Union veterans on the national political scene. Endorsement by the GAR became a critical prize for aspiring politicians. Of the first seven presidents elected after the Civil War, only one was not a member of the GAR. The GAR's openness to Union veterans of any rank added to its muscle and led to a democratization of veterans' disability pensions. The Consolidation Act of 1873 based pensions on the degree of a veteran's disability, not on his rank while in service.[14] The act also provided for a disabled veteran to hire a nurse or housekeeper if he lacked a caretaker. The GAR's political power climaxed in the Dependent Pension Bill of 1890, which provided disability pensions for Union veterans whether their disability was acquired in the war or not. By that year, the GAR had grown to almost half a million members and benefits for Union veterans were the largest item in the federal budget. "By 1932, the amount paid to Union Civil War veterans and their survivors amounted to twice the cost of the war."[15] At the end of the nineteenth century the mechanisms were in place to provide for disability benefits for future veterans, if not to determine their scope or amounts.

Needless to say, Confederate veterans did not enjoy the benefits of the triumphant Union vets. Rebel vets received what scant support their families and devastated communities could muster. Those due pensions from America's earlier wars forfeited them because of their disloyalty to the Union. Only many years later did some Southern states eke out meager pensions or burial sites for Confederate veterans.

The Spanish-American War

In 1898, the U.S. battleship *Maine* deployed to Havana to protect U.S. interests during Cuba's uprising against its Spanish colonizers. When an explosion sank her in Havana harbor, major American newspapers blamed Spain in a frenzied call for retaliation. An official investigation found the explosion an accident and Spain offered to pay compensation for the *Maine*, but neither action could slake the thirst for war. Congress authorized U.S. military intervention on behalf of Cuban rebels provoking Spanish and then U.S. declarations of war in April 1898. Congress gave no thought to benefits for returning veterans.

Military units in Cuba lacked the knowledge, resources, and medical staff to treat yellow fever, malaria, dysentery, and typhoid, and five times as many soldiers died of disease as died in combat.[16] Fevered men packed ships returning to abysmal medical facilities in quarantined army camps in New York and Virginia. War Secretary Russell Alger blamed the soldiers for their illnesses. "The official policy of shifting blame to them was more than just avoiding embarrassment.... The War Department still paid all disability claims out of the defense budget and he [Alger] didn't want the liability to increase." Alger required physicals before the men were released, "not to identify and treat service connected physical problems, but to establish a basis for denying future claims."[17] In its sunset, the GAR saw the demands of the Spanish-American War veterans as a threat to their own benefits and resisted legislation to help them.

Teddy Roosevelt prophetically warned his Rough Riders "that the world would be kind to them for 10 days, but after that they would be considered tainted just for having gone."[18] Spanish-American War veterans received a pittance at separation and were on their own for transportation home, whether home was around the block or two thousand miles away. They were eligible for disability payments but, since there was no system of veterans' medical care, they had to find and pay for their own medical care. The decision to expand the goals of the Spanish-American War to also "free" the Philippines from Spain reflected our worst imperial tendencies. Rather than aid Philippine independence (with the probability of gaining a U.S. naval base from a grateful Philippines), President William McKinley supported total acquisition of the islands. He later claimed to be inspired in this decision by a wish to "Christianize" the predominantly Catholic colony.[19] American forces suffered almost no casualties freeing the Philippines. A treaty negotiated with Spain in 1898 officially ended the war in April 1899. When Filipinos began to experience their American "freedom" as Spanish colonialism with a new face, they rose in bloody revolt. Almost all American casualties in the Philippines resulted from suppressing the insurrection that persisted for fourteen years beyond the time of the treaty. When modest benefits were ultimately offered to veterans of the Spanish-American War, veterans of the "post-treaty" Philippine insurrection were excluded. Soldiers and sailors who participated in a range of "small wars" after the Spanish-American War and before World War I—actions in the Caribbean, Central America, and Russia—were similarly not acknowledged with veterans' benefits.[20]

World War I and the Bonus

No veterans' benefits were more bitterly contested than those following World War I. Finally provoked into a war the country had hoped to avoid, Congress authorized massive conscription in 1917 to supplement voluntary enlistments. The draft brought over two million men into the armed forces, many destined for France, where brutal trench warfare exacted casualties in appalling numbers. Wary of postwar costs, Congress passed "war-risk life insurance for American soldiers and sailors who voluntarily signed up and paid the premiums through deductions from their pay."[21] Although most soldiers were paid a dollar a day, postwar pension demands were not anticipated.[22] At this paltry wage over a quarter of the U.S. armed services risked life and limb turning the tide of battle in Europe. Even enlistees who never left American soil suffered financially. After deductions for necessary expenses a soldier might earn as little as $21 a month.[23] For those who held jobs before the war, enlistment usually meant a sizable pay cut. On return to civilian life, these men not only struggled to find jobs but also found that most who did not serve had fared well economically. An average farm laborer in 1917 earned $1,641, but by 1919 the average was $2,302.[24] Factory workers saw larger jumps in wages and war profits produced 2,100 new millionaires.[25]

Growing sentiment regarding the veterans' plight prompted Congress to award returning troops $60 at discharge to resume their lives. "The $60 was an acknowledgement of the problem rather than a solution to it."[26] For a vet returning to a lost job, a delinquent mortgage, or a foreclosed farm, $60 was small comfort. For those returning with severe wounds, lungs compromised by gas warfare, or "shell shock," the new term for "soldier's heart," the payment was no comfort at all. Veterans and their advocates clamored for meaningful compensation, a lump payment soon named the "bonus." In 1920 a significant bonus bill passed the House but failed in the Senate. As historians of the period noted, "America's elected leaders were not disputing the veterans' claim to back pay for wartime service. They just didn't want to write the check."[27] In that same year Warren Harding campaigned for the presidency on a platform favoring a bonus. Once in office he reversed himself, favoring tax cuts instead, and vetoed a bonus bill that passed Congress handily. Efforts to override Harding's veto fell just short in the Senate.

As the volume of ill and wounded World War I veterans overwhelmed military hospitals, responsibility for treating veterans was transferred to the Public Health Service (PHS), as were several military hospitals and funds for new hospitals. During the two years the PHS was responsible for veterans it realized a threefold increase in hospitals and an eightfold increase in patients.[28] In 1921, Harding signed legislation consolidating formerly uncoordinated veterans' programs into the Veterans Bureau. This brought together the War Risk insurance program, the Federal Division of Vocational Rehabilitation, and Public Health Service hospitals. It also provided funds to develop additional hospitals and medical treatment for veterans. In response to subsequent wars, these veterans' services would become the largest hospital system in the world. Sadly, the system had a rocky start. Harding appointed Charles Forbes, a crass opportunist, as the first director of the Veterans Bureau. Forbes exploited his post by reaping huge kickbacks after overpaying for land to build hospitals and by selling freight-car-loads of hospital supplies as surplus after creating massive overstocks. All told, Forbes diverted between 200 and 250 million dollars to himself and his cronies.[29] Tried and convicted, he served twenty months in federal prison. Subtracting a $10,000 fine from the lower estimate of his booty, Forbes served *one day in prison* for every $322,580 he embezzled from funds intended for wounded World War I veterans—men who risked their lives for a dollar a day.

Harding died a little over halfway into his presidency, and his vice president, Calvin Coolidge, succeeded him. Coolidge openly opposed the bonus. In clear opposition to a president of his own party, Representative Hamilton Fish, Jr. (R-NY), a veteran himself, proposed compromise legislation in 1924. Each veteran was to be awarded a dollar a day for every day he had served (minus the $60 discharge payment). Those who served overseas merited $1.25 a day. However, the bonus, with accrued interest plus another 25 percent, would not be available until twenty-one years later, in 1945. This would allow Congress to set aside funds incrementally to meet this future obligation. The bill sailed through both houses straight to Coolidge's veto. Coolidge, known as a man of few words, added an ill-considered flourish to his veto, asserting, "Patriotism which is bought and paid for is not patriotism."[30] His remarks infuriated enough of his own party for Congress to override the veto. Bonus legislation finally passed, but, as historians Paul Dickson and Thomas Allen clarify, "The so called bonus was neither compensation nor a bonus. It was a twenty-one year endowment life insurance policy payable at death or in 1945, which ever came first."[31] Those whose bonus was $50 or less received immediate payment. The rest received certificates reflecting their anticipated final payment, on average about $1,000.

The First Bonus March

In 1929, a few months after Herbert Hoover assumed the presidency, the stock market crashed, plunging the country into the Great Depression. In 1930, the Veterans Administration itself was born of Hoover's efforts to stretch the starving federal budget. To reduce administrative costs, he combined the Bureau of Pensions, the National Homes for Disabled Veterans, and the Veterans Bureau into the Veterans Administration. The budgets of World War I veterans were also stretched. As hordes of veterans joined the financially desperate, a bonus deferred so far beyond immediate needs seemed a cruel joke. Pressure for early payment of the bonus was intense and in February 1931 Congress responded with legislation allowing its immediate payment. Hoover felt the federal budget could not support such demands. He vetoed the bill but consented to legislation the next day allowing veterans to borrow up to 50 percent of the face value of their bonus certificates at 3 percent compound interest. Such loans would reduce the final value of the certificates, but more seriously, "No veteran who needed the money in loan form could conceive of being able to pay the loan back."[32]

As economic conditions worsened, all manner of protesters began to descend on the nation's capital. Some demanded federal programs to create jobs; others marched against hunger. A relatively small march from Philadelphia urged early payment of the bonus. This first bonus delegation had little impact, but it forecast a coming storm. In January 1932, Father James Cox, a Catholic priest, mobilized eighteen thousand of the unemployed to converge on Washington. After initial reluctance, President Hoover briefly met a delegation of marchers. Foreshadowing his difficulty in personally engaging protesters, he read them a statement explaining that the depression was nearly over and new government job programs were unnecessary.[33] A month later, veterans' groups secured a permit for another march of their own. When it appeared that unmanageable numbers might join this march, the Hoover administration met with the organizers and persuaded them to cancel it. The genie, however, was out of the bottle. In April 1932, a thousand members of the Veterans of Foreign Wars (VFW) marched to the Capitol and presented over two million veterans' signatures to Congress supporting early payment of the bonus. Hoover remained firm and early bonus legislation remained locked in House committees.

What came to be known as the Veterans Bonus Army began in Oregon in early May 1932. Veteran Walter W. Waters announced he was leading a veterans' contingent to Washington to demand payment of the bonus. Nearly three hundred men began the journey from Portland in a cluster of boxcars. Obstacles thrown in their path by railroad management or police were regularly subverted by railroad workers, other police, or local politicians sympathetic to their cause. When they stopped in big or small towns they marched and spoke. Supportive citizens turned out with sandwiches and encouragement. By the end of May the Oregon contingent was outside Washington. Press coverage of their journey mobilized thousands of veterans, all heading to Washington. They rode the rails in coal cars or the roads in convoys of trucks; some walked; vets among the wandering homeless brought their wives and children.

Pelham Glassford, a retired army brigadier general and supporter of the bonus, commanded the Washington, D.C., police force. He managed the earlier demonstrations in the capital well. Unable to defuse the veterans' march by encouraging bonus legislation, Glassford worked to accommodate the vets as well as possible. He arranged an encampment on the flats across the Anacostia River from the Capitol, fought for resources the veterans needed, and frequently dipped into his own pocket to help with food. Many others, in and out of Washington, contributed to support the Bonus Army. The veterans raised tents and shanties on the flats and occupied several other areas in the city. Their numbers grew to almost twenty thousand.[34] They vowed to stay until early bonus legislation passed.

Opponents of the bonus sought to discredit the marchers as inspired by Communist agitators, but the main body of the Bonus Army zealously purged known Communists from their ranks. A small, openly Communist contingent of veterans led by John Pace camped in their own area of the city. Communists also claimed undue credit for the march, but few in the press or public accepted such propaganda. Still, the communist threat did resonate inside the Hoover administration and the military, particularly with General Douglas MacArthur, U.S. Army chief of staff.

Shortly after the Bonus Army was established in Washington, the House of Representatives passed a bonus bill. Two days later, on June

17, Waters led over six thousand veterans to Capitol Hill to await the Senate's action. He called for double that number to join them from the Anacostia flats, but, without consulting Glassford, city officials raised the Anacostia drawbridge and blocked other bridges offering access to the Capitol. The bridges were later opened, but the maneuver guaranteed that the veterans who finally joined Waters would be in a foul mood. In the early evening, the Senate rejected the bill. Waters announced the decision to a crowd in which the tension was palpable. In a spur-of-the-moment evocation of nonviolence, Waters shouted for the veterans to "Sing *America.*" Supported by the quick response of the U.S. Army Band, the veterans broke into song. With the edge off their anger, they milled back to their camps.[35] The veterans' response in song to their frustration won glowing praise in the press.

The veterans did not go away. In fact, after the adverse Senate action their numbers may have swelled.[36] On July 7 Congress approved $100,000 to help the bonus marchers return home. Congress also set a deadline of July 15 for the vets to be out of town. The deadline passed with few veterans taking the travel assistance. Demonstrations continued and tension grew. Congress adjourned until December. President Hoover, who steadfastly refused to meet with even a delegation of veterans, ordered their eviction. Veterans residing in partially razed government buildings on Pennsylvania Avenue had a deadline of July 22. The Anacostia flats were to be empty by August 4.[37] On the morning of July 28, police began evacuation on Pennsylvania Avenue. It was marred by a brief charge, brick throwing, and a small fight. There were minor injuries and several vets were arrested. That afternoon a more serious incident injured two policemen and gunfire in return killed one veteran and left another mortally wounded. In a backup plan not coordinated with Glassford, federal troops under General MacArthur were massed on the Ellipse ready to take over the evacuation. In late afternoon, mounted cavalry with drawn sabers and infantry with fixed bayonets (backed by several tanks) cleared the downtown camps.

The troops rested for supper and then, though it was several days before the ordered evacuation of the flats, MacArthur turned his forces toward Anacostia. Troops massed at the drawbridge near the camp and at 10:00 p.m. a leader from the camp begged for "an hour's truce so he could evacuate the camp."[38] An hour was, in fact, impossible. Many veterans, especially those encamped with their families, had their worldly belongings in the camp. When the hour was up, MacArthur's troops surged into the camp, driving those who had not fled before them and setting fire to shanties as they went. At a post-eviction news conference, MacArthur declared, "if there were one man in ten in that group today who is a veteran, it would surprise me."[39] The administrator of the Veterans Bureau had earlier reported the opposite proportion—that 90 percent of those included in the Bonus Army were veterans.[40] The military eviction of the Anacostia camp, which Hoover had not ordered but never disavowed, probably doomed his already tenuous prospects for reelection.

A Second Bonus March and a Hurricane

Franklin Roosevelt became president on March 4, 1933. Also opposed to early payment of the bonus, Roosevelt quickly roused the ire of veterans when he sought to provide jobs through a Civilian Conservation Corps (CCC), for which only men younger than the World War I veterans were eligible. Committed to balancing the budget, Roosevelt's Economy Act of 1933 voided all prior veterans' benefits and allowed him to determine benefits by executive order. He dramatically cut the pensions of veterans disabled in combat and eliminated the pensions of most whose disability was related to mental health or disease. A new veterans' march, organized to coincide with a May convention of the Veterans of Foreign Wars, was soon brewing. Restoration of disability payments was added to demands for an early bonus. The management of the 1933 Bonus Army was a tribute to Roosevelt's political skills if not his compassion. The army arranged a tent city for the veterans at Fort Hunt in Virginia, well away from Washington's center. The new marchers were deeply divided between left- and right-wing political groups and the White House helped shape the veterans' leadership by granting selective access to their staff. In sharp contrast to Hoover's cold shoulder and use of troops, Roosevelt arranged for his wife, Eleanor, to visit the veterans' camp and listen to their concerns. Roosevelt also opened the CCC to twenty-five thousand veterans. With these concessions and offers of free transportation home, the still-divided second Bonus Army drifted away from Washington.

Roosevelt's apparent political coup was soon literally blown away. Several hundred newly employed veterans were assigned to build roads in the Florida Keys, where their camps on the island of Matecumbe were soon decimated by a narrow but incredibly powerful hurricane. By the time rescuers reached the islands, the sandblasted and bloated bodies of veterans were found in rancid estuaries, underbrush, and even trees. Author Ernest Hemingway joined the early rescue parties and wrote a devastating description of the disaster, questioning why veterans were not evacuated in a timely manner when most Floridians managed to leave or find shelter.[41] The Roosevelt administration and its congressional allies produced a shameless whitewash of the tragedy while suppressing more factual reports, including one by the American Legion titled "Murder in Matecumbe." The hurricane disaster was added to the Bonus Army evictions in evoking national sympathies in favor of veterans. Historians Dickson and Allen contend that these events created a fertile climate for the generous GI Bill of World War II.[42]

World War II and the GI Bill of Rights

The Japanese attack on Pearl Harbor in December 1941 precipitated U.S. entry into World War II and united the nation as no other conflict had. Over sixteen million Americans ultimately volunteered or were caught up in a draft that made few social distinctions. Most Americans had a family member in the service and their attention to the progress of the war in Africa, Europe, and the Pacific was highly personal. When the press documented staff shortages in VA medical facilities or offered accounts of horribly wounded men who returned to face bureaucratic obstacles to critical care, the public could readily imagine it happening to someone they knew. Members of Congress may have feared the specter of a bigger, nationally destabilizing Bonus Army, but their constituents feared for loved ones. Support for a range of veterans' benefits was broad and deep.

Veterans' organizations lobbied vigorously for extensive veterans' benefits and many details of the final GI Bill legislation were developed by veterans' organizations. A year of unemployment benefits allowed vets to take time to find work or survey their prospects. Educational benefits had never been offered to veterans before. Veterans' organizations lobbied hard for them, though they were strongly opposed by some university elites (the president of the University of Chicago warned against turning universities into "educational hobo jungles").[43] Aside from helping veterans there was concern that the return of millions of veterans during the shift from a war to a peace economy could provoke a huge recession. Generous educational benefits could both delay and enhance the return of veterans to the workforce.

When the Servicemen's Readjustment Act of 1944, the GI Bill, became law, it not only provided well for veterans, but it transformed the nation. Educational benefits allowed men and women for whom college was not even a dream to realize potentials that surprised even themselves. Over half of World War II veterans took advantage of their educational benefits and the maturity and diligence of veterans as students became legendary even at the most prestigious universities. Their performance opened doors and hopes for millions of Americans whose previous educational horizon was high school graduation. Combined with education, GI loan benefits helped veterans start new businesses, achieve home ownership for themselves and their families, stimulate the postwar economy, and substantially enlarge the U.S. middle class.

World War II saw an unprecedented entry of women into the armed services. Though women who enlisted in the army or navy were eligible for the same benefits as men, societal expectations limited their use of those benefits. Other deserving women were simply excluded. In World War I, General John J. Pershing put out a call for women to serve as bilingual telephone operators in France. The women wore army uniforms and some served in France. Yet at war's end they were told they were contract civilian employees, not veterans (though they had no contracts),[44] and they found themselves ineligible for veterans' benefits. In World War II, women who served in the Women's Auxiliary Army Corps (WAAC) or as Women's Airforce Service Pilots (WASP) found themselves in the same position. The WASPs in particular had performed crucial wartime duties, flying military aircraft (including bombers) from factory to duty stations and helping to train military personnel. They had lost thirty-eight of their sister pilots in the performance of these duties. They too were considered civilian contractors.[45] This injustice was rectified by Congress two decades later. A more egregious exclusion involved soldiers and sailors exposed to radiation during atomic tests in the immediate aftermath of World War II. Many suffered multiple maladies, but as will be detailed in Chapter 3, most were denied access to veterans' medical care and benefits.

Post–World War II Changes in the VA

President Harry Truman was a World War I veteran and serious about addressing the needs of World War II veterans. Truman was politically at odds with Frank T. Hines, a former general who had led the VA from its inception. A scandal in the treatment of returning vets at the VA hospital in Northport, Long Island, provided Truman with the opportunity to replace Hines. Suggesting that veterans might prefer "a general of their own war," Truman made the popular appointment of General Omar Bradley to direct the Veterans Administration.[46] Bradley, a major army commander in North Africa and Europe and a national hero, strove to reduce red tape and to strengthen medical care for veterans. He called in army surgeon Major General Paul Hawley to assist him and supported Hawley's initiatives to create a Department of Medicine and ally VA hospitals with major medical schools.[47] This alliance immediately brought desperately needed doctors into the VA health care system. Doctors in their training residencies often added critical specialties. Concurrent appointments for staff physicians to medical school faculties enhanced recruiting and gave VA doctors regular access to a range of highly trained colleagues and information on the latest medical advances. Medical residents who enjoyed their VA experience might also be recruited into the VA health care system. In a little over two years, Bradley oversaw the regional reorganization of the VA, increases in VA staff and efficiency, and the addition of twenty-nine new VA hospitals. At the urging of mental health advocates the VA made unprecedented steps to include mental health specialists among those addressing the needs of returning World War II veterans and became a leader in training and employing clinical psychologists.[48] This pioneering focus on mental health was slow to be matched in response to the needs of veterans in subsequent wars. Historian Davis Ross carefully traced the policies and political intrigues that shaped the national response to home-coming World War II vets— veterans' advocates generally triumphed. "The new Ulysses of 1945 and 1946, unlike his classical ancestor, had not been forsaken."[49]

The Korean Conflict

Sometimes called the "Forgotten War," the Korean War was part of a United Nations "police action" to defend South Korea after a North Korean invasion. North Korean troops nearly pushed American and South Korean troops to the edge of the Korean peninsula before U.S. forces resumed the offensive in a daring amphibious landing at Inchon. In the fall of 1950, American forces were pushing deep into North Korea when Chinese forces entered the conflict in support of North Korea. The Chinese drove U.S. forces south again in bitter winter battles. The struggle swung back and forth until halted by an armistice in July 1953. American troops are still stationed at the 38th parallel, the same border established in 1945 between North and South Korea. The Korean War did not mobilize the nation as did World War II, and its veterans did not receive comparable benefits. The GI Bill of 1952 offered Korean veterans less in unemployment and educational benefits than did the GI

Bill of 1944. Eight percent fewer Korean veterans availed themselves of GI educational benefits than did World War II veterans.[50]

Korean veterans also fell under the pall created by Chinese treatment of American prisoners of war (POWs). It is estimated that over 40 percent of U.S. POWs died in Chinese captivity. Subjected to cold, deprivation, brutality, and constant indoctrination, a number of U.S. soldiers made anti-American statements that were filmed and distributed as propaganda by the Chinese. In World War II, the nation elevated its fighting man to mythic status. The "brainwashing" of U.S. soldiers by the Chinese, no matter how harshly achieved, was a blow to national pride, and a basis for excluding a number of veterans from benefits.

> Former POWs were especially distrusted, considered stained by captivity, or contaminated with communist ideology. Even veterans' organizations combed their rolls for potential communists infiltrating their posts. The army issued less than honorable discharges to anyone accused of leaning to the left, even if their records were clean and sent a suspect list of former prisoners to the Federal Bureau of Investigation. The VA rescinded benefits of anyone on the FBI suspect list, denying help to those most in need.[51]

Korean veterans suffered another blow when a controversial report by an army psychiatrist suggested that as many as a third of U.S. POWs in Korea may have been brainwashed.[52] Neither were they aided by a subsequent movie, *The Manchurian Candidate,* a fictitious thriller in which a brainwashed soldier is "programmed" by communists to assassinate a presidential candidate, only to be stopped at the film's climax.

Vietnam

Other than the Civil War, no war divided the nation like the one in Vietnam. An undeclared war, it grew in steps, or missteps, to a massive commitment. Many of those steps involved deception by Presidents John

F. Kennedy, Lyndon Johnson, and Richard Nixon as well as senior defense and military officials. Dr. Martin Luther King, Jr. linked protests against the war with the struggle for civil rights. Citizens anchored in traditional values and allegiance to the nation became appalled as antiwar civil disobedience and destruction raged on college campuses and in cities. Many draft-eligible youth fled to Canada. Antiwar sentiment seemed to drive unsettling cultural shifts among the young—in dress, art, music, drug use, gender roles, and sexual behavior. The turmoil split the electorate, the military, institutions, church congregations, and families. Many divisions persisted for decades.

Some returning veterans became vigorous supporters of the antiwar movement, especially through Vietnam Veterans Against the War. Traditional veterans' organizations were more attuned to the medical needs of aging World War II and Korean veterans. Steeped in anticommunism and the patriotic fervor of World War II, they were less-than-avid advocates for vets who were the first to "lose" an American war and whose ranks included truculent protesters. These negative attitudes were also evident in the VA.[53] Vietnam veterans generally received fine initial care in military hospitals. Those transferred to the VA for continuing care were often not so fortunate. The VA was again ill equipped for the influx of damaged Vietnam veterans. The Paralyzed Veterans of America (PVA) may have been an exception to other veterans' organizations. The needs of paralyzed veterans remain similar across all wars. The PVA helped sneak a *Life* magazine photographer into the VA hospital in the Bronx, New York,[54] and the shocking photos and story in May of 1970 provoked a national scandal. Captions in the article read:

From Vietnam to a VA Hospital
ASSIGNMENT TO NEGLECT

and

Staff shortages, overcrowding, dirt and leaky roofs in a medical slum.[55]

Paralyzed veteran Mark Dumpert described vets lying unattended for hours while urine bags overflowed. He told of calling attendants to no avail and then screaming to encourage a rat to slink off his immobilized hand. He said he preferred his dirt bunker at Khe Sanh to the Bronx VA hospital. *Life* quoted VA director Donald E. Johnson as proclaiming that veterans receive "care second to none," but concluded that "The evidence is overwhelmingly against him."[56]

Still, improving the VA was not a priority of the Nixon administration. In such circumstances, lobbying assumed radical forms. In February 1974, disabled veterans, many with serious paralyses, occupied the California offices of their advocate, Senator Alan Cranston (D-CA), and commenced a hunger strike until VA director Johnson met with them.[57] After resisting, Johnson succumbed to public pressure and flew to California. Seeking some measure of control, he went to the seventh floor of the Westwood California Federal Building and insisted on meeting there with the veterans, who occupied Cranston's offices on the thirteenth floor. When the vets refused to leave the thirteenth floor, Johnson returned to Washington. His stubbornness precipitated a public relations disaster[58] and drove him to meet the protesting veterans two days later, when he proved poorly prepared and promised a follow-up meeting. Johnson entered the follow-up meeting with three bodyguards and a nine-page report of VA services, but was overwhelmed by the array of veterans' advocates and firsthand accounts of poor treatment.[59] Continuing revelations regarding Johnson's management of the VA prompted his resignation in April 1974.

Among the priorities of Vietnam veterans was improved mental health care. In August 1974, President Gerald Ford appointed Richard L. Roudebush, Johnson's deputy and a highly patriotic World War II vet, to direct the VA. Roudebush had earlier been quoted as saying "Vietnam veterans were 'crybabies' whose problems stemmed from losing their war."[60] Barely a week after Roudebush's appointment, several strongly aggrieved vets leafleted the lobby of the VA headquarters, while three others entered Roudebush's office and nailed the door shut. Having gained his undivided attention, they proceeded to indoctrinate him on the needs of veterans, especially their mental health needs. One of the advocates, Jack Smith, was both a veteran and a researcher into the severe stress reactions of Vietnam veterans. Roudebush was soon freed by the police but refused to press charges. It is not clear how much Roudebush profited from his forced orientation. He and Smith would actually later become friends.[61] Roudebush did add medical facilities, fight for more funds for home loans, and urge President Ford to sign a bill increasing educational assistance for Vietnam veterans. Still many services lagged behind veterans' needs.

Vietnam veterans hailed President Jimmy Carter's 1977 appointment of Max Cleland to direct the VA. Cleland had lost two legs and an arm in Vietnam and experienced the shortcomings of VA care on his return. During Cleland's tenure the malady with so many aliases—soldier's heart, barbed wire disease, shell shock, battle fatigue—finally won medical recognition as PTSD. The VA planned and won funding for almost a hundred vet centers across America, which relied heavily on informal peer counseling for vets to share their concerns and trauma. The emphasis on peer counseling made the vet centers controversial but with key congressional support they expanded to over 180 centers by the late 1980s. World War II and Korean vets still composed the bulk of VA patients and a 1977 study by the National Academy of Sciences (NAS) concluded that the VA was caring for aging veterans whose disabilities were unrelated to their military service to the detriment of veterans disabled in Vietnam. One of the recommendations of the NAS study was that many veterans be treated in the existing civilian health care system.[62] That recommendation became the focus of Cleland's response, and he vociferously defended the VA system. Ironically, for all Cleland's passion and advocacy he became the target of veterans beset by the curse of Agent Orange, a defoliant dropped in abundance in Vietnam. Agent Orange was subsequently blamed for multiple cancers and birth defects in the offspring of those exposed to it (see Chapter 4) and any resolution of the Agent Orange issue was years away.

During the Vietnam War, the armed services issued almost half a million military discharges under less-than-honorable conditions.

Over half these discharges excluded the veterans from medical care or benefits. Several factors contributed to this high rate of what veterans called "bad paper." Trapped in what increasingly appeared a fruitless and morally questionable war, thousands of soldiers in Vietnam balked at both routine and life-threatening assignments, especially once the end of the war was under negotiation.[63] Also, as the military struggled to fill its ranks for an unpopular cause, they resorted to enlisting tens of thousands of young men who were previously deemed unqualified for military service.[64] Not surprisingly, a number of these recruits did not measure up. Vietnam veterans fought a protracted battle to gain review and reversal of many of these discharges, discharges that denied so many comrades VA benefits.

Veterans and Racism

Racism remains an enduring force in American life and has resulted in the exclusion of many active service members and vets from access to rights they deserved. Our attitudes toward minorities are shaped by our prevailing beliefs about the intellectual capacities and moral qualities of those minorities as well as the higher calls of our American ideals—that all men are created equal. The inclusion or exclusion of racial minorities in the American military reflects attitudes in the larger society as well as tensions particular to the military. More specific to the military are tensions between their needs for manpower and their worries about discipline and morale when disparaged minorities are included in the fighting forces. Among some whites, there was a historical fear of providing military experience to African Americans, whose maltreatment and social exclusion might tempt them to violence. This fear, and doubts about black "competence," made the army slow to use their black units in combat roles in the two world wars.

Still, black Americans participated in all our crucial armed struggles. In our fight for independence, they joined the Continental Army (the need for recruits and the fact that the British enlisted black soldiers in their cause may have enhanced their acceptance). Black soldiers also fought with Jackson to defeat the British at the Battle of New Orleans. In these ventures they fought at the sides of white soldiers. However, from their participation in the Union Army in the Civil War through World War II, black soldiers served in segregated units, almost always commanded by white officers. In the navy, blacks constituted between 20 and 30 percent of the enlisted ranks and served with white sailors through much of the nineteenth century. This level of involvement dropped sharply at the beginning of the twentieth century. Blacks were less likely to be recruited into the navy and their assignments were usually to ranks performing dirty or menial tasks. Cumbersome administrative procedures made it difficult for blacks to transfer to duties with better prospects for advancement both in the military and afterward. The black vote was important to President Franklin Roosevelt and black leaders pressed him throughout World War II to integrate the military and use black troops in combat roles. The military made some accommodations, but generally argued that war was no time to be simultaneously conducting "social experiments." Roosevelt deferred to their stand.[65]

Black leaders continued to press President Truman, whose ultimate action was influenced by a rash of appalling violence against black veterans. In 1946, a black vet named Isaac Woodard, still in uniform, was returning to his home by bus after being honorably discharged. In Batesburg, South Carolina, Woodard was removed from the Greyhound bus by local police, severely beaten, arrested, and beaten again in jail. His corneas were so battered that he was blinded for life. When Truman belatedly learned the details of this incident he was furious. He initiated a federal investigation that resulted in the indictment of the Batesburg police chief. The trial, however, was conducted in the U.S. District Court in Columbia, South Carolina, hardly a sympathetic venue for Woodard. Asserting that he beat Woodard in the eyes in "self defense," the police chief was acquitted after a local jury deliberated for only thirty minutes.[66] One historian described the period when Woodward was blinded as "the bloody spring of 1946."

Black GIs returned from World War II, having faced bullets and bombs and—despite their segregated, second-class status in the army—having lost arms, legs, and buddies while fighting for freedom and democracy, only to find that at home the war was far from over. The enemy appeared simply to have changed uniforms: it now wore sheets or sheriff's badges—or both. In the first fifteen months after Hitler's defeat, a wave of antiblack terror, mostly but not only in the southern states, killed fifty-six African Americans, with returning veterans the most frequent victims.[67]

In July 1948, Truman integrated the armed forces by executive order, requiring that "equality of treatment and opportunity ... be put into effect as rapidly as possible, having due regard to the time required to effectuate any necessary changes without impairing efficiency or morale."[68] But, as illustrated in the story of Robert Yancey, the meaningful implementation of that order dragged for years. Yancey served in World War II as a navy steward, essentially a servant for commissioned officers. When called from the reserves to serve in Korea, he knew he wasn't going back to such service and enlisted in the army, hoping to better control his destiny. Yancey was assigned to a segregated unit of the army's Twenty-fourth Infantry Division (two years after Truman's desegregation order). That unit bore much of the frontline action early in the Korean War and suffered massive casualties. When he returned to the United States, some white officers, apparently offended by the stripes Yancey earned in combat, belabored him with threats and unreasonable assignments. Only because he carried his complaints to senior officers did he avoid several courts martial. Before he finished his twenty-one years in the army, Yancey earned a Bronze Star for bravery, treating seriously wounded soldiers under fire in Vietnam.[69] In spite of his difficulties Yancey may have been wise to choose the army. The navy was the last of the services to change its discriminatory practices.[70]

Black vets also profited little from Truman's order. It wasn't until the appointment of Harvey Higley (VA administrator 1953–1957) that the VA began the vigorous desegregation of its hospitals. As in the active military, top-down changes come slowly while racism remains pervasive. Ethnic differences in the provision of quality health care are often attributed to the limited economic resources of minority groups. Economic barriers to VA health care are minimal, yet studies since the "desegregation" of VA facilities persist in showing racial and ethnic disparities. Currently, the data and quality care revolutions in VA health care (described in Chapter 8) allow the VA to systematically research, track, and confront these disparities. A 2007 VA study reviewed disparities in VA care across a broad range of medical conditions with the goal of determining what policies, follow-up, and training might improve care for minority veterans.[71] The findings suggest that complex interactive factors, rather than simple racism, may contribute to differing patterns of care. For example, blacks may be more reluctant to accept remedial heart surgery than whites, and some blacks may express a preference for prayer to the risks of surgery. Addressing such issues may require more time and sensitivity on the part of VA staff. Is a preference for prayer a cultural value that must be respected, or does a particular vet lack a clear understanding of his or her condition and the recommended procedures? Is a vet's decision grounded in a concern that poor blacks have often provided the learning experiences for surgeons in training, eroding levels of trust in surgical procedures in the black community? Still, recent studies[72] indicate that treatment disparities are a continuing problem with possible negative consequences for black veterans. VA administrators now look at this data with new sophistication and take it as a serious issue.

Theoretically eligible for the generous benefits of the GI Bill, in practice black vets were virtually excluded. Segregation barred blacks from living in most middle-class residential areas, from employment in many jobs, and from access to most centers of higher education. In *Crabgrass Frontier,* a classic account of the post–World War II explosion of suburbia, Kenneth Jackson describes how federally backed loans from the VA and the Federal Housing Authority produced an explosion of new homes in the sprawl of American suburbia. These loans favored whites and discouraged blacks (often explicitly encouraging restrictive covenants against reselling houses to blacks and denying loans in areas where one or two black families resided for fear of underwriting homes that would lose their investment value). Loan policies stripped the inner cities of the white middle class and subsequent public housing initiatives concentrated minorities in unworkable inner-city slums.[73] Only in 1962 did President John Kennedy issue an executive order banning segregation in federally supported housing programs. The VA is not insulated from the pernicious prejudices present in the larger society and too often black vets suffered within the VA. Similar stories unfolded for many Latino, Asian, and Native American vets. The scenario playing out in the military in the twenty-first century, focused on volunteers who are gay or lesbian, bears a striking resemblance to the debates about black inclusion in the military during the mid-twentieth century.

More Recent Veterans

Vietnam veterans may have felt compelled to resort to drastic measures in a time when their needs were unmet and their national status seemed ambiguous. Still, the saga of veterans with real but unacknowledged problems has continued. Veterans of the 1991 Gulf War in Iraq won a quick victory and returned acclaimed as heroes; however, as described in Chapter 5, these veterans began reporting a range of troubling symptoms that were initially dismissed by the government and the VA. As was the case with Agent Orange, after more than a decade the VA recognized the legitimacy of some serious and even lethal conditions possibly contracted in the 1991 Gulf War. As with all our wars, the returning wounded regularly overwhelm the medical resources awaiting them. Veterans of Operation Iraqi Freedom and the conflict in Afghanistan provided challenges that the renowned Walter Reed Army Medical Center was ill equipped to meet and that hospital officials were unwilling to admit until they were exposed in a Pulitzer Prize–winning series in the *Washington Post*.[74] The VA faced similar challenges as a new wave of veterans passed from military hospitals into VA care. While conducting wars in Iraq and Afghanistan the United States maintained its commitment to an all-volunteer military. This placed enormous strain on a limited number of personnel. Troops endured repeated deployments with little respite between combat tours. The stress of these repeated tours and the massive injuries produced by the improvised explosive devices (IEDs) used against U.S. troops posed new challenges to veterans' care (see Chapter 8). There is a growing awareness of the strain a volunteer military places on families and how vets who return with profound disabilities exhaust their caretakers. Current veterans return to a health care system that comprises almost 180 major medical centers and scores of outpatient clinics as well as mobile clinics and vet centers. How will these resources provide the help vets and their families need?

Throughout history, countries have gone to war with enthusiasm and visions of easy victory while grossly underestimating the costs, the devastating casualties, and the lives lost. America is no exception. The First Battle of Bull Run in the Civil War is the classic example. Washington society carried picnics to the battlefield to watch Union troops rout the Confederacy. When the rout went the other way, the partygoers fled in greater disarray than the Union troops. The ultimate cost of the war was immense. More recently, on May 1, 2003, President George W. Bush stood on the deck of the aircraft carrier USS *Abraham Lincoln* under a huge banner proclaiming "Mission Accomplished" and declared an end to the combat phase of operations in the second U.S. war in Iraq. Over 97 percent of U.S. casualties in that war occurred after that premature declaration.[75] Nobel Prize–winning economist Joseph Stiglitz and Harvard finance expert Linda Blimes have estimated that the ultimate cost of the incursion into Iraq, including veterans' benefits and medical costs, will be close to three trillion dollars.[76] That is a stunning price tag for a venture that Ken Adelman, a policy analyst and aide to the secretary of defense, had predicted would be a "cakewalk" in a 2002 guest editorial in the *Washington Post*.[77] The enthusiasm that leads to wars fades for the returning veteran. As another Washington columnist observed, "Although war spending was never considered inflationary, veterans' benefits are."[78]

After wars, the heavy lifting to help veterans and ensure their care falls to their families and the major veterans' organizations. While these established organizations have sometimes been less welcoming to newer veterans or at political odds with each other, they remain the backbone of veterans' advocacy. Today, though their collaboration is not total, the American Legion, the Veterans of Foreign Wars (VFW), AMVETS, the Disabled American Veterans (DAV), and the Paralyzed Veterans of America all work diligently on behalf of veterans. Veterans' organizations and the body politic have learned from the aftermath of Vietnam. The second Iraq War to replace Saddam Hussein had strong opposition in the United States. In contrast to Vietnam, however, even those who vehemently opposed the war in Iraq generally respect the troops who fought it. Veterans' organizations, in which Vietnam veterans now hold a prominent place, have been highly responsive to the needs of new veterans returning from Iraq and Afghanistan.

The history of veterans' benefits and care demonstrates that budgets, political will, and public support for veterans wax and wane. In whatever climate, it is the comrades and families of men and women who serve and sacrifice who become their prime champions. America's veterans' organizations provide the clout, political expertise, and experience to effectively channel the collective effort of these advocates. They are the linchpin of future victories on the behalf of America's veterans.

CHAPTER THREE

Atomic Veterans

Radioactive poisoning "is a very pleasant way to die."

General Leslie Groves

T HE GI BILL FOLLOWING WORLD WAR II offered unprecedented benefits to America's veterans, but the postwar experience of a group of "atomic veterans" was one of betrayal rather than appreciation. These men felt used recklessly, sometimes harmed, and uncompensated for their roles in supporting America's drive to develop nuclear weapons.

Late in World War II, as Nazi Germany faltered, its scientists raced to develop a nuclear bomb. The United States joined that fervid race, enlisting its best scientific resources in the top-secret Manhattan Project. Germany fell to the Allied forces before it could produce a bomb, and, on July 16, 1945, one hundred days after the Nazi surrender, the United States tested an atomic device in the New Mexico desert. America was still locked in mortal struggle with Japan. Capturing islands closer to Japan, the United States suffered high casualties. Facing Japan's implacable opposition and a prospect of even greater troop losses,[1] President Harry Truman authorized nuclear strikes on the cities of Hiroshima and

Nagasaki. These attacks and a Soviet declaration of war forced Japanese leaders to an unconditional surrender.

Victory left America the world's sole nuclear power, but it did not end the arms race. Soviet Russia, an essential U.S. ally in World War II, moved to impose Communist regimes on the lands it occupied as it repulsed the invading German forces. Ensconced in Poland, Hungary, Czechoslovakia, and East Germany, Russia imposed its Communist systems and replaced Germany as a threat to the freedom of Western Europe. World War II gave way to a Cold War—decades of threatened confrontation between the United States and Russia with clashing ideologies, provocative geopolitical maneuvers, and the flexing of military muscle. In this atmosphere the U.S. Department of Defense (DOD), officially the War Department until 1947, conducted a range of nuclear tests that placed thousands of U.S. soldiers and citizens at unwarranted risk. Four months after Russia detonated its first nuclear device in August 1949, the DOD released a "ton of chemically treated, highly radioactive uranium" into the atmosphere from its Hanford, Washington, plutonium facility. The DOD wanted to test its ability to detect Russian weapons tests over long distances,[2] but, due to adverse weather, the "plume stagnated in the local area for several days," exposing parts of Washington and Oregon to unanticipated levels of fallout. The exposure of these U.S. citizens remained secret for nineteen years.[3]

The United States military continued nuclear tests from the closing of World War II until the 1963 Nuclear Test Ban treaty ended all but underground tests.[4] In the course of these tests and U.S. troop deployments to the destroyed Japanese cities, up to 380,000 American service personnel were exposed to varying levels of radiation. Perhaps the mass deaths of World War II and the potential for even more lethal Cold War conflicts hardened U.S. officials to the radiation risks to American servicemen. Certainly the tensions of the Cold War only increased during the testing period. The 1950s witnessed the specter of nuclear spies,[5] the paroxysm of anticommunism culminating in the shameful hearings conducted by Senator Joseph McCarthy (R-WI), and the shock of Russia's launch of the first space satellite. In this ferment, the U.S. Army,

Navy, and Air Force often exaggerated Soviet threats in an interservice competition to enhance their respective arsenals with nuclear weaponry.[6] Only the near nuclear confrontation of the 1962 Cuban Missile Crisis began to temper the nuclear arms race.

The DOD and the Atomic Energy Commission (AEC), which took control of atomic research and development in 1947, were keenly aware of the hazards of radioactivity to which they exposed American troops. The radioactive fallout at the initial New Mexico atomic test surprised American scientists.[7] Colonel Stafford Warren, commander of the medical section of the Manhattan Project, worked to cover up the effects of radiation after World War II. In a classified briefing in 1946 he warned, "You need only to absorb a few micrograms of plutonium and other long-life fission materials, and then know you are going to develop a progressive anemia or a tumor in from 5 to 15 years. This is an insidious hazard."[8]

The dangers of radiation became horribly evident after the August 1945 bombings of Hiroshima and Nagasaki. The Hiroshima burst killed some seventy thousand Japanese and twenty-three American POWs held in the city. But the bomb had a more deadly legacy—by the end of 1945 radioactive fallout and diseases resulting from degraded immune systems raised the city's fatalities to over 100,000. By 1950, the Hiroshima death count was estimated at 200,000. The same lingering threats stalked the exposed residents of Nagasaki.[9] Yet when American veterans, exposed to radiation by the DOD for test purposes, expressed alarm and sought relief, the VA responded defensively.

Exposure of Atomic Veterans—Tests and More Exposure

Within weeks of the U.S. atomic attacks, some 200,000 American troops deployed to Hiroshima and Nagasaki to aid in the occupation of Japan. Almost from the day American forces arrived, the U.S. military downplayed the impact of radiation on the Japanese. Afraid the growing radiation deaths in the two Japanese cities could foster the perception that America had utilized a "horror weapon," the military launched a concerted effort to conceal the atomic aftermath. Censorship became so all-encompassing that the supreme Allied commander in Japan, General Douglas MacArthur, closed two Japanese news agencies that reported fallout casualties. Within days of Japan's surrender, he "imposed a ban on *any* articles dealing with reports of atomic bomb damage."[10]

Resistance to later claims of radiation-induced sicknesses by American troops deployed to Hiroshima and Nagasaki began in this atmosphere of secrecy. Such censorship would cast doubt on all subsequent government claims that American military personnel suffered little or no radiation exposure in Japan. The desire for secrecy came from many directions. American scientists first believed that the blasts would cause 85 percent of the casualties and were dismayed at the levels of radiation poisoning in the weeks after the bombing.[11] Eventually scientists like Shields Warren concluded that radiation caused the majority of fatalities in Hiroshima and Nagasaki.[12] Army general Leslie Groves, who commanded the Manhattan Project, helped lead the deception campaign. Although "aware that thousands of Japanese were dying from medical complications caused by radiation," he assured the American public and the U.S. Congress that no Japanese suffered aftereffects from fallout. At one point he even claimed that radioactive poisoning "is a very pleasant way to die."[13] This was a bitter dismissal of Japanese pain and the pain of many U.S. veterans who would later suffer from maladies they attributed to their radiation exposure during deployments or nuclear tests.

In July 1946, the United States commenced postwar atomic weapons testing at the Bikini Atoll in the Pacific Ocean. In an operation dubbed Crossroads, the navy deployed two weapons against a fleet of mothballed and captured enemy ships while hundreds of naval vessels and thousands of men waited nearby to observe the blast or later enter the blast area, inspect the target ships, and collect data. One blast (Shot Able) occurred in the air and the second (Shot Baker) underwater. Baker gained a reputation as a dirty blast for its contamination of the testing area. The blast produced "a chimney of water half a mile in diameter" that rose from the middle of the lagoon. According to one veteran, "The flash seemed to spring from all parts of the [target] fleet at once," while at its "base a tidal wave of spray and steam rose to smother the fleet and move towards the island."[14]

Some forty-two thousand military personnel witnessed the Cross-roads explosions.[15] Although the DOD and the VA refused for decades to acknowledge that radiation exposure at Crossroads exceeded AEC standards, a number of participants reported contact with elevated radiation. Indeed, "not far from the blast, sensors on one of the islands registered 1,000 roentgens/hour, a spectacular level of radiation."[16] Naval commanders sent military personnel scrambling onto the target ships shortly after the detonations to clean up the radioactivity without the benefit of decontamination clothing. Other sailors drank tainted water because their ships' filtration systems could not fully eliminate all the radioactive particles. Some untargeted ships that entered the area remained so hot that the navy delayed their return to the United States until they "cooled off."[17] A few were sunk since they were too hot to scrap. Crossroads' veterans saw themselves as unwitting "guinea pigs" of a government focused on developing powerful weapons.[18] High-level military leaders, fearful of the liability that might be incurred from the Crossroads tests, soon scheduled secret meetings to discuss damage control.[19]

The outbreak of the Korean War and the precipitous initial retreat of the U.S. 8th Army after massive Chinese forces entered the conflict in the fall of 1950 fueled a call to develop and test tactical nuclear weapons. Fear that the war could spread beyond the Korean peninsula added to this urgency.[20] In an effort to assess how quickly troops could take advantage of an atomic battleground, the DOD pushed to move troops ever closer to test blasts or "until thresholds of intolerability are ascertained." Staff of the Armed Forces Special Weapons Project rejected the proposal, emphasizing that such a threshold could only be determined once troops suffered immediate, acute reactions.[21] Eventually, a group of volunteers witnessed an explosion from a mere fifteen hundred meters and troops deployed to ground zero within minutes of an atomic detonation.[22] In assessing risks, both the AEC and the DOD remained extremely closed-mouthed about the effects of breathing contaminated air, even though the AEC "knew internal doses posed a serious hazard" to the troops.[23]

Testing and Measurement

Early on, the DOD and the AEC determined that veterans would require exposure to more than five rems of radioactivity to suffer any ill effects (a rem is a measure of absorbed radiation multiplied by a factor determined by the type of radiation to gain an estimate of potential damage to human tissue). This standard represented a best guess with no scientific evidence of long-term effects. The VA's subsequent rationale for granting or denying medical treatment or compensation almost always rested on dose reconstructions based on the radiation badges worn by soldiers, sailors, airmen, and marines during the tests. Many vets never wore badges or reported that their badges were seized and discarded shortly after the tests.[24] According to one soldier who witnessed a 1952 blast,

> We waited for a couple of hours and then we were trucked to within one mile. At this point we were all issued film badges. They were pinned onto the front of our uniforms, chest high. We then marched toward ground zero.... We walked all around the ground zero area and were amazed at the destruction.... When we got back to the pickup area, Army personnel retrieved our film badges and threw them into a box. If there had been any irregularities with the badges, they would have never known who wore the badges. They were given out randomly without any type of identification as to who received which one.... That night we were debriefed, telling us what we could say and what we couldn't. We were allowed to express what we saw when the bomb went off, our feelings about it, but nothing about the size and power of the bomb and absolutely nothing about the paratroopers and what we saw at ground zero. We were told it would be a court

martial offense to do so. They also told us we hadn't received enough radiation to matter.[25]

Like many of his fellow paratroopers, Stanley Cook maintained that there was no effort to accurately measure the levels of radiation each man experienced. This failure became critical for later compensation claims. According to Cook, "Most of us were given film badges.... As I remember we walked right through ground zero.... We remained in the area for a couple of hours. We then walked past a Sgt. with a Geiger counter, if your reading was too high, two men with brooms swept you off. At that time the film badges were taken, never to be seen again."[26]

Sailor Tom Bair served aboard the USS *Curtis* and observed nuclear tests in 1952 and 1954. According to him, after each blast,

> The radiation measuring team would load up in small personnel boats and proceed to measure the amount of radiation on various flat barges and floats in the area.... On one mission, I jumped on a flat barge to measure radiation and all of my instruments pegged, then I jumped in the escape boat and we sped away. When I checked to see how much radiation I had been exposed to, they said my film badge and dosimeter both were so overexposed they could not determine how much radiation I had received. They recorded that I had been issued a defective film badge and a defective dosimeter.[27]

James Harmon assisted in the decontamination of the planes that dropped nuclear bombs. "Most of the time was spent in the open atmosphere, with the exception of when I would fly in the plane to observe and record the blast from the bomb. We would fly as close to the explosion as permitted for a period of approximately 15–20 minutes. Some members of our team were given a film badge, but only selected members of our unit got the device, on the assumption that the rest of the outfit would likely receive similar radiation exposures."[28]

Navy photographer Donald Byers claimed that after he got back to his vessel "we were checked with geiger [sic] counters. The counters had speakers and you could hear it, and they had a scale and you could see the needle go up.... We were told to turn in our clothes to the laundry and take showers.... I never had a film badge."[29] A declassified U.S. Air Force report cites a number of radiation injuries to servicemen recovering test filters following Operation Sandstone. The report notes that "No one had much faith in the dosimeters" and that several went "off scale."[30]

Veterans' reports, navy reports, and a later study by the Government Accounting Office (GAO) challenged DOD and VA assertions that no sailors received excessive radiation. Sailor Whitey Coker went "aboard the blasted ships checking on the damage and reading the instruments for the scientists" shortly after the atomic explosion. When he reboarded his own ship, he was checked with the Geiger counter. "The counter would start clicking and the needle would swing way over." He was ordered to take his clothes off and other personnel hosed him down with salt water from the radioactive lagoon. He then resumed checking the radioactive ships.[31] Second Class Petty Officer Edward Cushing served on the first ship that entered the lagoon after Shot Baker. He reported that "the large green dot on their badges had turned black" as they collected water samples. One sailor asked, "What number do I put in the book when the Geiger counter needle is higher than the meter's printed numbers and it's against the stop?" Sensing the great danger from fallout, an AEC observer aboard warned the ship's captain, "It's very dangerous for us to stay a minute longer.... I'll take all the responsibility for leaving." The captain quickly ordered the ship to leave the lagoon but the vessel was so badly contaminated that the navy later sunk it.[32]

Dennis Bentley maintained, "We were one of the first three or four ships to return to ground zero after the explosion of both Able and Baker.... When we stopped at 'Pearl' on our way home we had to flush all our salt water lines with acid. They were still radioactive. The civilian crew that was suppose [sic] to do the job refused to come aboard."[33] The fleet's own Radiological Safety Section reported that in 1946 "many persons received more than the permissible degree of radiation on a number of days, as indicated by the records of film badges."[34] This report was quantified when a GAO study released in 1985 estimated that some seventeen thousand personnel, or about 41 percent of those who served Crossroads, received heavier doses of radiation than claimed by the DOD in the 1980s. Moreover, only about 15 percent of the sailors wore radiation badges and few wore protective gear. The GAO found that the greatest risk arose for the sailors who actually went into the lagoon. In the words of the report, "Water in the lagoon was still radioactive down to 8 feet deep for two weeks after the blasts but it was still used by nearly 2,000 Navy personnel to 'scrape, scrub and wash the ships in an effort to get them down to acceptable radiological levels.'"[35] The Defense Nuclear Agency (DNA) rejected the report's conclusions.[36]

The Advisory Committee on Human Radiation Experiments (ACHRE), appointed by President Bill Clinton in 1994, later sharply criticized the AEC and the DOD for their claims that radiation badges demonstrated that most military personnel received minimal doses of fallout. The commission acknowledged that many soldiers did not carry badges and that in some cases they recorded higher doses than allowed by DOD or AEC standards. The commission also acknowledged that accurately determining the long-term health implications of radiation exposure of such a large group remained daunting due to the paucity of records.[37] As one atomic ex-marine quipped, "No one knows how to 'reconstruct a radiation dosage' estimate any more than we know how to reconstruct Sara's dosage at Sodom, before she became a pillar of salt."[38]

Cold War Pressures and Excessive Secrecy

The Pentagon transferred jurisdiction over atomic research and testing to civilian control with the creation of the AEC in 1947, but the military continued to push for experiments. The AEC insisted that the DOD scale back its demands for troop exposure, but army and marine officials asked the AEC to raise the acceptable levels of radiation exposure to demonstrate that troops could enter an atomic battlefield quickly.[39] Military leaders wanted many American soldiers to witness atomic blasts in order to "demystify" the process and conquer the almost-universal fear of radiation.[40] While exposing over 200,000 personnel to atomic explosions, the DOD also threatened participants with ten-year prison terms if they ever related their test experiences.[41] Such intimidation played a part in delaying claims by atomic veterans. Some feared retribution or even prison if they sought compensation from the VA over illnesses they considered radiation induced.

With many soldiers experimentally exposed to radiation, the issue of informed consent troubled some civilian military leaders. At the Nuremburg Trials of Nazi leaders, the United States championed the cause of informed consent. Given this precedent, in 1953 Secretary of Defense Charles Wilson ordered that soldiers must assent to participation in atomic experiments.[42] But informed consent is problematic in a military setting, where commanders expect troops to follow orders without question and "volunteering is often seen as a matter of duty and honor."[43] In the end, a relatively small number of "volunteers" formally consented to participation in nuclear tests.[44] In a "Catch-22" only the military could generate, the DOD classified Secretary Wilson's directive "Secret," effectively ensuring that military personnel would remain unaware of their right to consent to radiation exposure.[45] Given the VA's policy of granting veterans "the benefit of the doubt" in cases where conflicting evidence clouds the issue, does failure to warn American troops of potential risks support a presumptive right to compensation for their later health problems?

The unwavering denial by the DOD that veterans could have received dangerous levels of exposure is striking given the vigorous debate between the DOD and the AEC during the testing period. Atomic explosions that occurred at ground level produced high levels of local radioactivity and fallout. The ACHRE later discovered that the AEC warned the Pentagon that "no one should approach ground zero for three or four days" after a surface shot. Despite such warnings, some U.S. troops approached ground zero within four hours of surface detonations and remained there for over an hour. In another test, "Five days after the shallow underground shot, men crawled across contaminated ground, again to determine the effectiveness of protective clothing. Other men drove armored vehicles through contaminated areas to check the shielding effects of tanks and to check the effectiveness of air filtering devices."[46] Unfortunately, AEC leaders ultimately threw in the towel and allowed the military to "assume full responsibility" for exposing U.S. soldiers to levels of radiation beyond AEC recommendations.[47]

In the early 1980s, an atomic vet conducting research at UCLA discovered the secret papers of Stafford Warren. The account detailed his severe criticism of the military during and after the tests for its disregard of the dangers that radiation exposure presented to American forces. At one point, Warren railed about the "blind, 'hairy-chested approach to the matter of radiological safety'" by naval officers eager to measure the extent of radioactive contamination in the target ships just hours after their saturation with fallout. Warren pointed out that navy negligence allowed men to eat and drink contaminated food and water given that "every ship may have received significant doses of radiation."[48]

The ACHRE report noted the deep divisions within the government over radiation testing on human beings. Shields Warren and others asserted that it remained just as easy to test on animals and that tests like Crossroads were unnecessary to discover the effects of radiation. Of the two physicians named Warren, Shields emerged as the strongest advocate for troop safety. Colonel Stafford Warren, with the Manhattan Project, was less public in his criticisms and came under ACHRE scrutiny for his involvement in later plutonium experiments on uninformed human subjects. During all these discussions, government officials remained concerned with avoiding embarrassment and financial liability for harm to veterans. Clearly, secrecy to avoid Soviet intelligence gathering was not the sole guide for the DOD and AEC. Leaders in both organizations feared a future when thousands of down winders, veterans, and Pacific Islanders might successfully petition the U.S. government for compensation for their contact with fallout.

In the late 1980s, journalist Eileen Welsome of the *Albuquerque Tribune* began investigating radiation testing throughout the Cold War. Her work was greatly enhanced in 1993 when President Clinton directed the Department of Energy to declassify and make public a huge volume of documents from the testing era. Welsome published her findings in 1999 as *The Plutonium Files*. She argues that nothing is more destructive to democratic institutions than excessive state secrecy.[49] More than any other factor contributing to the immense disillusionment of atomic veterans and others exposed to ionizing radiation was the overweening confidentiality that surrounded the experiments. Many patriotic veterans could scarcely believe that their government would withhold information critical to their health on the basis of dubious national security interests.

Atomic Veterans Suffer

Almost from the beginning, some veterans exposed to atomic tests exhibited serious health problems, but more would suffer years later. It is easier to attribute health problems to radiation when illness occurs on the heels of exposure, but radiation damage may only manifest itself over time. Some servicemen experienced both immediate and later symptoms. In 1946, within two days of going ashore immediately after an atomic detonation, Anthony Guarisco experienced diarrhea, fever, and blood in his urine. When numerous welts appeared on his torso, he was admitted to a hospital ship. By age fifty-six, Anthony's symptoms were different; he had spinal, heart, prostate, bladder, and kidney problems.[50] Robert Stroup stated that two days after witnessing an atomic blast, "My eyes felt like I had sand in them and they were sore and I had floaters or spots go across my field of vision, which I still do at times. The fourth day after the blast I began to get sick, throwing up and diarrhea with a lot of blood." The military quickly discharged him. Nevertheless, he later reported, "severe PTSD, and severe ear problems, also, eye problems, bone and cartilage deterioration, and a nervous disorder. Five years after the test [he developed] a tumor in a testicle sack."[51]

Atomic vets displayed a wide range of ailments as they approached middle age. Andy Hawkinson, a military policeman who observed Pacific tests, reported that by age thirty-nine, physicians had removed seven cataracts from his eyes that he attributed to radiation exposure. Sailor Gerry Brauninger recounted that he acquired a malignant tumor in his mouth at age forty-three.[52] Sailor Ken Wessels went blind at age forty-six, developed cardiovascular problems, and lost most of his teeth by 1983. A physician from the National Institutes of Health (NIH) informed Wessels that his symptoms mirrored those of atomic survivors Wessels had studied in Japan after World War II.[53] Second Class Petty Officer Edward Cushing served on the USS *Barton* as it led the way into the lagoon after Shot Baker. He spent most of the time with his left side facing the water. His clothes became soaked with water from the lagoon as he took water samples. Like so many atomic veterans, he developed numerous health problems in later years. Cushing recounts:

> I have had several medical problems, on my left side. My left ear went dead. I had a growth removed from my left chest. My left testicle shrunk to half the size. I had a left hernia. I had a cancerous melanoma removed from my left leg. I went through a very serious mental depression, diagnosed as a chemical imbalance in the brain. I had my cancerous prostate removed. My left wrist aches. Both feet ache.... But the Navy would not acknowledge the Barton's crew having higher then normal medical problems. If the USS *Barton* wasn't still radioactive and a health hazard, it could have been used for scrap metal. But the USS *Barton* was used for target practice and was sunk.[54]

As the atomic vets grew older, the frequency of their bouts with cancer rose. Air force weatherman George Schultz participated in Operation Ranger in the Nevada desert in 1951 and later developed topical cancers and leukemia.[55] Army engineer Al Kelsch observed a blast from a close distance and then quickly moved to ground zero. In 1996, he developed prostate cancer, and attempted unsuccessfully to have his claim linked to his military service.[56] Paratrooper Marty Jacek witnessed an atomic detonation in 1951 in Nevada. He later experienced larynx cancer.[57]

Korean War vet Charles Christian also witnessed Nevada explosions. He later developed four diverse types of cancer. The VA denied his requests for compensation.[58]

By 1983, sailor John Smitherman had suffered from multiple cancers that resulted in the amputation of both of his legs. He had a large growth on his back and doctors speculated about amputating one of his hands. Smitherman argued that his introduction to fallout caused his many health problems. Two physicians concluded that his exposure to radiation injured his lymphatic system. His health problems began shortly after witnessing an atomic blast and the U.S. Navy granted him a medical discharge less than two years later. With the "burden of proof" squarely on his shoulders, Smitherman traveled to Hiroshima, where doctors who specialized in radiation-related illnesses supported his suspicions that fallout destroyed his health. Still, the VA rejected his claims for compensation five times, weighing the experts from Japan lightly while relying on two consultants who earned $200 to judge his assertions unworthy. "I don't think there is any compassion at the VA," Smitherman declared.[59]

The VA declined his seventh application for benefits several days after physicians diagnosed him with terminal cancer. The outside consultant who helped deny his claim, Harvard Medical School's Dr. William Bloomer, argued that Smitherman's cancer was common for his age group and that "on a statistical basis, there is no compelling evidence to indicate that it's radiation-related. I feel sorry for the guy, but the government and VA basically have to protect themselves in the long run."[60] Probably no statement better expressed the VA's attitude toward the atomic vets. "Compelling" evidence is hard to produce when a time bomb has a secret fuse. It is even harder to produce when the petitioned organization has its own compelling interest in avoiding claims for radiation-induced illnesses.

Tom Eberspecher served as a marine during the 1946 tests. He "experienced periods of fluctuating feeling from extreme heat to extreme cold" within two weeks of his discharge in September 1946. The condition disappeared after a year. In 1950, he developed a skin disorder and discovered "ulcers and canker sores in his mouth." In 1984, a pre-cancerous tumor was removed from his bladder. In 1987, he suffered a heart attack that required angioplasty and subsequently required eight additional angioplasties and open-heart surgery with four bypasses.[61] Could any of his later conditions be linked to atomic exposure? Was he predisposed to conditions that were exacerbated by radiation? How does one resolve one's suspicions when DOD and VA records are lost, destroyed, or kept secret or when radiation-detecting badges were not used, were discarded, or were collected so haphazardly that they cannot be matched with a veteran?

Evidently more than evidence of atomic exposure was required. Atomic marine veteran Charles Donahue contracted chronic myeloid leukemia and died in 1978. His wife continued to press his claim for damages. The VA denied her compensation in 1982 despite the fact that, in this unusual case, she could prove he experienced greater radiation exposure than the DOD's five-rem limit.[62] As the stories of the atomic veterans became public, more Americans supported their cause and more veterans came forward to report health problems developed after the atomic tests. Tom Eberspecher was not alone in spilling his bitterness: "The Japanese were compensated for the atomic bombs dropped in 1945. Felons at Washington State Prison in Walla Walla, Washington were compensated for radiation that they were exposed to during tests. The Bikini islanders were compensated. The servicemen I worked with were not compensated."[63]

Organized Veterans Meet Organized Resistance

By 1979, some atomic veterans realized that the government would take no action without concerted efforts to mobilize public and congressional support. They formed the National Association of Atomic Veterans (NAAV). The NAAV sought to advise atomic vets of the health dangers they faced from radiation exposure decades earlier and urged recognition and compensation by the Veterans Administration. By 1981, the NAAV counted 4,000 members, a mere 1 percent of the personnel exposed to radiation during Cold War tests.[64] By Memorial Day 1983, the NAAV boasted nearly 12,500 members and maintained that 39 percent suffered from cancer.[65]

If atomic veterans organized in the early 1980s, DOD resistance organized three decades earlier. In 1947, VA director General Paul Hawley met with several key government leaders, including Groves. In the meeting, Groves warned of the possibility that Crossroads personnel might file claims against the U.S. government for radiation exposure. The group formed the Central Advisory Committee to conceal "the fact that the Veterans Administration might have problems in connection with atomic medicine, especially the fact that there might be problems in connection with alleged service-connected disability claims."[66] The committee created a Veterans Administration Atomic Medicine Division, classified the committee's work, and endeavored to keep its labors secret. In the 1950s, Dr. George Lyon became special assistant for atomic medicine to the VA's medical director. Lyon erected a wall of doubt and evasion regarding the potential dangers of radiation exposure to American military personnel. The ACHRE uncovered an August 1952 letter to Lyon from the DOD that "called for comment on the Army's proposal to eliminate the requirement for maintaining detailed statistical records of radiological exposures received by the Army personnel." The DOD wanted the rule waived "to protect the government's interest in case any large number of veterans should attempt to bring suit against the government based on real or imagined exposure to nuclear radiation during an atomic war." Lyon ensured that no record of veterans' radiation exposure would surface. In 1952, he declared it "unwise to publicize unduly the probable adverse effects of exposure to radioactive materials." Lyon "maintained records of [a] classified nature emanating from the AEC and the Armed Forces Special Weapons project which were essential to proper evaluation of claims of radiation injury brought against [the] VA by former members of the Armed Forces engaged in the Manhattan Project." When the ACHRE sought such records it discovered that the VA had lost or destroyed most of the details from the era. In the words of the committee, "While mystery still remains, the documentation that has been retrieved indicates that prior to the atomic testing conducted in the 1950s, the government and its radiation experts had strong concern for the possibility that radiation risk borne by servicemen might bear longer-term consequences."[67] On stepping down, Lyon received the VA's exceptional service award. Was it for guaranteeing that thousands of atomic veterans would be denied benefits for decades to come?

The NAAV aimed much of its ire at the government's negligent record keeping. A large (one former high-ranking VA employee characterized it as "suspicious") fire in 1973 at the U.S. government's National Personnel Records Center (NPRC) in St. Louis, Missouri, destroyed sixteen to eighteen million military records, 80 percent of them records of U.S. Army personnel released from duty between 1912 and 1960. They included the accounts of many soldiers subjected to atomic testing and LSD experiments in the 1950s and 1960s.[68] At one point, a federal judge fined the VA $150,000 for destroying records in the midst of litigation over compensation for the atomic vets. As *Newsday* pointed out, it was the military's job to maintain military records. But when vets made claims for compensation and medical treatment, the government that lost their records denied their requests.[69] In 1998, Dr. Rosalie Bertell testified regarding the lost records of atomic veterans before the U.S. Senate Committee on Veterans' Affairs, "Normally, failure to retain evidence results in the assumption of maximum wrongdoing. I doubt that the IRS would forgive all back taxes if the taxpayer lost the records."[70]

As of 1983, of the 3,325 claims made by atomic vets since 1978, the VA had granted the benefit of the doubt to a mere 69 veterans.[71] While utilizing local and questionably qualified VA doctors to determine whether a veteran's illness resulted from ionizing radiation,[72] the decentralized VA lacked a consistent response to veteran claims. At one time, it cited "five different standards when resolving claims … leaving veterans hopelessly confused." Senator Alan Cranston (D-CA) characterized the VA approach to compensation as "schizophrenic."[73]

In 1985, as the VA continued to deny over 98 percent of atomic veterans' claims, Senator Paul Simon (D-IL) cited reports that one thousand atomic veterans were dying a year when he called on the U.S. government to take full responsibility for the health and future of the atomic vets.[74] The general counsel for the VA, Donald L. Ivers, denounced Simon's prescription as "a wicked extravagance," claiming that it would cost the government "an alarming $23 billion." *Washington Post* columnist Mary McGrory countered that the VA based its monetary estimate on *every* atomic veteran filing a claim, an absolutely unrealistic position.[75]

Based on a review of numerous official records and interviews with atomic vets and nuclear testing officials, *The Orange Country Register* concluded in 1987 that the DOD had "altered or discounted official descriptions and eyewitness accounts of troop movements at nuclear tests to support its position that radiation exposures were low." It also cited GAO conclusions that many troops wore defective film badges during the detonations, which "allowed the Pentagon to underestimate radiation exposure to troops." In a startling conclusion, the newspaper reported that the Justice Department, while agreeing that many veterans suffered excess radiation exposure, suggested that the government could invoke the shield of sovereign immunity because it had "the legal power to sacrifice lives to benefit national security."[76]

Frustrated with constant VA foot dragging, the atomic vets questioned that legal power in court. Their suit hit a brick wall—the Supreme Court's decision in *Feres v. United States* (1950). In *Feres,* soldiers or their families sought relief in cases of death or injury due to truly astonishing military negligence. In response the Court asserted, "We know of no American law which ever has permitted a soldier to recover for negligence, against either his superior officers or the Government he is serving."[77] As the atomic veterans pursued their claims, civilian personnel exposed to fallout in the western United States launched numerous lawsuits against the American government, as did Marshall Islanders, who reported alarming rates of thyroid cancer following the Pacific tests.[78] Both groups would eventually receive compensation.

Taking a cue from Vietnam veterans who sued the manufacturers of Agent Orange and received a settlement for their health problems (see Chapter 4), the atomic vets attempted to take legal action against the contractors who conducted the tests. They were thwarted in 1985 when, in a conference committee, Senator John Warner (R-VA), at the behest of the Reagan administration, inserted a clause into a defense bill that denied atomic vets the right to sue the contractors who directed the atomic blasts.[79]

There seemed to be no limit to the barriers constructed to deny atomic veterans. After Congress passed in 1984 the Veterans Dioxin and Radiation Exposure Compensation Standards Act, which aimed to compensate vets who received over five rems of radioactivity during the tests, the VA continued to rely on discredited government estimates of radiation exposure. Even if accurate badge data were still available, it would not measure the amount of radioactive material inhaled by troops, and later research confirmed that that atomic veterans suffered a higher-than-expected rate of nasal cancers.[80] In 1988, Congress passed further legislation to compensate atomic vets, but the legislation limited claims to certain cancers. On the same day that the VA announced it would finally provide medical treatment for atomic veterans, the deputy chief medical director of the VA, Dr. D. Earl Brown, acknowledged that the VA approved about 2 percent of atomic veterans' claims. The VA would maintain a compensation rate of fewer than 2 percent for the next decade.

Data Wars: The Struggle over Exposure Moves to Research

At the time that U.S. servicemen were exposed to atomic radiation there was no research on the long-term effects of exposure to low-level radiation—neither the claims of the government nor those of veterans benefited from good research. In 1983 claims and counterclaims heated up. The Defense Nuclear Agency (DNA) admitted to being contacted by forty-five thousand vets about radiation-related health problems, but continued to assert that the vets were exposed to "negligible amounts of radiation."[81] A 1983 study by the Centers for Disease Control (CDC) reported "significantly higher" levels of leukemia than expected among veterans who participated at Shot Smoky in Nevada in 1957.[82] On July 16, 1983, the day that President Ronald Reagan proclaimed "Atomic Veterans Day,"[83] the U.S. government released a report by the NAS that argued that there was no abnormal rate of bone cancers among vets who occupied Hiroshima and Nagasaki. The NAAV struck back immediately, arguing that it provided the NAS with information on thirteen known sufferers of the disease and six of them were ignored. In response, VA physician Victor Herbert accused the NAAV of lying about the information. The vets countered that the report was "medically criminal."[84]

Within days, the NAS and the VA came under withering criticism. The DOD paid a mere $19,000 for the study of less than twelve hundred atomic vets while refusing to conduct a large-scale epidemiological study of all atomic vets. Dean Emeritus Bernard Greenberg of the University of North Carolina School of Public Health, while not disagreeing with the report's conclusions, characterized the NAS methodology as "slovenly." Emeritus Professor Sidney Cobb of Brown University argued that no "self-respecting epidemiologist" could reach the report's conclusions.[85] The NAS only studied people who volunteered for the study and made no effort to examine the record of dead vets or those who had yet to come forward about their medical problems. Expressing the skepticism of many vets, a NAAV spokesman suggested that the Reagan administration and the DOD showed no desire to hear about radiation exposure while in the midst of launching a major increase in the American nuclear arsenal. Several members of Congress called for an independent analysis of the NAS report and, in December, the Office of Technology Assessment (OTA), the research arm of the U.S. Congress, argued that the NAS constructed its study in a way likely to underestimate the number of vets affected by radiation while finding fault with just about every aspect of the investigation.[86]

In response to the barrage of criticism the NAS returned to the drawing board and produced a study of forty-seven thousand "atomic veterans." The study concluded that atomic vets actually experienced lower rates of cancer than the general population. The second study may have been worse than the first. The study included fifteen thousand veterans never exposed to radiation and omitted some twenty-eight thousand who were exposed. In an article in *The Bulletin of Atomic Scientists,* sarcastically titled "No Matter What, Says NAS, Atomic Vets Are O.K.," the author noted that the NAS explained the huge discrepancies as "unintentional—the result of pressure to complete the work, the inexperience of the data gatherers, and the difficulties in obtaining complete and accurate records."[87]

The Advisory Committee on Human Radiation Experiments

The story of atomic veterans received its first comprehensive review when President Bill Clinton appointed the ACHRE in 1994. The commission took a broad approach, including all humans exposed to radiation by the U.S. government.[88] With respect to atomic veterans, the commission faced the dilemma of determining exactly what constituted an experiment, as opposed to normal training exercises. Risk remains inherent in military service and one could argue the U.S. government's right to perform experiments on military personnel in the name of national security. Still, the committee concluded that the exposures of atomic veterans did not meet modern standards of informed consent or some of the standards that existed at the time of the experiments. The committee also questioned the scientific value of the risky test exposures: "The bomb-test research illustrates the significance of the position that bad science is bad ethics."[89] With faint praise, the committee acknowledged that "The military took precautions, with great success, to preclude exposure to radiation at levels that might produce acute effects," but concluded that troops were exposed to long-term risks without precise record keeping or tracking and follow-up.[90] In one of its more damning statements, the ACHRE contended that the U.S. government entered into these experiments with no illusions. Indeed, the commission argued, "the government acted with full knowledge that the use of individuals to serve the ends of government raised basic ethical questions."[91] This declaration supported the contention of the atomic veterans that the U.S. government remained aware of the risks of fallout while accepting dubious ethical standards in deciding on the experiments. Many atomic vets and victims of radiation experiments found the committee's conclusions tepid given the damning information available to it. Internal friction within the committee had led to a compromise; they agreed that actions, not persons or institutions, would be judged wrong.[92] In accepting the committee's findings, President Bill Clinton issued a broad apology to all Americans exposed to radiation because of Cold War fears. In his statement on receiving the report he cautioned, "Let these pages serve as an internal reminder to hold humility and moral accountability in higher esteem than we do the latest developments in technology."[93]

Six years after the ACHRE report, the NAS produced their final study of the medical condition of atomic veterans, *The Five Series Study: Mortality of Military Participants in U.S. Nuclear Weapons Tests*. The study was *retrospective*; it looked backward, depending on the quality or lack of quality of data collected, or not collected, by others with no awareness of the needs of the research. A *prospective* study would have been much stronger. That would have required the VA or the DOD to have good records and to track exposed veterans and an appropriate sample of unexposed veterans going forward following their health histories, treatments, and any cause of death using well-constructed protocols. The option of a responsible prospective study was never considered by the DOD or undertaken by the VA.

The number of atomic veterans in *The Five Series Study* was huge and the methodology careful, but the findings could be no better than the data. The controversial "dose data" was considered unsuitable for research and health and death records were less exact than wished. While the study reported "no statistically significant differences are evident in all-cause, cancer" between the sample of atomic veterans and a sample from the general population, the researchers did find more cases of leukemia in the sample of atomic veterans (with a greater incidence in veterans exposed to land tests rather than sea tests). The researchers acknowledged that the increase in leukemia was "consistent with a radiogenic cause,"[94] but noted that the sample would need to be much larger to establish a statistically significant rise in leukemia among the veterans. The atomic veterans did show significantly elevated rates of death due to external causes of injury, nasal cancer, and prostate cancer as compared to the general population. Because these were not conditions that the researchers would have predicted from radiation exposure, they were cautious about making any linkage.

The researchers noted that the failure to find statistically greater mortality in the overall comparisons "might be a comfort to those veterans who are not sick and to their families," although they acknowledged they could not rule out possible increased risk among distinct subgroups. The researchers also noted that the data they used was not going to get any better and that it was "unlikely that another cohort study of this type and magnitude would provide more precise answers."[95]

In retrospect, although thousands of servicemen suffered unnecessary atomic exposure, the number of radiation casualties was not as great as might have been feared. This is of no solace to the veterans who suffered serious illnesses and whose personal conviction was that their illness was related to their exposure. The ACHRE report noted that the government's obligations "to limit risk, to consider who should bear the risk, and to inform the public, while recognized, were often subordinated to concerns for national security, which were sometimes joined or melded with concerns for public relations." They note the damage "caused by the initial secrecy, however well motivated, and by subsequent failures to deal honestly with the public thereafter." The ACHRE describes the ultimate result for the DOD and the VA as a "legacy of distrust."[96] In many ways the legacy became mutual. Many veterans and much of the public learned that the government was quick to put other interests, including public relations, before the health of veterans. The VA bureaucracy also became quite practiced in distrusting veterans' claims and compromising their principle of granting veterans the "benefit of the doubt." Sadly, the legacy of distrust developed in the era of atomic veterans was preserved as subsequent veterans came forward with complaints resulting from their service in Vietnam or the First Gulf War. The VA also failed to observe the most critical lesson to be learned for the atomic veterans—the need for research on veterans' claims and health problems—Epidemiology 101. Such an approach could have helped enormously in addressing the critical needs of Vietnam and Gulf War veterans. The care of veterans, not collusion in Defense Department errors, is the primary mission of the Department of Veterans Affairs.

CHAPTER FOUR

Agent Orange

By Peter Berres

I contacted my wife and told her that I had just spent my worst day in Vietnam,
and that for the first time, I had cried in Vietnam....

Bob "Doc" Topmiller[1]

MY FRIEND DOC TOPMILLER did not write the quote above during one of his horrific days at Khe Sanh, but in an e-mail to his wife Terri after he visited Thuy By (School of the Beloved), a Buddhist treatment center for children handicapped by Agent Orange. In 2002, Doc worked up the courage to confront the ravages of Agent Orange on the children of Vietnam.[2] It was a pivotal experience. Thich nu Minh Tanh, the dynamic, compassionate Buddhist nun who directed Thuy By and its rural outreach, guided Doc into villages and homes where he was moved to his core by the children he met and by their families' efforts to care for them amid deprivation that challenged their own survival. Doc wrote of a teenager who could only flop along the floor like a fish to greet him. He remembered four disabled children at Thuy By from one family.[3] The effort and concern he witnessed in Vietnam contrasted sharply with his own experience in seeking an evaluation at the VA for possible Agent Orange symptoms. He wrote:

VA health care workers remained more interested in convincing me that no health risk could be linked to Agent Orange than in discovering if I had any significant physical problems. I had to wait for months for an appointment and the doctor who examined me would not answer my questions or communicate with me in any meaningful way. At one point during the physical, VA employees required me to view a video that claimed no evidence existed that Agent Orange caused health problems, a statement that flew in the face of a substantial body of opinion and the VA's own acknowledgement of Agent Orange linked diseases.[4]

Doc discovered that such resistance and cynicism was familiar to many veterans seeking relief from the VA. His efforts to educate fellow veterans and the public about Agent Orange redoubled after his exposure to the damage wrought in Vietnam. Doc wrote bitterly that "the massive ecological attack carried out against the Vietnamese people in the form of chemical defoliants represented the most egregious American wartime action and an undertaking for which the US never acknowledged much responsibility."[5]

In subsequent trips to Vietnam, Doc "adopted" the Thuy By school, providing it with financial support and visiting it to replenish his commitment to his classroom lectures and presentations. He dedicated *Red Clay on My Boots* "To the Sick Children of Vietnam." The present volume continued his concern for Vietnamese children damaged by Agent Orange—half of the eight pages he sketched for this chapter focused on Vietnamese victims of Agent Orange, particularly those born with defects three generations removed from the war.[6]

History of Agent Orange

Agent Orange burst into world consciousness with the war in Vietnam. The United States and (to a lesser extent) South Vietnamese forces began using herbicides in 1961 to defoliate forests and mangroves that hid the

North Vietnamese and Vietcong, to clear protective perimeters around U.S. or South Vietnamese military installations, and to destroy crops needed by the enemy. Eventually they released nearly twenty million gallons in Southeast Asia, mostly in Vietnam, but also in border areas of Cambodia and Laos. Along with napalm and blanket bombing, the use of herbicides came to symbolize a "total war" mentality that tolerated massive "collateral damage"—civilian and environmental.

In the heady era of post–World War II progress, America enjoyed the fruits of many scientific and technical advances. Among these advances were new chemicals that promised everything from easy cleaning to insect control. Some of these chemical promises later proved to have serious downsides. In the case of the herbicides later known as Agent Orange, problems came early, but for reasons of profit, military advantage, and politics, key players gave little attention or publicity to the problems. In 1955, the German chemical company Boehringer contacted Dow Chemical Company about disfiguring chloracne and liver problems in their employees at a plant that made 2,4,5-T, a key ingredient in Agent Orange. The source of the problem was dangerous dioxins created as a by-product of 2,4,5-T. Unlike U.S. chemical companies, Boehringer halted production and conducted a thorough study. By 1957 they discovered they could limit dioxin contamination in the herbicide by cooking the chemicals at lower temperatures. Such cooking slowed production. Dow purchased Boehringer's proprietary information on slow cooking in 1964 and started using it in 1965. They failed to notify other manufacturers or the government about the technique until 1967.[7] Like the chemical companies, military scientists began experimenting with herbicides in the 1940s, but changed priorities in the late 1950s curtailed some of the government programs and left the military dependent on chemical companies for assessment and technical guidance.

The herbicides used in Vietnam were nicknamed for the colored bands painted on their 208-liter storage barrels. Agent Orange contained one of the most dangerous of the chlorinated dioxins, 2,3,7,8-TCDD (or TCDD). A diabolical toxin that attaches itself to the fat cells of humans and animals, TCDD can remain in the body for decades. A cell's nucleus is normally protected by a defensive perimeter that prevents molecules lacking the right structure from entering the nucleus. But within cellular cytoplasm, dioxin blends with a component that is naturally present in every cell, the aryl-hydrocarbon receptor, and is able to enter the nucleus by "passing itself off" as a hormone.[8] Scientists think that once present, TCDD binds with cell proteins known as Ah receptors, which can trigger molecular events that affect cellular growth, potentially leading to cancer and other illnesses. Researchers also hypothesize that dioxins can alter the regulation of genes, leading to changes in DNA and therefore genetic defects.

About 65 percent of the herbicides used in Vietnam contained the active herbicide 2,4,5-T,[9] which was contaminated with varying levels of TCDD.[10] White, Blue, Purple, Pink, and Green agents used in Vietnam also contained 2,4,5-T, while Agent Blue contained arsenic. The dioxin TCDD is so toxic that it is often measured in parts per billion or trillion while many other agents are measured in parts per million. Reports suggests that TCDD is capable of killing some species of newborn mammals and fish at levels of five parts per trillion (or one ounce in six million tons).[11] Since Agent Orange constituted the majority of mixtures used, *Agent Orange* will be used here to refer to the class of herbicides containing dioxins.

Agent Orange in Vietnam

My dad, John Berres, a retired army colonel, was with the Fourth Infantry Division at Pleiku, Vietnam, in 1967. He remembers watching the planes spray Agent Orange around his firebase: "They would turn off the spray at the perimeter, fly overhead, and resume the spraying on the other side of the perimeter. Due to the momentum of the aircraft and wind, I would feel the liquid fall on me."[12] Apart from their historical dedication to independence and reunification, perhaps the best asset for North Vietnamese and Vietcong forces was Vietnam's landscape, particularly the triple-canopy jungle, which hid movements and provided cover for ambushes. To neutralize the vegetation advantage, defoliation efforts were concentrated around American firebases, along the northern demilitarized zone (DMZ) and the Ho Chi Minh Trail borders of Laos and Cambodia. Earlier dubbed Operation Hades, the defoliation effort later became Operation Ranch Hand;[13] it is not clear whether the change to a less ominous name was to soften growing awareness of the herbicide's dangers. Even as the United States ratcheted up troop levels and the spraying of Agent Orange over South Vietnam in 1965, "the government and the chemical companies that produced the defoliant knew it posed health risks to soldiers and others who were exposed."[14] What the military knew and when they understood the dangers associated with dioxin-contaminated herbicides is still being uncovered and debated, though it is clear that the military did have sufficient information to realize that Agent Orange involved risks early in the 1960s as it commenced its use in Vietnam.

> When we initiated the herbicide program in the 1960s, we were aware of the potential for damage due to dioxin contamination in the herbicides. We were even aware that the "military" formulation had a higher dioxin concentration than the "civilian" version due to the lower cost and speed of manufacture. However, because the material was to be used on the "enemy," none of us were overly concerned.
>
> —*James Clary, former scientist with the Chemical Weapons Branch of the Air Force Armament Development Laboratory*[15]

If scientists weighed the dangers of toxins, there was little or no concern among U.S. troops in Vietnam about Agent Orange. The 3.2 million American soldiers who served there had a general trust in science, understood the military use of the herbicides, and expected judicious use of chemicals by their government. Spraying DDT to control mosquitoes was a daily summer occurrence in many towns and army bases in the 1950s. Many troops, especially second-generation vets, could remember riding their bikes through mists of DDT when they were kids. One could smell, taste, see, and feel the spray of Agent Orange, but it provoked little alarm and was valued for its potential for saving American lives. The immediacy of combat creates a myopic perspective in which it is unrealistic for soldiers, even their commanders, to consider long-term environmental impacts or illnesses in later life, much less long-term generational birth defects. A pervasive racism, tendency to dehumanize the enemy, and anger at being in Vietnam[16] all helped minimize American concern for any long-term effects of defoliants in Vietnam. American soldiers were unaware that the defoliants could have a devastating, even lethal, reach into their own futures, even into succeeding generations.

> Former Marine Danny Gene Jordan remembers sitting on Hill 549 near Khe Sanh in the spring of 1968, waiting for night and cooking his C-rations. Jordan had been in country just a few weeks and was still learning his way around, so he wasn't sure why the five C-123s approaching his unit would be flying so low and in formation. "They're defoliating," one of his buddies told him. Then came the mist, like clouds floating out of the back of the C-123s, soaking the men, their clothes and their food. For the next two weeks, the men of Jordan's unit suffered nausea and diarrhea. Jordan returned from Vietnam with an unusual amount of dioxin in his system. More than 15 years later, he still had 50 parts per trillion, considered abnormally high. He also had two sons born with deformed arms and hands.[17]

Unfortunately, Danny's story would be told again and again in later years by U.S. veterans who were seriously ill or whose children were born (and died or survived) with major deformities. Similar stories would also be told by huge numbers of Vietnamese.

The United States reduced use of Agent Orange in late 1969 when the following message was sent to the operational commanders for Vietnam:

A report prepared for the National Institutes of Health presents evidence that 2,4,5-T can cause malformation of offspring and still-births in mice, when given in relatively high doses. This material is present in the defoliant (Agent) Orange. Pending decision by the appropriate department on whether this herbicide can remain on the domestic market, defoliation missions in South Vietnam using Orange should be targeted only for areas remote from population. Normal use of White or Blue herbicides can continue, but large scale substitution of Blue for Orange will not be permitted.[18]

Operation Ranch Hand ended in 1971, soon after the U.S. surgeon general halted all domestic use of 2,4,5-T.

The VA's Response to Agent Orange

The story of VA reactions to veterans' health issues begins with the discharge process. My own experience at the point of discharge from the U.S. Army in August 1970 involved a separation physical. Troops, eager to expedite their last days in the service, lined up for physicals and rushed through documents standing between them and civilian life. Each soldier was directed, without explanation, to sign the bottom of a one-page form and then proceed to a line where the physicals began. Having suffered wounds in Vietnam and experienced a violent physical reaction to pain meds for the wound, I, unlike most in front of me, chose to read the form. It stated, "I verify that I am departing the military in the same health condition with which I entered the service." The exit physical, which began with a waiver of military responsibility for my health, consisted of the standard drill—weight and height measurements, a look at ears, nose, and throat, and a check of heart rate and blood pressure. At best, the assessment was cursory. There was no opportunity to discuss my history, any wounds I suffered, or future health issues. We surrendered our documents to the file clerk and happily cleared the building to begin our lives as veterans of the United States military. Some vets had already compromised the paper trail needed to establish later claims with the VA. I still had the waiver form in my pocket.

With the end of the war, any lingering "concerns" about the use of Agent Orange seemed to subside. The story of the VA and Agent Orange resembles the VA's negative response to atomic veterans. Veterans seeking help or redress for exposure to toxic herbicides were initially treated as "free-loaders" and rarely afforded the "benefit of the doubt." Then, in the 1970s, Maude de Victor, a VA benefits counselor in Chicago, became concerned about a veteran who died of cancer he attributed to Agent Orange. She began to gather data that suggested a pattern of illnesses related to Agent Orange. Chicago papers picked up the story and in 1978 a special report, "Agent Orange: The Deadly Fog," aired on CBS.[19] Agent Orange inquiries and disability claims mushroomed at the VA and concerned groups began to meet. Agent Orange emerged as a new specter from a war that most Americans, and the VA, wanted to forget.

In many ways 1978 was a watershed year for the Agent Orange controversy. In response to the "Deadly Fog" story, the VA reported that only 27 of the 2.5 million claims it processed in the previous year were herbicide related. In May of that year the VA issued a memo stating that only the skin condition chloracne could be accepted as related to herbicide, that reported neurological symptoms were "fully reversible," and that staff should avoid making file entries connecting veterans' complaints and herbicides.[20] Also in 1978, Paul Reutershan, suffering from stomach cancer:

- Hired a lawyer and initiated the first lawsuit against makers of Agent Orange;
- Helped found and organize Agent Orange Victims International (AOVI);
- Recruited a dynamic veteran, Frank McCarthy, to lead AOVI after his death;
- Inspired McCarthy's much-publicized Memorial Day confrontation with President Jimmy Carter regarding the need for a thorough study of Agent Orange; and[21]

- Died on December 14 in deep debt from his medical bills and organizing efforts.

Ironically, Reutershan's core supporters were organized out of the Veterans of Foreign Wars (VFW) office in Stamford, Connecticut. At that time the national VFW, dominated by World War II vets, strongly supported the VA's denial of claims for injury due to Agent Orange.[22] Still, late in 1978, the VA established a computerized Agent Orange registry to track illnesses related to Agent Orange. It is not clear whether they directed their claims staff to ignore their earlier memo prohibiting file entries linking illness with Agent Orange.

The Growing Indictment of TCDD Dioxin Poisoning

In 1979, pressure by veterans helped move federal legislation requiring an epidemiological study of veterans exposed to Agent Orange and create a National Veterans Commission on Agent Orange. The study was assigned to the CDC. That same year, the Environmental Protection Agency (EPA), the government agency that had no problem taking TCDD seriously, banned the use of Agent Orange due to an alarming rise in stillbirths in an area of Oregon where the herbicide was being liberally used.[23] In addition, employees of the Norfolk and Western Railway won a suit related to dioxin exposure in which thirty-two of forty-six plaintiffs were awarded at least a million dollars apiece. By 1979 the initiative begun by Paul Reutershan and pursued by Frank McCarthy had enlisted the services of Victor Yannacone, Jr., the lawyer who had led the fight to ban DDT, resulting in the filing of a class action suit against five herbicide manufacturers in U.S. District Court for the Southern District of New York.[24] In 1983, the EPA confronted the contamination in Times Beach, Missouri, where dioxin-laced oil was used to spray the town roads. The EPA bought 801 homes for $33 million and fenced the area, turning Times Beach into a ghost town. Later in the year the EPA identified 200 locations nationwide for critical dioxin cleanup. The year 1983 also saw the number of state commissions to study Agent Orange rise to nineteen; the publication of a Swedish study linking TCDD to soft tissue sarcoma and non-Hodgkin's lymphoma;[25] and the publication of *Waiting for an Army to Die: The Tragedy of Agent Orange*—Fred Wilcox's compelling account of the impact of Agent Orange on Vietnam vets and their failed struggles with the VA.[26]

Meanwhile, the growing consortium of plaintiffs and lawyers in the federal suit were pushing forward and the chemical companies were pushing back. Ironically, the chemical companies were forthcoming about many dangers of Agent Orange, but only to protest that they had warned the military in a timely fashion and therefore exonerate themselves by placing liability on the military. For example, Dow told the *Chicago Tribune* it had shared information with the military as early as 1949 and throughout the 1960s.[27] Although the federal government is subject to some suits, the military is protected from liability claims by the *Feres* doctrine discussed in the previous chapter. The chemical corporations also alleged that they were protected from suit as government contractors, although that legal stratagem did not succeed on this occasion. In 1984, federal judge Jack Weinstein brokered a controversial agreement in which the chemical companies provided $180 million in compensation to the Agent Orange plaintiffs.[28] The decision was immediately appealed by a number of parties.

Ultimately the 1984 court decision withstood the challenges of appeal, but the apparent victory soon gave way to disappointment. Judge Weinstein had made provision for inclusion in the settlement of both those veterans and their families who had opted out of the original settlement and those whose illness would become manifest only after the suit. The inclusion of this last group limited new cases to those manifest before 1994. The volume of claims was so high (in the range of 50,000), that individual claimants rarely received more than $5,000.[29] This figure stands in sharp contrast to the million-dollar settlements awarded most plaintiffs in the Norfolk and Western Railway suit. The subsequent history of veterans' efforts to find relief through the courts, including the efforts of the many whose illnesses became evident after 1994, is complex, but the bottom line is that they have proved expensive but futile. Most simply put, the courts have granted the chemical companies protection from further suits from vets based on the companies' status as government contractors. Such immunity has developed over the years to protect companies that enter into major contracts with the military, some of which may require risky innovations. Immunity, of course, does not encourage responsibility.

Still the growing evidence of the dangers of TCDD did not seem to touch the VA. Perhaps they were bolstered to stand firm by the Reagan administration, which seemed determined to avoid paying Agent Orange compensation. Further support came from an air force study published in February 1984. The air force research, named Operation Ranch Hand II, tracked the health of a small number of military personnel who personally handled and sprayed the chemicals during the war. The air force study concluded that 1,269 pilots and crewmen involved with the spraying of Agent Orange suffered no higher death or serious illness rates than the general population. The study did not include representatives of the large number of U.S. soldiers or Vietnamese soldiers and civilians who were exposed, directly and indirectly, to the spraying. "To Vietnam veterans, studying aircrews who had handled drums of Agent Orange, and not the soldiers exposed to it, was like testing the Enola Gay [the plane that dropped the A-bomb] for the effects of radiation, not the survivors of Hiroshima."[30] Meanwhile, the CDC made no progress on the epidemiological study mandated by Congress in 1979. Their researchers repeatedly cited problems in finding the necessary data to proceed, although the military insisted the necessary data was available. In 1987 the CDC would "exonerate" Agent Orange on the basis of inadequate data. The NAS and the Institute of Medicine (IOM) were highly critical of the CDC's efforts. It was later discovered that staff of the Reagan administration edited incriminating material out of the air force report. In 1990 the U.S. House Government Operations Committee released a report charging that the Reagan administration also purposely "controlled and obstructed" the CDC study. On the heels of the House report, the American Legion and the Vietnam Veterans of America filed suit in the U.S. District Court in Washington, D.C., in August 1990. They alleged a White House cover-up of the cancellation of the CDC research and sought to have the research go forward.

Congress Steps In

Besieged with complaints from veterans and veterans' organizations and frustrated with questionable research, Congress passed Public Law 102-4, the Agent Orange Act of 1991. The law sought to resolve growing confusion about the long-term health effects on Vietnam veterans who during their service in Vietnam were exposed to herbicides 2,4,5-T and its contaminant 2,3,7,8-TCDD. The legislation created a list of "presumptive illnesses" for which veterans could be compensated and directed the secretary of Veterans Affairs to ask the NAS to perform a comprehensive evaluation of scientific and medical information regarding the health effects of exposure to Agent Orange, other herbicides used in Vietnam, and the various chemical components of those herbicides, including TCDD. The resulting committee report, *Veterans and Agent Orange: Health Effects of Herbicides Used in Vietnam* (VAO), was published by the NAS in 1994. That report evaluated and integrated the scientific evidence regarding statistical associations between health outcomes and exposure to the herbicides and TCDD, based on published literature that had accumulated prior to 1994. As required by the law, the secretary also asked the NAS to review studies on the chemicals found in the herbicides, to update their reviews every two years for ten years from the date of the first report, and to recommend additions to the list of covered conditions. Diseases or birth defects were to be added if exposure to defoliants was more likely than not to increase a person's risk. Between 1991 and early 2010, the VA added to the list fifteen diseases and seventeen birth defects in the children of female veterans, but veteran groups say as many as a dozen additional illnesses could be associated with the herbicides, as could numerous birth defects in the offspring of male vets. In 2003, the VA began providing disability compensation to the children of veterans who suffer from any of the recognized birth defects.

After updates on Agent Orange conditions in 1996, 1998, and 2000, the Veterans Education and Benefits Expansion Act of 2001 extended the biennial updates until 2014. The 2008 report was the second of the second ten-year series. The review committee assigned each health outcome to one of four categories of relative certainty of association with exposure to the herbicides that were used in Vietnam or to any of their components or contaminants. Based on the 2008 report, retired army general Eric Shinseki, the new secretary of the Department of Veterans Affairs, announced in 2009 that three new illnesses would be added to the list of Agent Orange conditions for which veterans could be presumed eligible for benefits—Parkinson's disease, B-cell leukemia, and ischemic heart (or coronary artery) disease. The last addition produced a strong reaction on Capitol Hill. Senator Jim Webb (D-VA), a Vietnam veteran and strong veterans' advocate, expressed concern that "presumptions have expanded to include common diseases of aging," and that the costs could be enormous. In connecting ischemic heart disease to Agent Orange the NAS had moved it from the category of "insufficient evidence" to "limited or suggestive evidence."[31] To some, that seemed too weak to justify the costs. Senator Webb succeeded in requiring the delay of such payments until sixty days after implementation of new VA regulations for ischemic heart disease. The VA published regulations allowing Vietnam vets to be compensated for ischemic heart disease on October 30, 2010.

Breakthrough Research

After many failed efforts to develop data that could tie TCDD exposure to veterans making claims, Dr. Jeanne Stellman, professor emeritus at Columbia University's School of Public Health, led a study that the CDC had earlier suggested was impossible. Stellman also improved on the 1974 data used by the NAS as a basis for challenging the CDC's pallid efforts. Aside from her research skills, Stellman brought to the task a determination and persistence apparently lacking in the 1980s efforts. Critical of earlier methodology, Stellman utilized the previously ignored daily logs filed by pilots after missions. By developing maps of spraying and time frames, researchers could tell whether particular military units or populations were present in a given zone on a day of spraying or whether they arrived later. It was now possible to assess direct exposure and indirect exposure to Agent Orange.[32] In the course of exploring flight records in the Armed Services Center for Research of Unit Records, Stellman's team discovered a wealth of other useful data. Most importantly for veterans, using the most sophisticated computerized maps ever produced of herbicide spraying in Vietnam, it became possible to calculate an exposure index accurate enough for epidemiological research linking Agent Orange with health data. Stellman's team calculated the index by compiling a computer database that overlaid staggering amounts of data, including flight-path information, the amount and type of agents delivered, troop locations and movements, the location of Vietnamese populations, land features, and soil types. The data even accounted for exposures caused by leaks, crashes, and dumps of excess herbicide. Stellman also estimated that millions of Vietnamese were directly exposed to Agent Orange. In 2010, Stellman expressed concern that the critical studies connecting the best data on the spraying of Agent Orange and the health status of exposed troops have yet to be done.[33]

Even with Stellman's sophisticated data, the potential exposure of many veterans remains undocumented, especially in the areas where the herbicides were stored or spilled, or where storage barrels were misused by unsuspecting troops. Both reports by the *Chicago Tribune*[34] and the *U.S. Veteran Dispatch Staff Report*[35] describe the creative uses of barrels that stored the herbicides. Barrels that contained allegedly "harmless" defoliants were cut in half and used for barbecuing; they were used to store water for showers or filled with fuel or lubricating oil for motor vehicles. Exhaust from vehicles using contaminated fuel was suspected in an investigation of defoliation along many roadways near the air base at Da Nang. Only in October 1969 did army scientists at Fort Detrick,

Maryland, forward an urgent message to the military command in Vietnam providing instructions on the cleaning of herbicide drums, particularly warning of the need to clean Agent Orange drums.[36]

Does Good Research Really Help?

Although Stellman's research makes it possible to evaluate soldiers and civilian populations on the receiving end of the spraying, providing important verification for both military and civilian claims, the VA has not officially accepted her work as a basis for guiding their claim decisions. Research challenging the devastating impact of Agent Orange also persists. In 2004 a team of researchers drawn from several disciplines argued:

> The historical record does not support the position that Vietnam veterans were widely exposed to Agent Orange.... The circumstances in which spraying occurred were carefully controlled, and as a result, spraying of troops with Agent Orange in Vietnam was highly unlikely.[37]

The report goes on to assert that "much of the Agent Orange sprayed was intercepted by the upper forest canopies, and that under most conditions, the TCDD in the material sprayed had a half-life of a few hours. Moreover, applications of herbicides were spatially precise and involved optimal amounts of herbicide necessary to achieve the desired result. Thus, the opportunity for widespread chronic exposure of civilian populations to TCDD was limited." The authors were not above adding barbs for those who disagreed with them, "A wider view of potential causative factors and recognition that TCDD exposure may be much less than generally assumed can release medical resources and scientists from the grip of the 'Agent Orange problem' and re-focus resources toward the real causation of health problems."[38] Those of us who served in Vietnam or have studied it carefully can attest to the chaotic, imprecise nature of the war. Accuracy, precision, and truth are complicated by accidents, misunderstandings, in-difference, contrived data, and even malicious intent. It is not surprising that such a sanitized version of the problem should emerge in research that acknowledges the "financial support of the Dow Chemical Company and the Monsanto Company" in the "preparation and publication of this article." Amazingly, no reference is made to Stellman's work.[39]

The slowly growing list of conditions for which veterans can be compensated reflects an increased understanding of dioxins and their action on exposed victims. As was the case with atomic veterans, scien-tists are starting to understand the latent nature of illness due to toxin exposure. For many exposed veterans, the reality is that diseases are becoming manifest in themselves and their children. Some vets lament that VA policy, reflected also in the experience of atomic veterans, is based on waiting for veterans to die. New and pending claims for com-pensation related to Agent Orange are now competing with the huge influx of claims from veterans returning from Iraq and Afghanistan. As described later in Chapter 8, the VA's claims backlog is daunting. Agent Orange claimants worry that their cases will get lower priority, especially since the slow processing of Iraq/Afghanistan claims is already causing congressional unrest.

In 2009, Secretary Shinseki announced a new three-year study of Agent Orange by the VA. He acknowledged that an adversarial relation-ship has developed between many veterans and the VA. Hopefully the study will make the best use of the best data and finally provide a better basis for compensating veterans and their offspring victimized by Agent Orange. As mentioned above, the secretary's addition of a common heart disease to the Agent Orange list produced congressional pushback. Secretary Shinseki may improve the VA's response to Agent Orange, but the system will not be efficient or just; the statute of limitations for using those adjectives expired some time earlier. As many veterans who suffer from Agent Orange maladies approach old age and the end of a "natural" life expectancy, they still fear their illnesses may persist in their children and grandchildren, either in the form birth defects and deformities (some unfolding only gradually) or in the fear of such defects.

Research indicates that the children of exposed veterans have a small but significant likelihood of suffering birth defects and that such likelihood may be increased based on a parent's TCDD level.[40] The National Registry of Birth Defects (www.birthdefects.org) maintains a section on veterans with links to research information. The VA does provide compensation for some defects and a Health Administration Center (HAC) provides a toll-free number where families can obtain information and additional help (1-800-820-1756). Sharon Perry, who watched her husband succumb to a cluster of Agent Orange–related illnesses, also raised two daughters with bewildering handicaps and worries about problems in a new grandson. Sharon and her oldest daughter have created a website (www.agentorangelegacy.ning.com) "to unite the children of Vietnam veterans who have AO related illnesses, and others who want to advocate for more research and resources for them."[41]

The Devastation of Vietnam

The Vietnamese estimate that 2.1 to 4.8 million Vietnamese civilians were exposed to toxic herbicides by the end of the war and over a million Vietnamese have physical disorders brought on by Agent Orange. According to officials from the Dong Nai Health Service, there are 1,333 cancer patients for every 100,000 residents in the Bien Hoa area of Vietnam.[42] In the emotional wasteland of postwar realities, many Vietnamese tend to rely on Agent Orange's legacy to account for any birth defect. The 2009 *Chicago Tribune* series on the legacy of Agent Orange documents the profound impact the toxin has left in South Vietnam. The series describes the early emergence of birth defects through the eyes of Dr. Nguyen Thi Ngoc Phuong, a young obstetrician working in a hospital in the former Saigon:

> In 1968, two years after U.S. forces expanded the use of herbicides by millions of gallons, Phuong said she delivered a baby born without a brain or a spinal cord. In the next few months, she said, she

delivered dozens of infants with equally severe deformities, three or four a week—babies born with organs on the outside, with no arms, no legs, no eyes. "It was very horrible for me and my colleagues," she said, her voice cracking as she wiped away tears. "The first case happened on my duty. I didn't show the mother because I was afraid she would go into shock. But the father and other family members demanded to see, and it was horrible."[43]

The *Chicago Tribune* series goes on to describe almost unimaginable tragedies in Vietnamese families—families who suffered multiple stillbirths in efforts to have a child only to have one, two, or more children with profound deformities. In a culture with a great emphasis on ancestor worship, the desire for children is great, and some families persist in the face of such frightening outcomes. Unlike U.S. troops, who left their risk of further exposure when they left Vietnam, in a number of areas of Vietnam TCDD exposure has been both intense and sustained. In 2000, Hatfield Consultants, a small, independent Canadian environmental firm, identified twenty-eight "hot spots" including three highly contaminated sites around population areas in Da Nang, Bien Hoa, and Phu Cat. These names are familiar to most veterans as points of arrival and departure for so many and as the airbases where chemicals were stored and spraying was initiated. At Bien Hoa, the largest air base, seventy-five thousand gallons were spilled by accident in 1970. Vietnamese and American scientists measured toxic levels in soil on the base at levels one thousand times higher than the globally acceptable standards—the highest ever measured in Vietnam.

The Hatfield group traced toxins through the food chain, from soil and sediment of nearby ponds to the fat of ducks and fish to the blood and breast milk of villagers living on the contaminated site. They found dioxin levels in the blood and breast milk of workers at Da Nang airport that were one hundred times higher than World Health Organization safety guidelines. Considered to be the most persistent toxin known, dioxin has a half-life of decades in the environment and in the human body a half-life of about 7.5 years.[44]

The United States now has normalized relations with the united Vietnam, but financial assistance from the United States to help clean up toxic sites or help suffering Vietnamese is sparse. Vietnamese efforts to secure help through the U.S. courts have failed. The EPA provides significant technical assistance as a way of contributing to efforts in Vietnam. In June 2009, the Congressional Research Service quoted cost estimates to clean up the Da Nang air base at $17 million; while Vietnamese authorities estimated it will take about $60 million to clean up the war-related hot spots. Several nongovernmental agencies and charities, including the Ford Foundation, have made Agent Orange a focus and provided $11.7 million to date. Cleanup costs and compensation are clearly far beyond what the United States in any form, public or private, will ever provide.

In a country currently involved in Iraq and Afghanistan and where few news stories can hold public attention for long, America has moved well past concerns with Vietnam. This makes continuing efforts to secure help for Agent Orange vets and their families more difficult. America's concern with the suffering of the people of Vietnam is even more remote. Doc's personal pain was deeply linked to Vietnam's children of Agent Orange and his was a lonely crusade. When Doc first decided to return to Vietnam, it was for personal and scholarly reasons, but his exposure to the children of Agent Orange changed him. "As I fought my way through a firestorm of guilt, disbelief, and depression, I became determined to find a way to confront Agent Orange."[45] Doc embarked on an emotional, a financial, and a physical journey to lend a hand to the sick children of Vietnam. His healing became inextricably linked to theirs and he came to link America's own cultural and national healing to Vietnam. It was a perspective rooted in Doc's soul, but that few others could share. His work with Agent Orange issues in Vietnam and his personal dedication to several schools and orphanages became a center for his scholarship and personal commitment.

In the United States we can scan maps of areas of Vietnam impacted by Agent Orange, but in Vietnam, the legacy of Ranch Hand is still visible in environmental degradation and in shocking human deformities, especially the birth defects of children. Like Doc, this chapter's author has returned to Vietnam a number of times. In December of 2008, I accompanied a group of students on a study tour from the University of Kentucky as we drove (south) from Hue to Hoi An. North of the former Da Nang air base the incredibly green and rich foliage suddenly gave way to sand and scrub vegetation. The students were stunned by the change. We stopped and, as they walked gingerly on the dead sand, our guide recited depressing statistics for the abnormally high rates of cancer and other illnesses around Da Nang, rates linked to Agent Orange. Agent Orange was to be the focus of the students' next step. After learning of Doc's visits to Thuy By and his subsequent adoption of the school (reading *Red Clay* was a trip requirement), the UK students prepared to risk what they expected to be their most challenging experience, to visit the school.

In Doc's tradition, we purchased candy, cakes, and juice to take with us, along with a DVD player, a gift in honor of Doc. I introduced myself as Doc's friend, which brought tears to the teachers who fondly recalled his gentle presence. The children duplicated their attempts to entertain us, much as Doc described in *Red Clay*. We returned the favor by dancing the Hokey Pokey, to their confused delight and applause. We sat with them on the floor, helped them open their packages of treats, and felt their hands all over our bodies, seeking human contact. It transformed the experience for us from dreadful to extraordinary. I presented a copy of *Red Clay on My Boots* to Thich nu Minh Tanh, the intrepid nun Doc so admired. She turned the pages featuring photos of the school, teachers, and children and tears came to this stoic woman who had more reasons to cry than most of us ever will. At that moment she needed to mourn the loss of a friend of the children, the school, and her country. As the children eagerly posed for pictures with their visitors from Kentucky, we felt emotionally drained, but surprisingly uplifted. In the parting ceremony, we were taken to the shrine erected in Doc's honor. Following the nun's lead, each student lit incense and offered up a private prayer. The author emptied a spice jar containing Doc's ashes into the incense bowl before the shrine.

CHAPTER FIVE

Gulf War Syndrome

For it's Tommy this, and Tommy that, an' "Chuck him out, the brute!"
But it's "Savior of 'is country" when the guns begin to shoot;
An' it's Tommy this, and Tommy that, an' anything you please;
An' Tommy ain't a bloomin' fool—you bet that Tommy sees!

From *Tommy* by Rudyard Kipling

KIPLING'S POEM ABOUT BRITISH SOLDIERS hailed in wartime and scorned in peace may resonate with many veterans of America's Persian Gulf War of 1990 to 1991. Their actual predicament, however, might be captured in a brief science-fiction scenario. Imagine that our government sends an exploratory team of two hundred skilled specialists to Mars in 2050. On returning, a fourth of these well-screened men and women suffer a strange disabling sickness. How should the nation respond to these space pioneers? Certainly, their symptoms should be taken seriously. Thoughtful research should focus on possible causes and cures for their illnesses. They should receive the best treatment available and be compensated for any disabilities that persist. Officials might not understand their disease, but given their previous health and the numbers affected, it would be foolish to assume their suffering was unconnected to their Mars venture. Yet space officials of 2050, obsessed with their image and potential liability for ill astronauts, publicly exonerate themselves and challenge any link between the

Mars mission and the illnesses. Because current medical books cannot account for these maladies, space agency doctors give short shrift to the astronauts' accounts, award them psychiatric diagnoses, and imply that they are slackers looking for benefits.

In a nutshell, this science-fiction tale mirrors the story of thousands of American veterans of the 1990–1991 Persian Gulf War. The strange planet they visited was Iraq. Not the everyday Iraq in which the people experience the troubling illnesses and hardships of a hot, arid Middle Eastern country, but a more hazardous wartime Iraq replete with toxic environments—external and internal. Among toxins in the external environment are chemical warfare agents, insecticides, depleted uranium (DU), and windborne residues from burning oil wells. Hazards carried inside the troops include vaccines to prevent anthrax and pyridostigmine bromide (PB) to blunt reactions to the nerve gas sarin. These substances, not tested to U.S. Food and Drug Administration (FDA) standards,[1] were administered to unprecedented numbers of servicemen and women in the 1990–1991 Gulf War. Many veterans who visited "planet Iraq" came home ill. The military and the VA were painfully slow to take their reports seriously or investigate the nature of their illnesses. Doctors evaluating the veterans doubted that they could be dealing with anything unexplained by "current medical knowledge" so they stretched existing diagnoses to fit, especially psychiatric diagnoses—often with clinical notes suggesting the vets were malingering.

The First Signs of Gulf War Syndrome (GWS)

Although forces from 34 nations participated in the Persian Gulf War, the large majority were from the United States. Iraqi forces were soundly defeated while 148 U.S. troops were killed in direct combat and 467 were wounded.[2] The outcome was considered a triumph for American forces, their strategy, and their weapons systems. In the wake of victory celebrations, however, it became apparent that the conflict generated a huge number of delayed symptoms—affecting "at least one fourth of the

697,000 U.S. veterans who served in the 1990–1991 Gulf War."[3] The varied collection of symptoms displayed by veterans of the First Gulf War came to be known as Gulf War Syndrome (GWS).

In her book *Gulf War Syndrome: Legacy of a Perfect War,* Alison Johnson recounts a litany of such casualties—military personnel who returned home with an array of physical problems, many of which increased in severity over time. Some of these veterans remembered in great detail when their symptoms first occurred. Staff Sergeant Willie Hicks, a Vietnam veteran and former teacher, heard a loud explosion early one morning in January 1991. He assumed it was an incoming missile. He instantly felt sick and soon discovered his urine was pink with blood. Members of his outfit also became ill. Hicks estimated, "Of the unit's 100 soldiers, 85 later suffered medical problems." When he returned to the United States and reported his symptoms, the VA claimed that he suffered from PTSD. Despite the psychological diagnosis, his symptoms included "headaches, blood in the urine, insomnia, joint and muscle pain, disorienting vision, loss of mobility in his left arm, night sweats, and diarrhea (sometimes bloody)."[4] Petty Officer Sterling Symms, a member of a U.S. Navy Seabee unit, reported a thunderous detonation in January 1991 followed by a "sharp odor of ammonia in the air." He said, "his eyes burned and his skin stung." Though members of his outfit donned chemical gear for close to two hours, officers assured him it was only a sonic boom, not a missile. Symms later "experienced fatigue, sore joints, runny nose, a chronic severe rash, and open sores which have been diagnosed as an 'itching problem.'"[5] A member of the same outfit, Mike Moore, experienced more serious symptoms, which emerged after he returned from the war—"a severe thyroid problem, a heart attack, memory loss, tired and aching joints, rashes on his feet, nervousness, and muscle cramps."[6] Terry Avery, another Seabee in the area, heard the same blast. Like Hicks, he had served in Vietnam and doubted the explosion was a sonic boom. On returning home, Avery "began feeling tired and having headaches, and later endured fatigue, headaches, weight gain, itching, muscle and joint pains, and memory loss."[7]

The DOD feared that forces entering Iraq might run afoul of chemical or biological agents. Many units had chemical weapons detectors. A number of veterans insisted the detectors indicated the presence of nerve or mustard gas in their campsites and that some soldiers suffered physical reactions immediately or soon after. Within two or three days of such an incident, Roy Morrow claimed, "unit members began to suffer from rashes, diarrhea and fatigue." After the conflict, Morrow suffered "swollen lymph nodes, fatigue, diarrhea, night sweats, low grade temperature, weight loss, aching joints, muscle cramps, rashes, (transient) blisters, welts (2–3 times a month), a permanent hand rash, and short term memory loss."[8]

In February 1991, a sergeant awoke Specialist Valerie Sweatman. He told her the unit was on alert and ordered her to put on her chemical gear. She heard no explosion, but the next morning, "her hands were itching from the wrist on down" and she "developed little blisters which went away about a week later." Like a number of vets who suspected they were exposed to chemical agents, Sweatman's initial symptoms were followed by "nausea, diarrhea, and bloody stools." Back in the United States, she endured "headaches, exhaustion, fatigue, memory loss, nausea, muscle and joint pain, rectal and vaginal bleeding and rashes." The VA eventually diagnosed this collection of complaints as arthritis and PTSD.[9]

Retreating Iraqi soldiers set fire to many of Kuwait's oil wells. Soldiers struggled to breathe as they moved through areas near the burning oil fields. At times the smoke was so thick that headlights of military vehicles could not penetrate beyond ten feet. Drivers stopped to wipe oil from blackened windshields. Troops could only breathe through "doubled-up scarves."[10] A number of these veterans reported nagging to severe respiratory problems after the war. British sergeant Ann Shelby grieved, "I can't walk for long distances without my lungs filling up with fluid because your lungs try to protect you by producing more fluid. So basically what happens is that I start choking or coughing on the fluid after I've walked a little while."[11]

Beleaguered by biting insects, which could carry infectious diseases, soldiers often sought relief by lathering themselves with pesticides, either what they were issued or what they could find. They bought pesticides in Saudi Arabia, Bahrain, or other rear areas, where many of the insecticides sold were banned as hazardous in America. Some even resorted to wearing flea collars or used industrial strength DEET. Used in most insect repellants, physicians caution against concentrations of DEET because of its toxicity. A RAND Corporation study reports that overuse of pesticides was common and in some cases "extreme." In an area with large numbers of biting insects the study's authors suggest it is no surprise that soldiers would "be tempted to use whatever means was available to remove the pests."[12]

One group of soldiers blamed their later illnesses on chemical-resistant paint utilized by U.S. forces during the war. When American forces arrived in the region they repainted their vehicles to desert camouflage with CARC (Chemical Agent Resistant Coating). The 325th Maintenance Company, untrained in the use of CARC and without protective gear, rushed to spray paint vehicles in enclosed tents. Some painters suffered almost immediate health problems, complaining of "headaches, nausea, vomiting, and dizziness, along with respiratory problems."[13] Of 200 members in the unit who took part in the painting, 163 reported postwar health problems. Later investigation suggests that most illnesses related to CARC were within the 325th, but the VA did not track or summarize the CARC data. The Research Advisory Committee on Gulf War Veterans' Illnesses (abbreviated as RAC) found that CARC could be a contributing factor to some GWS, but CARC exposure was far too limited to account for the large volume of Gulf War illnesses.[14]

A final suspect in the mystery of GWS is depleted uranium (DU). A byproduct of enriched uranium, DU is denser than lead and has properties that enable shells to penetrate armored vehicles like tanks and then ignite. When a DU round detonates it produces uranium oxide, a deadly carcinogen. Smaller particles of uranium oxide can be inhaled. While humans discharge some 90 percent of the substance in a few days, "The 10% of DU in blood that is not excreted is retained by the body, and can deposit in bones, lungs, liver, kidney, fat and muscle." The kidney is particularly vulnerable to ingested uranium and uranium can lodge in the bone marrow and other major organs.[15] Exposure to DU is hard to substantiate and the path to longer-term consequences is hard to track. In the Gulf War, the United States reintroduced the risks of radiation exposure onto the battlefield with uncertain repercussions.

Tragically, the threat to U.S. forces did not abate with the end of hostilities. Seeking to limit Iraq's future military capacity, the army continued destroying Iraqi weapons, including the huge weapons depot in Khamisiyah. Soldiers from engineering units of the 82nd Airborne took several days to destroy the Khamisiyah stockpile. They were instructed that any chemical weapons would be specially marked but didn't find such markings. They also never received a CIA warning that the Iraqis did not use special markings—a notice sent as they were in the midst of the destruction process. Low on explosives near the end of their work, the engineering units chose to disable rather than completely destroy some munitions. Munitions that were broken up rather than totally incinerated probably released more chemical agents.[16] A number of troops near or downwind from explosions triggered at Khamisiyah developed severe health problems. For five years, the DOD denied there were any chemical arms in the Khamisiyah dump, even though military leaders were informed by the CIA and the UN that the storage area contained chemical weapons.[17]

Soldiers who served in or around Khamisiyah received letters six or more years later divulging their possible exposure to the deadly nerve gas sarin. Many were suffering well before their exposure was acknowledged. In his book *Veterans Under Siege,* journalist Martin Schram recounts the story of Army Specialist Bill Florey of the 82nd Airborne. Parked near the site of the Khamisiyah explosions four days later, Florey was given the day off because of continuing fallout from the infamous "plume" that followed the multiple Khamisiyah explosions. He "figured he'd wait it out near his tent." After the dust and debris got worse, he moved inside his tent and "when the dust and bad air seeped into and filled the tent, he pulled a tarpaulin over his head."[18]

Four years later, Bill Florey commenced his battle with a rare and aggressive cancer that began in his parotid gland. As it spread, Florey endured an open hole in the side of his neck, lost part of his jaw, and was left with a gaping hole in his skull that required constant dressing as the cancer continued to assault his brain. During the eighteen months before he died, Florey and his advocates tried repeatedly to obtain disability benefits from the VA. Payments would have permitted Florey to help his grandparents, who provided constant care over his last year. The VA, however, like the imaginary government doctors of our opening Mars mission, asserted that "current medical literature does not support an association or a relationship between environmental hazards found in the Gulf War and mucoepidermoid carcinoma of the parotid gland." Florey's claim was denied and his further efforts also failed. Maybe the VA response to Florey was worse than the Mars example. Schram reports that, "at the very moment that the VA was sending Florey his routine claims denial" it already had research demonstrating that brain cancers were linked to nerve agents released at Khamisiyah.[19]

Nature of Symptoms

Symptoms reported by veterans of the First Gulf War vary greatly and no symptom clusters seem firmly connected to particular agents or experiences. There are, however, many commonly reported symptoms—skin rashes, burning sensations, nausea, diarrhea, and blood in the urine are among early symptoms. Prominent among later symptoms are fatigue, intestinal and respiratory problems, joint pain, and a range of neurological and memory problems. Symptoms of GWS were also reported by veterans from other nations. Czech troops reported similar symptoms but a monitoring system for them was shut down in 1994. Though chemical alarms sounded in many Czech units, the possibility of illness due to low-dose chemical exposure was discounted by both Czech and U.S. officials. In a statement that Alison Johnson says "might have been scripted by the Pentagon," a Czech military doctor explained that the Czech soldiers' problems were "80% psychological" because, "these chemicals either kill you or leave you alone."[20]

More serious is the high rate of terminal tumors and neurological diseases among veterans of the First Gulf War. An increase in brain cancers occurred among those exposed to Khamisiyah fallout, but such serious illnesses have not been confined to that group. Retired Gulf War veteran U.S. Air Force brigadier general Thomas Mikolajcik was diagnosed in 2003 with ALS, the fatal, degenerative nerve condition known as Lou Gehrig's disease. General Mikolajcik said a 2001 study shows that Gulf War veterans are twice as likely to have ALS as the general population.[21]

Problems the Military Anticipated

Unlike the planners of the imaginary Mars trip, the DOD anticipated some of the hazards experienced in the First Gulf War. Anthrax inoculations were given on a large scale.[22] The DOD sought a waiver from Food and Drug Administration safety standards to permit its massive use of PB.[23] The PB capsules were issued in case of exposure to soman, a lethal nerve gas for which preventive measures are critical. Troops were also issued protective clothing and chemical weapons detectors. Coalition forces established fourteen thousand chemical detection stations in the region, which reportedly averaged two alarms per day during the war.[24] Doc Topmiller's oldest son, who served in the Gulf War, told his dad that chemical alarms went off almost every day. Though PB was to be used only on orders from superior officers, alarms may have sent many troops to their blister packs of PB capsules. Troops from France and the Czech Republic reported frequent dangerous readings on their chemical weapons detectors.[25] In some areas the chemical weapons alarms sounded so often without apparent reason that troops began to ignore them.

In January 1991, before the Gulf War ground attack started, U.S. Army intelligence warned:

The danger of oil fires, toxic gases, and smoke in the Kuwaiti Theatre of Operations (KTO) is very serious.... By far the greatest danger is from disassociated hydrogen-sulfide gas and highly volatile light ends [gases] released from well head blow-outs. In the KTO, the prevailing wind generally blows from north northwest, southward toward Saudi Arabia. Smoke and gases from Kuwaiti fires and blowouts will most likely be blown in the face of northerly advancing forces along the southern front of the KTO.[26]

Army studies showed the danger of inhaling smoke and hydrocarbons from oil fires. One report warned, "an extensive literature review by the author has found petroleum exposure associated with the following symptoms: cancer, fatigue, breathlessness, cough, skin rash, headache, diarrhea, weight loss, memory loss, immune suppression, chemical sensitivity."[27]

Large-scale use of inadequately tested medications, chemical alarms, masks and protective clothing, burning oil in the KTO, the continued use of controversial depleted uranium—what other risks did the military anticipate on planet Iraq only to later deny as possible causes of GWS?

Early Investigations Flawed by Military Denials

Information on the large number of Gulf War veterans suffering from a "mystery illness" began to emerge slowly, but by 1992, the press referred to "Gulf War Syndrome" and Congress mandated a study of the phenomena by medical experts. The study by the National Association of Science's IOM was not funded until late in 1993 and their work did not begin until 1994, the same year that the DOD and the NIH published reports of their own. The study by the DOD's Defense Science Board (DSB) trumpeted the low casualties of the Gulf War, which the authors suggested, "probably put into relief the residual health problems" reported by veterans after the war. The report also concluded that

There is no scientific or medical evidence that either chemical or biological warfare was deployed at any level against us, nor that there were any exposures of US service members to chemical or biological warfare agents in Kuwait or Saudi Arabia. We are aware of one soldier who was blistered, plausibly from mustard gas, after entering a bunker in Iraq during the postwar period.[28]

What the report failed to mention was that there was considerable "intelligence evidence" of such exposures.[29] Considering the high levels at which this report was approved, it is hard to assume that suffering vets were not betrayed by official deception. If not at the level of the DSB, information about Khamisiyah must have been available to those who provided data to the board or to those who authorized the report. The NIH panel, operating in similar darkness, made recommendations for better data collection and studies providing for the "retrospective simulation of exposures of possible health interest; research into potential stressors;" and "development of effective responses to diagnosis and treatment of stress-related conditions."[30]

The DOD offered no better information to the congressionally mandated studies conducted by the IOM. In its first report, the IOM echoed a refrain from studies of atomic vets—that the DOD failed to provide sufficient data to document veterans' possible exposures. The IOM considered most of the environmental factors mentioned at the beginning of this chapter—fumes from burning oil (their initial charge), vaccines, PB capsules, and insecticides. The report identified important areas for further investigation, including the need "to resolve uncertainties about whether PB, DEET, and permethrin have additive or synergistic effects ... suggestions that they may have chronic neurotoxic effects need to be tested in carefully controlled studies in appropriate animal models."[31]

The second IOM report proceeded with considerable caution. It noted that "individuals would have experienced illness during this period whether or not they were in the PGW [Persian Gulf War], whereas the health complaints of others might be a result of their PGW service. However, there is no way to determine which veterans fall into the former group." The report repeated another mantra that recurs in studies of veterans' health issues, the need for ongoing epidemiologic studies.[32] The experts who prepared the report were clearly aware that this was a long-standing need:

> As far back as World War I, and perhaps antiquity, every war has left a proportion of service personnel and veterans with serious medical complaints that cannot be explained on the basis of known health hazards or identified physical illnesses. This pattern is so consistent, and the health problems are so important, that databases and health information systems should be designed and implemented now to deal with and mitigate similar problems that are likely to arise in future conflicts.[33]

The IOM traced the concerns over Gulf War illnesses beginning with reports of individual veterans, proceeding to "outbreak" studies that looked at military units where there was a high incidence of symptoms, and then moving to registries created by a VA call for veterans to come forward voluntarily and report symptoms. This approach continued to underestimate the scope of Gulf War illnesses, but did not alter a tone of skepticism in the IOM report:

> Veterans who have voluntarily participated in these registries have not been found to have any unusual rates of diagnosable conditions but do report a pattern of symptom complaints similar to that seen in the outbreak studies.[34]

Early Clinical Responses by the VA

The IOM report explored the possibility that "'Gulf War Syndrome' may result from leishmania infection." This is a serious illness in the Gulf region transmitted by sand flies (one reason troops were supplied with powerful pesticides). The report noted that a dozen veterans were diagnosed with leishmaniasis, although there are no good blood tests for leishmania and the veterans' symptoms only partially matched those in the literature on leishmaniasis.[35] But it was not the leishmaniasis diagnosis that VA clinicians stretched most often to fit Gulf War illnesses; it was psychiatric diagnoses. The Defense Department's DSB report, the NIH report, and the 1996 IOM report all suggested that stress could be involved in many of the veterans' symptoms. The DSB report emphasized the mix of great heat and the need to wear protective combat gear as a primary stress, while the IOM report provided an extensive list of stresses for those deployed in the Gulf, which "creates a picture of an extremely stressful environment, filled with the dangers and trauma of war, combined with a hostile living and work environment."[36]

Faced by symptom arrays with which they had little experience, VA clinicians fell back on the familiar. Psychiatry has a history of sweeping unexplained physical symptoms into the psychiatric realm. Indeed, there is a psychiatric diagnosis named "somatization disorder" that readily covers broad collections of unexplained symptoms similar to GWS.[37] A problem with that diagnosis is that onset is usually in the early teens and it is diagnosed almost exclusively in females. But if such symptoms were psychological, who was to say they could not be engendered by stress? Some military psychiatrists suggested that the fear of chemical and biological warfare was so acute among vets that it could play a major role in the outbreak of post-Gulf VA referrals.[38] A common diagnosis among early vets presenting with GWS was PTSD.[39] Sometimes joint pain or intestinal problems received independent diagnoses such as arthritis or gastrointestinal labels. Still there was a measure of clinical suspicion often associated with the PTSD diagnosis, since the stresses of the Gulf War seemed so much less than those experienced by Vietnam vets. Alison Johnson speculated:

A party line seems to have disseminated throughout the VA system. Why else would ill veterans who went to VA hospitals in various areas of the country so frequently see the same language appearing in their medical evaluations, language like "Patient is malingering for secondary gain."[40]

Some VA staff clearly resisted this trend. Dr. William Baumzweiger, a neurologist and psychiatrist formerly at the VA outpatient clinic in Los Angeles, concluded that, because most Gulf War vets suffered insufficient stress "to precipitate PTSD," they suffered neurological conditions due to "environmental intoxication."[41] There was actually a tendency in some VA hospitals for mental health professionals to attribute GWS to medical problems while specialists in internal medicine assigned the problems to the realm of mental health.[42]

Low-Level Exposure to Chemical Agents

Apart from the exposure to sarin belatedly acknowledged at Khamisiyah, it was not unusual for Gulf War veterans to believe that they were exposed to low levels of chemical agents in the Gulf War theater. After all, they were issued protective equipment and medicines because of the threat of chemical agents. Chemical alarms sounded regularly in some areas. A number of veterans also experienced symptoms shortly after explosions or attacks believed to be Iraqi artillery or missiles. Such missile and artillery attacks did not constitute the only possible source of chemical warfare agents. At the onset of the conflict, American aircraft bombed Iraq's chemical weapon stockpiles and production sites.[43] In the process, the U.S. military introduced large quantities of nerve and mustard agents into the atmosphere. American personnel could have ingested traces of these lethal substances, given that thousands of U.S. troops camped in the region as they prepared to liberate Kuwait.[44] In 1996, before Representative Christopher Shays's (R-CT) House Committee on Government Reform and Oversight, the DOD assistant secretary for health affairs, Dr. Stephen Joseph, testified, "Current accepted medical knowledge is that chronic symptoms or physical manifestations do not later develop among persons exposed to low levels of chemical nerve agents who did not first exhibit acute symptoms of toxicity."[45] As with the Czech military doctor mentioned earlier, there were no shades of gray for the DOD. Among toxicologists, however, there is a maxim, "The dose determines the poison." Dr. Joseph's testimony was challenged by other medical experts and rejected by the committee.

Given the speculation in the IOM report about cumulative or synergistic effects of PB and pesticides, the possible presence of additional neurotoxins, even in small amounts, was critical health information. Veterans reported exposures, but the IOM report was clearly ambivalent about veterans' self-reports. The report encouraged clinicians to listen to soldiers for leads, but suggested they were poor sources for reliable data. An awareness of the potential for traces of neurotoxins in the atmosphere might have given some veterans' self-reports greater weight. Such lack of information about potential chemical exposures was not due to lack of effort. In early 1996, a committee of the U.S. House probingly grilled John Deutch, deputy secretary of the DOD, on whether there could even have been "accidental" exposure of troops to chemical agents in the Gulf. Deutch wavered briefly but stood firm in resisting any implication of troop exposure to chemical weapons.[46] Three years earlier, Deutch had suggested to a committee chaired by Senator Donald Riegle (D-MI) that DOD information on chemical exposures was classified. That testimony prompted Senator Riegle to send a letter to Secretary of Defense William Perry asking that any DOD documents regarding chemical or biological exposures be declassified. On May 4, 1994, the secretaries of Defense, Health and Human Services, and Veterans Affairs responded to the chairman's letter, stating that there was "no classified information on chemical or biological detections or exposures."[47] While the DOD remained emphatic in denying the presence of chemical warfare agents in the theater, they offered no plausible explanations for the frequent sounding of their own chemical alarms.

Research Initiatives from
Outside the Government

The plight of veterans suffering GWS symptoms concerned many outside the federal government. A research team headed by Dr. Robert Haley at the Texas Southwestern Medical Center in Dallas was pursuing investigations of GWS. In 1994, Texas billionaire and former independent presidential candidate H. Ross Perot was moved by the Gulf veterans' struggles. Perot, an ardent opponent of the Gulf War, donated $2 million to Haley's effort. In the January 15, 1997, issue of the *Journal of the American Medical Association (JAMA)*, Haley and his team published a meticulous evaluation of twenty-three veterans with GWS symptoms and twenty control subjects. He identified three patterns of symptoms among the GWS vets, all consistent with "a generalized injury to the nervous system."[48] In a second study in the same *JAMA* issue, Haley associated the patterns respectively with the wearing of flea collars, with PB use, and with a combination of PB and pesticide use.[49] A third article from the University of Iowa surveyed over thirty-six hundred vets and found highly significant differences between Gulf War vets and other vets in ten diagnostic areas, including chronic fatigue, cognitive function, bronchitis, and fibromyalgia.[50] None of these pioneering studies was supported by DOD or VA funds.

Dr. Haley's group has since garnered federal funds, but in August 2009, the VA cancelled a $75 million contract with the Texas Southwestern Medical Center to pursue further research on Gulf War Syndrome. The VA made allegations of "persistent noncompliance and numerous performance deficiencies" and the research team countered the allegations.[51] At the least, the dispute makes clear that research controversies over GWS are not going away. After hearings on the status of Gulf War research, the House Veterans' Affairs Oversight and Investigations Subcommittee issued a press release (July 31, 2009) in which Chairman Harry Mitchell (D-AZ) declared, "The future and direction of this research is vital because the questions surrounding the science continually impact the claims, benefits, compensation and treatment of veterans."[52]

Congressional Initiatives

As in the case of the atomic veterans, the United States Congress, the government branch that usually receives the worst public approval ratings, was most proactive in addressing Gulf War Syndrome. As early as 1992, congressional requests led to the 1995 and 1996 IOM reports.[53] A series of high-profile hearings called by different members of Congress highlighted the issues of Gulf War illnesses. The testimony and reports of these hearings—in small print, on flimsy paper, and unbound—sit in the archives of major libraries like collections of old magazines. These rarely read documents detail startling accounts of the betrayal of our fighting men and women, and unsparing critiques of agencies charged with responsibility for them.

In 1993, the Senate Committee on Banking, Housing, and Urban Affairs under Chairman Riegle launched an investigation into "the possibility that there may be a connection between the Iraqi chemical, biological, and radiological warfare research and development programs and a mysterious illness which was then being reported by thousands of returning Gulf War veterans."[54] It may seem strange for the Banking Committee to pursue GWS, but it has authority over U.S. exports and in October 1992 the committee heard testimony that "United Nations inspectors identified many U.S.-manufactured items exported pursuant to licenses issued by the U.S. Department of Commerce that were used to further Iraq's chemical and nuclear weapons development" as well as their missile systems.[55] A little over a year later, Gulf War veterans testified before the Senate Armed Services Committee that they were subjected to chemical attacks in Iraq. This caused Senator Riegle to wonder about connections between chemical agents and the growing reports of illness among Gulf War veterans. After extensive hearings, the committee issued a report in 1994 citing "significant evidence that coalition forces were exposed to mixed chemical agents." The report emphasized:

- Iraqi nuclear, chemical, and biological weapons plants and storage sites were priority targets for U.S. and Coalition forces and were repeatedly bombed.
- Chemical alarms began sounding and the servicemen were put on chemical alert simultaneous with the beginning of the air war.[56]

In spite of these conclusions, the DOD and VA took little action to address the problems presented by increasing numbers of veterans. In July 1996, on the verge of another hard congressional look at Gulf War illnesses, the DOD acknowledged the exposures at Khamisiyah, conservatively estimating that up to four hundred troops were "presumed exposed" to chemical warfare agents. Those next hearings were initiated by Representative Shays's Committee on Government Reform and Oversight. Their final report (issued November 7, 1997) minced no words in its title, *Gulf War Veterans' Illnesses: VA, DOD Continue to Resist Strong Evidence Linking Toxic Causes to Chronic Health Effects,* and was unsparing in its criticism of federal agencies:

> After 19 months of investigation and hearings, the subcommittee finds the status of efforts on Gulf War issues by the Department of Veterans Affairs [VA], the Department of Defense [DOD], the Central Intelligence Agency [CIA] and the Food and Drug Administration [FDA] to be irreparably flawed. We find those efforts hobbled by institutional inertia that mistakes motion for progress. We find those efforts plagued by arrogant incuriosity and a pervasive myopia that sees a lack of evidence as proof. As a result, we find current approaches to research, diagnosis and treatment unlikely to yield answers to veterans' life-or-death questions in the foreseeable, or even far distant, future.[57]

The report included eighteen findings and an equal number of recommendations. From the perspective of Gulf War veterans the first finding was the most damning—"VA and DOD did not listen to sick Gulf War veterans as to the possible causes of their illnesses." The committee found that the entire approach to researching, diagnosing, and confronting Gulf War illnesses was misdirected due to DOD and VA insistence that there was no exposure to toxic agents in the Gulf. The committee also found that, while treatment of Gulf War Syndrome has "largely focused on stress and PTSD," no credible evidence supports that "stress or PTSD causes illnesses reported by many Gulf War Veterans." Particularly discouraging was the finding that "Neither the VA nor the DOD has systematically attempted to determine whether sick Gulf War veterans are any better or worse today than when they first reported symptoms."[58]

The report offered detailed recommendations regarding diagnosis, treatment, and research of GWS. These included putting responsibility for coordinating all research into Gulf War veterans outside of the VA and the DOD. But, most critical to vets, the report's first recommendation declared that, "Congress should enact a Gulf War toxic exposure act establishing the presumption, as a matter of law, that veterans were exposed to hazardous materials known to have been present in the war theater."[59] In 1998, with the passage of the Persian Gulf War Veterans Act, Congress did just that. The act also created an independent advisory panel with respect to Gulf War illnesses. This panel, the Research Advisory Committee on Gulf War Veterans' Illnesses (RAC), produced a major report in November of 2008.

Research Advisory Committee on Gulf War Veterans' Illnesses (RAC)

In its December 2005 meetings, the RAC welcomed an impressive collection of research on Gulf War illnesses. By this time there was growing acceptance that a quarter of the 670,000 troops in the Gulf

War theater suffered from Gulf War–related illnesses. Tables of symptoms and exposures presented at the RAC meetings were striking.[60]

Between 56 and 72 percent of U.S. troops in the field reported either hearing chemical alarms or being required to don protective gear in response to a possible chemical attack. Percentages for British troops were higher. Between 5 and 12 percent of U.S. troops felt they were exposed to nerve agents. As many as 43 percent reported being close to the explosion of an Iraqi SCUD missile during their deployment. Tables showed similar patterns of Gulf War illnesses among U.S. forces and forces from the United Kingdom. Significant symptoms with some differences existed for other coalition partners. Danish troops, for example, reported respiratory and skin conditions similar to those of U.S. troops, but reported fewer neurological or joint symptoms. Australian troops reported a lower rate of problems overall. They used PB at equal or higher rates than U.S. forces, but reported lower use of pesticides. The patterns were highly suggestive of toxin-symptom connections. By the time the RAC's major report was issued in November 2008, stronger inferences were being made about a range of toxins on "planet" Iraq.

Psychological Stressors

Although psychological diagnoses held sway in early explanations of Gulf War illnesses, research reported by 2008 gave little support to such hypotheses. The report stated that "stress-related variables" were "consistently not identified as significant risk factors for Gulf War illness."[61] It is worth noting that a 2007 book by a group of British researchers arrived at very different conclusions than the RAC report.[62] They emphasize that no medically validated Gulf War illness has consistently emerged from considerable post–Gulf War research and suggest that early media reports of possible Gulf War illness fueled a persuasive narrative for service personnel suffering from a range of physical, posttraumatic stress, and readjustment problems following the Gulf War. Under the umbrella of the Gulf War Syndrome narrative, many former service personnel receive recognition as former soldiers, gain support from fellow sufferers or sympathizers, find a rationale for shortcomings in their functioning, and possibly gain compensation. The researchers do not challenge the reported experiences of the veterans, but worry that a failure to identify problems rightly can lead to a failure to seek or provide meaningful treatment. Like the RAC report, the British researchers fault medical personnel in both the United States and the United Kingdom for failing to take early reports seriously, and initiating meaningful research on the complaints of Gulf War veterans in a timely manner.

Kuwaiti Oil Fires

Research on the effect of veterans' exposure to oil fires is not as consistent as the findings regarding psychological stress. The RAC considered that oil fire exposures "are not likely to have been the primary cause" of Gulf War illnesses, but noted indications that a small group of heavily exposed vets may suffer from asthma and other symptoms.[63]

Depleted Uranium

The effects of DU exposure still remain controversial. Animal studies support the potential dangers of DU, but few Gulf War vets were exposed and troops with greater DU exposure in the recent Iraq War do not show GWS symptoms. Although the jury on the risks of DU remains out, evidence does not support DU as a significant factor in the large number of veterans suffering from Gulf War illnesses.[64] One VA doctor instigated a detailed study of a small group of symptomatic veterans who inspected damaged tanks and vehicles and could be considered to have greater DU exposure. He reported resistance to this research within the VA and attributed his later dismissal from the VA to his outspoken efforts to explore problems due to DU exposure.[65]

Anthrax Vaccine

Vaccinations are a routine ritual for world travelers and especially for troops preparing for overseas deployments. Most of the vaccines given to troops departing for the Persian Gulf were immunizations or boosters of frequently used and approved vaccines. The exceptions were vaccines against anthrax and botulinum toxin, thought by the DOD to be specific risks in the Gulf theater. The anthrax vaccine, generally used by veterinarians or others at high risk for exposure, is the most controversial. There was a single producer in the United States and its method of production changed after it received its first limited approval from the FDA. The FDA made its first-ever visit to the facility after the Gulf War and found numerous production problems. The specific vaccine used in the Gulf War was not approved for general use by the FDA. To be fully effective, the anthrax vaccine should be administered six times over a period of eighteen months. Limited time and supplies prevented such administration. The DOD estimated that 150,000 troops "received one or more shots."[66] Studies have not identified vaccines, including anthrax vaccine, as major risk factors for Gulf War illnesses, but use of the anthrax vaccine remains a contentious issue in the military.[67]

Cholinergic and Related Neurotoxins
(Pyridostigmine Bromide, Pesticides, Nerve Agents)

Nerve warfare agents, many pesticides, and PB "share a common toxic mechanism." These chemicals (acetylcholinesterase inhibitors) can produce excessive stimulation in various parts of the nervous system with differing results depending on the areas and the sensitivity of the individual. The additive or synergistic effects of these chemicals could collectively produce a wide range of symptoms encompassing most Gulf War illnesses.[68]

Data on all the possible exposures of troops to these neurotoxic agents can be estimated with various degrees of accuracy. Estimates of

PB use (66 percent of army vets)[69] are probably strongest. Estimates of pesticide use are about as high,[70] but not all pesticides have a similar chemical makeup and frequency and dose are hard to gauge. Possible exposure to chemical weapons is most problematic. Even the estimates from Khamisiyah vary greatly depending on the reconstructive models chosen.[71] Modeling efforts clearly suffer with the passage of time, another bitter fruit of earlier secrecy.

Research studies repeatedly associate the use of PB and pesticides with clinical symptoms of Gulf War illnesses. While veterans who participated in, or observed, the demolitions at Khamisiyah "experienced significantly higher symptom rates, nine years after the war" (brain cancer and cardiac dysrhythmias) than other veterans within 50 km of the demolitions, the overall relationship between exposure to chemical warfare agents and other Gulf illness symptoms remains ambiguous.[72] The RAC report concludes that "both PB and pesticides are causal factors in Gulf War illnesses," while low-level exposure to nerve gas emerges in some studies and "cannot be ruled out as a contributing factor."[73]

Infectious Diseases

Although a number of veterans experienced "acute respiratory or diarrheal diseases" while in the Gulf theater, no strong evidence links these to GWS. The extent of two other diseases, leishmaniasis and an infection by *Mycoplasma fermentans,* is hard to estimate. As of the report a variation of leishmaniasis had only been identified in twelve veterans and evidence of *Mycoplasma fermentans* DNA occurred in a number of symptomatic veterans, but results were too mixed to confirm these infections playing a significant role among Gulf War illnesses.[74]

Other Exposures

Other harmful exposures, such as the CARC paint fumes, affected small numbers of troops in the Gulf War, but no other factors were as widespread as PB and pesticides. The RAC report's authors emphasize, however, that it is impossible to rule out the potential interactive effects of other environmental factors in the cases of individual veterans.

Unfortunately, current research has not determined effective treatments for Gulf War illnesses. This remains the highest priority for ongoing research. As of 2005, 211,729 Gulf War veterans were receiving disability payments.[75] This is a huge cost in suffering, government funds, and compromised human potential. The RAC report states both its findings and its mandate:

> The extensive body of scientific research now available consistently indicates that Gulf War illness is real, that it is the result of neurotoxic exposures during Gulf War deployment, and that few veterans have recovered or substantially improved with time. Addressing the serious and persistent health problems that affect Gulf War veterans remains the obligation of the federal government and all who are indebted to the men and women who risked their lives in Iraq, Kuwait, and Saudi Arabia 17 years ago. This obligation is made more urgent by the length of time veterans have waited for answers and assistance.[76]

Clearly the DOD's failure to collect data, and to be forthcoming with what it knew, delayed the investigative work needed to help Gulf War veterans. The RAC report describes the announcement of the Khamisiyah exposure by the DOD as "a turning point in the federal response to Gulf War health issues." Certainly this opened up blocked avenues of research. Releasing information earlier may have prevented years of misdiagnoses and spurred earlier treatment efforts. Faced with the growing evidence that PB and pesticides strongly contributed to GWS, Lieutenant General Dale Vesser, acting special assistant to the secretary of defense for Gulf War illnesses, confessed, "although Saddam Hussein didn't use nuclear, biological, or chemical agents against coalition forces during the war, it never dawned on us ... that we may have done it to ourselves."[77] Sadly, in secrecy and embarrassment, the military continued "doing it" well after many veterans began suffering.

CHAPTER SIX

War and the Human Psyche
of America's Veterans

*And this I know: all these things that now, while we are still at war, sink down
in us like a stone, after the war will waken again, and then shall begin the disen-
tanglement of life and death.*

Remarque, *All Quiet on The Western Front*[1]

MANY TIMES WE HEAR that time heals all wounds. That may be true in some instances. However, it is often not true for those with scars seared into their psyche by war. Doc certainly felt that was the case. In *Red Clay on My Boots* he described the symptoms that pursued him throughout his life.

In 1968, I went to Vietnam for the first time as a nineteen-year-old hospital corpsman with the 26th Marines. As a result, for most of my adult life, I have experienced a profound sense of alienation from the society around me. I have often undergone feelings of isola-tion, immense survivor's guilt, bitterness, revulsion, uncontrollable emotion and remorse. But I have also been consumed with rage, an intense abiding anger that has affected the quality of my life and the existence of those around me, an often uncontrollable fury that I seldom understood and that resided just under the surface of my consciousness. Now, the ferocity of my rancor has turned into a dull ache, a source of unimaginable pain impossible to describe but nonetheless always lurking on the edge of my awareness. Even today, after so many years, memories of Vietnam trigger the most extreme reaction where my eyes fill with tears, my voice cracks and I have to exercise all of my self-control to avoid bursting into tears. Along with my emotional attachment to the war exists the most persistent sensation of all: a never-ending, pervasive, controlling anxiety. Indeed, for decades I have dreaded closed spaces, rats, failure, vulnerability, and others discovering the depth of my trepidation.[2]

The Scars

Trauma professionals tell us that "each trauma stressor is unique" and therefore the outcomes of trauma experiences may be "radically different."[3] Doc's experience was long and grisly, but still shares important parallels with those of other vets suffering from combat-induced trauma. This chapter focuses on the scars resulting from brutal encounters with war. PTSD is a recent diagnosis and the psychic injuries of America's Vietnam veterans played a significant part in its evolution. Though you can find the symptoms in Homer and early accounts of warfare, names for the malady as applied to warfare are recent—soldier's heart; shell shock; battle fatigue. In 1980 this ancient malady entered the psychiatric lexicon under the name of posttraumatic stress disorder. The entry wasn't easy. Dr. Robert Spitzer chaired the task force of the American Psychiatric Association that included the new definition in the association's third edition of the *Diagnostic and Statistical Manual of Mental Disorders* (DSM). When first confronted with data supporting the PTSD diagnosis he expressed serious resistance to the concept: "I don't care if it exists. If we recognize this disorder, do you realize what it's going to cost the federal government in terms of compensation?"[4] Nonetheless, the new diagnosis provided a focus for funding, for conducting research, and for developing innovative therapies.

Although PTSD became the "official" label for trauma reactions, the new term is no more stable than its predecessors. In 1994, "acute stress disorder" was added to the fourth edition of the DSM[5] to account for serious reactions to trauma that last less than a month, too short a time to meet the criteria for PTSD. Jonathan Shay, a psychiatrist who works extensively with veterans, proposes the modifier *complex*[6] to divide PTSD into two levels: "simple PTSD," which he believes can be treated by either group work or counseling and medication, and "complex PTSD," a reaction to prolonged and repeated trauma that "invades character" and compromises social trust and is so severe that it stays with a person for life.[7] Other terms such as "acute traumatic stress reactions" (short-term "normal reactions to abnormal circumstances")[8] or "posttraumatic stress symptoms" (a category that sought to encompass the anomalies of Gulf War Syndrome)[9] are also found in the professional literature. The PTSD diagnosis remains controversial. Elements of the diagnosis are expected to change with future revisions of the DSM. Research drives most changes, but prevailing opinions also play a role in naming war-related stress reactions.[10] Research showing that some vets fake PTSD in order to gain compensation further complicates attitudes toward the diagnosis, although research consistently supports the reality of trauma reactions in huge numbers of vets.[11]

Trauma as Moral Uprooting

Writing in the early 1990s, Jonathan Shay, a VA psychiatrist and winner of a 2007 MacArthur Fellowship for his work among combat veterans, expressed several criticisms of the PTSD criteria of that time. He challenged the specification in the DSM that the trauma victims "experienced an event outside the range of usual human experience." He found such a bland "ethically and culturally neutral" statement of little relevance.[12] The current version of the criteria doesn't include such a statement, but its emphasis still falls short of Shay's concerns. It specifies that the person experienced, witnessed, or was confronted with an event or events that involved actual or threatened death or serious injury, or a threat to the physical integrity of self or other.[13]

Such moral neutrality misses a huge element of trauma. It misses the betrayal of forcible incest and child abuse; it misses the shattering of belief in a sustaining, benevolent deity that may follow a natural disaster; it misses the profound erosion of moral sensibilities produced in the killing fields of war. Shay complains that the diagnostic criteria for PTSD fail to capture the "damaging personality changes that frequently follow prolonged, severe trauma" and he notes that the *Classification of Mental and Behavioral Disorders* by the World Health Organization includes a category for "Enduring personality change after catastrophic experience."[14]

Psychologist Edward Tick works intensively with traumatized vets. He chooses the "soul" as the locus of damage wreaked by combat trauma. *Soul* is a term absent from modern psychiatry and psychology, but Tick feels the need for a term that encompasses the moral and spiritual as well as the mental and physical ravages of combat trauma. Tick criticizes many approaches to PTSD for underestimating the assault of battle trauma on one's core identity. For him, "soul" helps reclaim the feel of such impact.

> In war chaos overwhelms compassion, violence replaces cooperation, instinct replaces rationality, gut dominates mind. When drenched in these conditions, the soul is disfigured and can become lost for life.[15]

For this reason Tick feels psychotherapy must address the veteran's "moral and spiritual" self if healing is to occur.[16] Fortunately, there is a growing recognition of the place of cultural, moral, and religious values in the conduct of mental health treatment.[17]

Lewis B. Puller, Jr. describes the erosion of compassion that war can generate. Puller grew up in awe of his father, a U.S. Marine general who won enough decorations to be a living legend in the corps. At the time of the Vietnam War, Lewis, Jr. completed training as a marine officer and his Vietnam assignment came quickly. Early in his combat tour he described his revulsion while restraining a marine from pissing on the decomposing body of a North Vietnamese soldier. Several months later he describes a changing reaction:

> A part of me had already begun to regard the enemy as some sort of inhuman cannon fodder. I realized that my reaction was a defense mechanism that allowed me to accept and dispense death and mutilation more readily, but I also knew that I was going to lose a part of my soul if that thinking progressed much further.[18]

Later still, Puller ordered his men to bury a North Vietnamese soldier killed in attacking their position. He later discovered that the men had decapitated the soldier and placed his head on a stake beside the road from which the enemy had come.

> I had none of the outrage over the desecration of the corpse I had experienced on first arriving in Vietnam, when one of my charges had tried to urinate on a dead soldier. I justified the difference in my reactions on the grounds that this particular soldier had tried to kill me, but I knew inwardly that ice was forming over my heart.[19]

Trauma Experiences

Hypermasculine or untested soldiers may assert that only the "weak" suffer from PTSD, and some people are clearly more vulnerable to trauma. The website of the VA's National Center for PTSD (http://www.ptsd.va.gov/) hosts the most recent research on PTSD. A brief spin through this large body of research reveals many predisposing factors for PTSD—a history of earlier trauma, prior mental health problems, female gender, lower education, low socioeconomic status, minority status, and being between ages eighteen and twenty-one. If all these risk factors eliminated military recruits, the enlistment pool would be too small to generate an army.

The horrors of combat can traumatize almost anyone. Studies of troops in World War I indicated that after 210 days in combat just about everyone was a psychiatric casualty.[20] Combat stress is often layered. Already-traumatized men may carry past trauma into new combat. Sometimes they are heavily stressed from the home front as well—family illness, marital breakup, a recent "Dear John" letter. Such anxieties are a huge risk. Soldiers may be asked to carry on in combat when they feel they have nothing to live for. A survey of returning troops after the Gulf War found that 25 percent of the men and 20 percent of the women "reported domestic stressors (e.g., dissolution of marriage, unexpected death of a loved one)" during their relatively short deployment.[21] The second author counseled a Vietnam vet who described his rage at news of multiple betrayals at home, none of which he could influence from Southeast Asia. He released his fury from a machine gun perch as his helicopter flew over "free fire zones," shooting civilians, women, and children as if they were targets in an arcade. Back in the States he collapsed under the dual weight of what he had done and the violent urges he felt when others offended him.

Some soldiers describe the bonds among troops who fight side by side as the most intense they ever experienced. These men are literally prepared to fulfill the biblical definition of "greater love" by dying for one another. They suffer the loss of comrades profoundly. The emotional numbing that comes with PTSD often begins with such losses. Men may carry guilt for not saving a friend or not dying in his place, especially if, in the madness of battle, they missed chances to support their comrades. In the chaos of a firefight they may even shoot each other. Estimates of death by "friendly fire" run as high as 20 percent in some engagements.[22] Men often report becoming wary of attachments to troops replacing lost comrades.

War involves high risk and little control. In some military units, poor leadership adds to the stress and sense of lost control. In the M*A*S*H

TV series, medical staff close to the Korean front managed unit tensions with pranks and humor. When men feel disrespected or incompetently led closer to the front, they may become bitter and violent.[23] In Chapter 1 Doc intervened when a soldier attempted to shoot a sergeant who both usurped his position and cheated him at cards. During the Vietnam War, "fragging," the killing or wounding of fellow soldiers or superiors, often with the use of grenades, became a serious problem. The army began tracking these instances late in the Vietnam War. Between 1969 and July of 1972 they recorded 551 such incidents, resulting in 86 deaths and over 700 wounded.[24]

Eric Maria Remarque, a German veteran of World War I, authored *All Quiet on the Western Front.* Starkly frank yet sensitive, many consider it the greatest antiwar novel. In one gripping episode, Paul, the German youth through whose eyes we see the war, is trapped all night in a shell hole in "no man's land," bewildered over which direction he must crawl to return to his own lines. An equally panicked French soldier plunges into the same shell hole and Paul stabs him repeatedly. As he goes through the dying man's pockets, he discovers a man with hopes and a family—a conscript with a simple trade who wants no more of war than Paul. Four years after coming to power, Hitler ordered all copies of Remarque's novel burned and Remarque fled the country.[25] In echoes of Remarque, a more recent book, *Wandering Souls,* tells the story of Lieutenant Homer Steedly, Jr., who came face to face with an armed North Vietnamese medic and instantly killed him. He searched the young man's body and took his identification and two notebooks containing meticulous writing and drawings. Homer sent them home, but remained haunted by the encounter. Thirty-five years later he set out to find the medic's family and return the notebooks.[26] Lieutenant Colonel David Grossman, former army ranger and West Point instructor, passionately researches the impact of war on soldiers. He believes that killing is a major component of combat trauma. The Londoners who survived the death and destruction of continuous Blitzkrieg bombings in World War II did not suffer nearly as much PTSD as troops in combat.[27]

As far as we know, Doc never killed anyone, but he layered trauma on trauma for seventy-seven days, desperate to save some comrades, forced to leave others, all the while under fire himself. Neither did Kenneth Kays shoot anyone.[28] As a young man he fled to Canada to avoid the Vietnam draft. His parents begged him to return and join the army if he could be guaranteed a role as a medic. Kays joined, became a medic, and deployed to Vietnam. His squad dug in for the night in a small previously abandoned firebase. The North Vietnamese knew it well. They had attacked it before and may have used it themselves. In the middle of the night, sappers crawled to their perimeter and threw explosive charges into their positions, followed by an intense assault. Wounded comrades screamed and Kays was running to their aid when a satchel charge flipped him in the air as it blew off his lower left leg. He calmly tied a shoelace tightly around his bleeding leg and hobbled on to treat his wounded brothers. When his base was relieved in the morning he was found nearly dead next to one of the men he was treating. Kenneth Kays was awarded the Congressional Medal of Honor, but never functioned well again. He suffered from PTSD, substance abuse, and depression, and spent time in civilian psychiatric hospitals. He may have been vulnerable to PTSD, but no one ever questioned his courage.

Stigma and Trauma Reaction as "Disorder"

The PTSD diagnosis is also under fire from persons concerned about its stigmatizing potential. A perceived stigma deters vets from seeking help they need and "causes individuals ... to lose respect for themselves whether or not they seek treatment."[29] In the recent conflicts in Iraq and Afghanistan, a RAND Corporation study estimates that a fifth of returning soldiers suffer from PTSD, but only half of those will seek help. The study does not tell us how long vets will sustain their efforts to seek help or whether the help will make a difference. We know that many vets drop out of treatment. As Doc said about sharing his fears,

"I have dreaded ... others discovering the depth of my trepidation." It is a tribute to Doc and his therapists that he took risks and gained the support that helped sustain him for many years.

In a 2009 article on the military's battle to cope with the stigma of mental health problems, a deployed psychologist describes how often men would sidle up to him outside his office seeking support or advice "off the record."[30] These same servicemen would hesitate to enter his office. They feared what their buddies would think; what their superiors might hear; that a psychological file could destroy their career; that acknowledging problems could cost them a security clearance or even lead to discharge from the service. The army is concerned not just about the future cost of untreated stress reactions, but about the preparedness of their current forces. They don't want soldiers distracted from their immediate mission. Given the machismo and traditions of the military culture, an air force colonel worries that the military is still "swimming upstream" against the stigma associated with seeking mental health treatment. In a sharp departure from the past, in May 2008 Defense Secretary Robert Gates announced the removal of the question "Have you ever consulted with a health care professional regarding an emotional or mental health condition?" from the security clearance questionnaire. The secretary did not say that such issues would remain irrelevant to military officials issuing clearances.

There are reassurances about mental health issues on the army's Behavioral Health website:

> Soldiers are being trained to look out for the mental health of their buddies in the same way that they look out for their physical health, and leaders are being trained to encourage soldiers to get help. The message is getting out that coming in to get help early is the best way to avoid long term problems. Our intention is to return soldiers back to duty.[31]

Still, the same website offers the comfort that most soldiers seeking help "do not receive a diagnosis of a mental health problem." It is not clear what such a statement does to mitigate stigma. A vet bedeviled by terrifying dreams of horrific events doesn't need to suffer the extra blow of a psychiatrically approved "disorder." In December 2007 a bereaved father testified before the House Committee on Veterans Affairs. He had lost his son, a National Guardsman, to suicide shortly after his return from a combat tour in Iraq. He observed that National Guard troops did not receive the mental health and peer support received by troops returning to military bases and that parents get little information about warning signs and how to access help if their sons or daughters are struggling. He recommended an "unboot" camp to prepare troops returning home from combat and training for the families to whom they return. He also eloquently addressed the use of the term *disorder*:

> We must all remove the stigma that goes with the soldier's admitting that he or she has a mental issue. Let these soldiers know that admitting they have a problem with doing the most unnatural thing that a human being can do is all right. Mental health issues from combat are a natural part of the process of war and have been around for thousands of years, but we categorize them as a problem.[32]

Penny Coleman's husband suffered severe PTSD and also committed suicide. She became a writer[33] and activist on the subject of veterans' pain. In testimony before the same House committee she was clear about where she stood:

> I use the term PTSD grudgingly. It is the official term, but it is deeply problematic. My husband did not have a disorder. He had an injury that was a direct result of his combat experience in Vietnam. Calling it a disorder is dangerous. It reinforces the idea that a traumatically injured soldier is defective, and that idea is precisely what keeps soldiers from asking for the help they need.[34]

Max Cleland, former director of the Veterans Administration and U.S. senator, lost two legs and part of an arm in Vietnam. He also suffered from severe posttraumatic stress. In the impassioned open letter to veterans with which Cleland begins his autobiography he observes that some of the deepest wounds of war don't leave a scratch, and urges his fellow vets, "No matter what you are feeling when you come home, no matter how crazy you feel inside, know that you are not mentally ill."[35] We can give trauma its due by calling the response to it a *reaction* and there are many specifications that mental health professionals can make that may be relevant for choosing an intervention—acute, complex, delayed onset, persistent, etc. Researchers Nash, Silva, and Litz trace the history of stigma associated with psychiatric battle casualties, and, after reviewing the growing evidence of neurological and brain changes that follow severe reactions to trauma, they make a persuasive case for removing the stigma by considering PTSD a literal form of brain injury.[36] The term *disorder* suggests a condition inherent in the person rather than an injury—it would seem strange to refer to a broken leg as a leg disorder. *Disorder* adds to stigma while contributing nothing of diagnostic or therapeutic relevance. For this reason the term *posttraumatic stress reaction* (PTSR) will be used where possible from this point forward. When quoting directly or citing a research study that uses the acronym PTSD we will use PTSD[R].

Negative Media Stereotypes

If there are problems with professional terminology, there may be greater problems with some popular conceptions of "battle-crazed" veterans. Many towns were apprehensive of accepting returning veterans after the Civil War for fear that they might pose a danger to the community. Doc was particularly concerned about rash reporting that fueled such stereotypes of Vietnam vets. In 2004, Kate O'Beirne,[37] writing in the *National Review*, cited examples of egregious reporting errors. In one story, a man killed fourteen employees in a post office in Edmond,

Oklahoma, before killing himself. The local news reported that he was a Vietnam veteran and repeated that assertion even after a navy spokesman clarified that the man had never served in Vietnam. Ironically, two of the victims were Vietnam veterans. Two years after the Oklahoma shootings, another "violent Vietnam veteran kills" story exploded in Texas. In fact, the accused entered the service seventeen months after the last combat troops had left Vietnam. One of the worst distortions of Vietnam veterans occurred in a 1988 CBS documentary, *The Wall Within*, hosted by Dan Rather. The hour-long special featured horrific accounts of murder and mayhem to which six purported Vietnam veterans were exposed and that provoked their postwar histories of drug abuse, alcoholism, homelessness, and despair. The dramatic stories were apparently too "newsworthy" to verify. Later checks revealed that only one of the vets actually served in combat.

Why So Much PTSR Out of Vietnam?

It would be hard to say that Vietnam produced more trauma than other wars, but the experience of Vietnam vets certainly brought combat trauma to a new level of awareness in America. Doc reflected on the contrast between his deployment and that of his father in World War II. Like many other soldiers, he was posted to Vietnam individually rather than deploying with a unit. He returned in the same way. Doc's father spent several months with his assigned unit coming back from England, including an ocean crossing on a ship full of bonded veterans telling war stories. Doc wondered if returning as a unit among men with a shared experience might have buffered his experience of trauma. Current military mental health interventions are closer to the front and the homecoming experience garners special attention. Present therapeutic wisdom suggests that the sooner one is free of danger and into treatment the better. For ten years after the Vietnam War, there was little understanding of trauma reactions, no closely relevant diagnosis, and virtually no discussion of the realities of Vietnam in the United States. Many Vietnam veterans wouldn't even admit that they had been in Vietnam in the years after the war. The stigma of mental health problems was compounded by the stigma attached to the unpopular war. When Vietnam veterans desperately needed understanding, and help, it wasn't there. Doc was acutely aware of how young he was when he entered combat—the average private in Vietnam was nineteen; in World War II, the average was closer to twenty-seven. He also believed that Vietnam veterans who carried severe PTSR into middle age also reached a point where recovery was unlikely.

PTSR Too Rarely Comes Alone

When PTSR is severe, other problems often accompany it. The huge study of Vietnam veterans completed by Kulka et al. showed that vets with PTSD[R] also suffered depression (20 percent), alcoholism (20 percent), or generalized anxiety (16 percent).[38] Depression may relate to memories, a profound loss of innocence, a collapsed worldview, and failure to escape the relentless mental consequences of trauma. Alcoholism and drug abuse may play a role in easing or blunting flashbacks and traumatic memories. Trauma also has physical consequences. VA data reveals that veterans subjected to "both combat and noncombat trauma appeared especially susceptible to health decline."[39]

The mental health costs of caring for traumatized veterans are high—"they require long term treatment and … have a greater tendency to develop physical health problems."[40] Joseph Stiglitz and Linda Bilmes estimate that the Iraq War will ultimately cost American taxpayers three trillion dollars. This is no rickety estimate; Stiglitz holds a Nobel Prize in economics and Bilmes, now at Harvard, is a former chief financial officer at the U.S. Department of Commerce. They put the range of treating PTSD[R] alone at between twenty-five and forty-four billion dollars.[41]

Confronting PTSR

On Return from a Combat Zone

The father who called for an "unboot camp" to help soldiers readjust might cite examples of readjustment support for persons returning from situations much less stressful than a combat zone. A number of corporations acknowledge that employees can face problems after overseas assignments. Religious missionaries may receive better transitional services on returning to the United States than returning troops do. The Peace Corps offers close-of-service conferences that may last for several days, a phone line for returning volunteers, health services for returnees who experience adjustment problems, a biweekly newsletter with reentry and job information, and local connections to former volunteers through the National Peace Corps Association.[42]

The military takes pride in the preparation of servicemen for duty. Boot camps are intense and communal. Completion is accompanied by celebratory rituals. Exiting from the military is too often solitary and bureaucratic. The military is working to identify potential transition problems, but much remains to be done. A Post-Deployment Health Assessment (PDHA) questionnaire is required of all returning troops. Because this questionnaire may miss important information (troops may fear that admitting problems can delay their return home), a Reassessment (PDHRA) is administered between three and six months later.[43] Still the handoff of medical care from the military to the VA is often problematic. The transfer of medical records from the military to the VA can be complicated and slow. There may be a significant shift in the quality of resources in going from one system of care to the other.

Home communities may offer welcoming parties, picnics, or even parades, but this doesn't compensate for the training and preparation servicemen and women need to make the homecoming adjustment. Recognition of post-discharge transition problems is growing and there is more helpful material to guide veterans and families through homecoming and beyond. Two recent books could be of special help to the returning combat vet and his or her family:

- *After the War Zone* is written by a psychologist and psychiatrist with the VA's National Center for PTSD[R] and offers practical advice ranging from addressing emotional reactions, reestablishing communication between vets and their families, changing roles of spouses, resuming a civilian job, and finances. It includes a twenty-one page listing of resources for veterans.[44] The authors utilize the acronym BATTLEMIND to introduce key points relevant to possible transition difficulties. The BATTLEMIND format was developed at the Walter Reed Army Hospital.
- *Back from the Front,* by psychologist Aphrodite Matsakis, is more directly focused on the homecoming of the soldier with significant combat exposure. Guidance is offered for both vet and family. Whether the veteran has current reactions to trauma or not, this is a compassionate and helpful read for veterans and spouses.[45]

These books might provide a core curriculum for a reverse boot camp, where important issues could be proactively addressed with returning troops. Active discussion of homecoming concerns among troops, a new spirit of post-discharge support, and a thorough orientation to services and organizations for veterans could be invaluable. Some professionals, for example, have reservations about the BATTLEMIND approach.[46] Open discussion can help clarify that a particular approach may work better for some veterans than others. Ideally families could be present and involved in the final stages of reverse boot camps or vets could designate persons vital to their homecoming to receive this information.

Family Involvement

Even families that could come to the final phase of a reverse boot camp may need further support. Vets often find that families are "clueless" with respect to what they have experienced and how they have changed. One might substitute "unprepared" for "clueless" and ask what preparation families need. Families may not understand a veteran's pain, but they often feel it. They agonize over whether to be patient or to push silent veterans to talk more; whether to broach the topic of counseling; whether to speak about the drinking; whether to ask the vet why he or she doesn't go places or do things they used to enjoy; whether to ask again about the faltering job search. What does a family say?

Aaron Glantz, a journalist who follows veterans' issues, writes:

> It's not easy to come home from war. Even if you're lucky enough to have survived mentally and physically, you still have to get used to the fact that most Americans can't relate to where you've been, what you think, what you've seen, how you feel, and what you've done.[47]

It is hard for families to realize that returning home can be more challenging than the deployment. When Remarque's character Paul returned home for a brief leave he could no longer connect:

> I breathe deeply and say to myself:—"You are home, you are home." But a sense of strangeness will not leave me, I cannot feel at home amongst these things. There is my mother, there is my sister ... but I am not myself there. There is a distance, a veil between us.
>
> I cannot get on with the people.... [Father] wants me to tell him about the front: he is curious in a way that I find stupid and distressing; I no longer have any real contact with him.... I realize he does not know that a man cannot talk of such things; I would do it willingly, but it is too dangerous for me to put these things into words. I am afraid they might become gigantic and I would be no longer able to master them. What would become of us if everything that happens out there were quite clear to us?[48]

Families must know that soldiers are changed by combat; that they need a new kind of support and understanding; that they may even need a caring friend or family member to watch them for signs of distress and, in more extreme cases, to seek help for them. As Slone and Friedman warn, families also change while troops are deployed. A soldier may return to a spouse who is more competent, has new supports, and is expecting a new role in their marital relationship.[49] Post-deployment telephone support for spouses using the BATTLEMIND model is being studied by the DOD and the VA.[50] The military needs to make major efforts to facilitate post-deployment reorientation to family and community.

At the VA

The VA has a major commitment to confronting PTSR. The Department of Veterans Affairs funds the National Center for PTSD. The VA also funds and encourages research and the use of the most promising treatments while recognizing that the needs of vets vary, and treatments should be flexible and comprehensive. Vets wary of stigma and mental health professionals may be more comfortable going to one of the VA's vet centers (locations can be found online), where fellow vets provide group support and counseling is less formal.

For a long time the VA was bound by locations in larger population centers. Now it offers small clinics or part-time clinics in small towns and rural areas. There are even clinics that operate out of mobile vans. In our huge country, however, large areas will always remain uncovered. This requires vigorous outreach to known sufferers and strong public information campaigns so that families and friends are not at a loss when a veteran needs help.

In his book *Uncle Sam's Shame*, former VA psychiatrist Martin Kantor stresses that "vets represent a unique group of patients with serious problems hardly shared by the general population."[51] He acknowledges that most of the VA care he saw was good or comparable to care in private clinics. He also cites a special aspect of the VA not shared with other medical systems:

One of the most important things was that the *clinic itself* provided the vets, many of whom were old and lonely, with a place to go or "hang." Some men had wives and some women had husbands who worked during the day, leaving them alone. Many had few friends.[52]

One cannot spend much time in a VA hospital or its cafeteria without becoming aware of the camaraderie that often develops among veterans and among their families in such settings. Such mutual support sometimes occurs in regular hospitals as families share time in special clinics or intensive care waiting rooms, but VA hospitals and clinics are a special venue for such supportive bonding.

Doc praised his care at the VA in Washington State and valued his therapist at the Lexington VA. He also recoiled at an insensitive interviewer during his first visit to the Lexington VA. Kantor also deplores occasional lapses in professionalism like those he witnessed in his VA clinic. At its most extreme he described staff who joked about serving, "red, blue, and white trash," and quoted one Vietnam vet who felt he was being judged by VA staff as though he "chose our nation's foreign policy."[53] Vets need to expect quality care and respect from the VA and to be comfortable speaking up if the VA falls short. Some vets have learned to be compliant and to accept authority in the military, and that can limit their ability to be active partners in their health care. Families can be encouraged to take an advocacy role as well.

Can PTSR Be Prevented or Cured?

"Curing" PTSR can be a huge challenge. The impact of trauma can depend on predisposing factors, the nature of the trauma (its seriousness, duration, and frequency), the reactions of the vet and those around him or her during or after the trauma, and how soon the veteran seeks help. Improvement can depend on the quality of the intervention, the veteran's social supports, and subsequent exposures to stress. In the case of a sexually abused child, it is clear that trauma will be much worse if the first response of an incredulous parent is to punish the child for accusing a "respected" perpetrator—father, uncle, priest. Veterans who are ridiculed by comrades or superiors, told to "shake it off," or even treated near the front and prematurely pushed back into combat may not be in much better shape. There is growing emphasis in the military on getting mental health support to men and women quickly and closer to the front.

> The principles of combat psychiatry that were applied in the Gulf War, involving proximity, immediacy, and expectancy, were originally developed in World War I. Nonpathological labels ..., simple interventions, and treatment in non-hospital-based facilities were used to promote recovery and return to duty.[54]

In the Iraq and Afghanistan wars such forward positioning of help has been stretched by the higher rate of trauma and a lack of sufficient mental health personnel. Often PTSR is late in onset, and there is no long-term data to determine whether this rapid-counseling/rapid-return-to-duty model prevents, reduces, or exacerbates later problems.

In a 1996 study of 486 veterans (most from Vietnam) with severe and persistent PTSD[R], Rosenheck and Fontana found high rates of comorbid (accompanying) illnesses including depression, substance abuse, and suicide attempts. They also found that these men made extensive use of health services and were more likely than Vietnam veterans in Kulka's national study to be involved with the law, lack employment, and suffer severe isolation, poverty, and homelessness. Rosenheck and Fontana followed these men over a year of treatment with some of the VA's best PTSD[R] clinicians. The treatment emphasized patience, attention to multiple problem areas, practical problem solving, flexibility, and continuity of care. The men in this program showed, at best, modest gains in most areas during the first four months. They then seemed to plateau or slide back slightly, with further therapy supporting but not adding to their gains. The study's authors concluded, "We do not have and cannot realistically expect to have clinical tools powerful enough to fully or even largely relieve these veterans of their sufferings."[55]

In the years since that study, our "clinical tools" have improved, but still have a long way to go. It appears that early intervention can ease or prevent later PTSR, especially with the use of cognitive behavioral therapies (CBT),[56] although the jury remains out. Combinations of therapies and medications can often improve a veteran's situation.[57] There is considerable data that PTSR can be eased by positive events and strong social supports.[58] A promising new variation on exposure therapy for PTSR is currently being explored by the DOD and the VA. The approach utilizes a virtual reality instrument (helmet with video, earphones, and scent-producing device). Employing carefully varied video formats that trigger traumatic memories, vets can learn to defuse their emotional responses to combat experiences.[59] Such treatment also poses ethical dilemmas—if used "preventively" could it provide a dangerous desensitization to violence? Dave Grossman decries the desensitization to violence that occurs in our violence-ridden media and video games.[60] Do we really want some form of "inoculation" against our natural inhibitions against killing?

Even with treatment, it is possible that PTSR may be aggravated by new stresses. When Doc was heavily stressed by the politics of a corporate office, his psychiatrist suggested he leave and find something less stressful. From his strong reactions to the oppression of former supporters of South Vietnam and Buddhist dissidents, and especially to the plight of victims of Agent Orange, it is likely that Doc's return visits to Vietnam added another layer of distress to his trauma. As we realized after his death, writing a book about something as personal as the betrayal and trauma of veterans was also a major stressor.

As will be evident in the following chapter, getting timely support to vets suffering from PTSR can be a matter of survival, yet the application of many desperate vets may languish in the VA's overburdened claims process. Claims delays have become a crisis for a number of vets returning from Iraq and Afghanistan. On July 12, 2010, President Obama announced new rules for streamlining veterans' claims for trauma reactions. The accounts of veterans who have PTSD[R] diagnoses from the VA, or psychiatrists and psychologists who perform evaluations under contract with the VA, will be accepted as valid evidence of trauma without a need for extensive review of service and related military records. The VA will also work to ensure that there are adequate professionals available for vets to receive timely evaluations. Only in the most questionable cases will further verification be required.[61]

We all have a responsibility to try and understand the stories of our returning vets, but the military and the VA play a special part in making homecomings work. The Vietnam War helped the nation learn an important lesson—how to distinguish between an unpopular war and the support that veterans need no matter the conflict in which they are called to serve. The psychic toll of war is reflected in thousands of veterans who suffer the ravages of PTSR. While an important improvement, the new regulations on PTSD[R] go only partway down the proactive path recommended in this chapter. The military needs to do a better job of preparing combat troops for the transition home. Consideration of how reservists and National Guardsmen are rotated home is particularly critical. Ideally, quality readjustment programs or reverse boot camps will be available to all combat vets and will include families and key members of a veteran's support system.

Continuing research to improve the understanding and treatment of PTSR is essential and the VA must offer welcoming, respectful clinics with well-trained staff that offer a range of therapies. The VA must also provide serious outreach for vets known to be suffering. Vets and their families need access to information and support and to be encouraged in their roles as advocates for the best care possible. It is up to Congress to provide funding for psychological health care and to prepare for long-term treatment for troops in the years to come. The country has a clear obligation to provide returning veterans with the medical benefits they have been promised. It will be very expensive, but it is hard to conceive of the nation walking away from such a commitment.[62] The country that put them in harm's way can do nothing less.

CHAPTER SEVEN

Veterans' Suicides

In every war American soldiers have fought in the past century, the chances of becoming a psychiatric casualty were greater than the chances of being killed by enemy fire.

Penny Coleman, *Flashback: Posttraumatic Stress Disorder, Suicide, and the Lessons of War*[1]

Suicide Rates and Suicide Realities

IN VIETNAM THE UNITED STATES suffered the loss of 58,220 U.S. servicemen.[2] In 1981, the *Seattle Times* reported that an additional 50,000 Vietnam veterans may have died by suicide after the conflict. Though not substantiated by credible research, the story assumed a life of its own. In some subsequent accounts the suicide estimate rose to 100,000. By 1985, such suicide estimates were cited on the CBS program *60 Minutes*. The figures were repeated in the 1988 CBS special *The Wall Within* (criticized for its poor research in the previous chapter).[3] The figures were not "official"; neither the DOD nor the VA tracked veterans' suicides, but the stunning figures sparked alarm. In 1991, a team of researchers, writing in the *American Journal of Psychiatry*,[4] reported their analysis of two studies of deaths among Vietnam veterans: the first, by the CDC, followed a random sample of 18,319 veterans (over half of whom served in Vietnam) for an average period of 13.7 years; the second study, by the Wisconsin Division of Health, tracked through December 31, 1984, 122,238 veterans in Wisconsin who had served in the armed forces for at least 180 days between 1964 and 1975. The Wisconsin study included over 43,000 Vietnam vets. Analyses of both studies produced an estimate of 9,000 suicides during the period. The researchers estimated that the suicide risk for Vietnam vets might be as high as one and a half times that of young men of comparable age in the general population. A rate over six times that of the general population would be required to reach the stunning figure of 50,000. Though this, and subsequent studies, debunked the most exaggerated suicide claims, a suicide rate among veterans that is significantly higher than a comparable civilian group is a grave concern. Candidates for the military are screened for health before enlistment and have access to military and often VA health care. They are generally healthier than the general population and (in peacetime) have a lower suicide rate as well.[5] This "healthy veterans" effect means that any higher-than-expected health problems among service members and veterans is cause for alarm, whether those alarms are sounded in the name of Agent Orange, Gulf War illnesses, or suicide rates. Ironically, during war, suicides among soldiers typically rise and suicides in civilian populations go down—possibly because the civilian population is more mobilized and purposeful in wartime.[6] Of course there is no "acceptable" rate of veteran suicides—the VA and the military must do their utmost to prevent them. Research shows that vets with PTSD[R],[7] who suffered serious and multiple wounds,[8] or who are notably depressed[9] are at higher risk for suicide. Such risk factors must inform the VA's care.

Two Brave Soldiers

In the previous chapter we encountered two veterans, Kenneth Kays and Lewis Puller, Jr., with exemplary records of military service. Both men agonized with the aftermath of their service. Congressional Medal of Honor winner Kays never functioned well after returning from Vietnam. He rejected the "hero" role, avoided the local press, and refused to participate (as guest of honor) in a local parade. In a brief poem he starkly expressed his inability to resume any intimate social life:

> I've seen too much and been too far
> To really love you when you're near
> For horrible visions haunt my mind
> Of bloody death and unchained fear.
> When I hold you in my arms
> I see men who've long since gone
> Guys who helped me through the night
> Blown away before the dawn
> To men who've shared a bloody hill
> And soaked up fire and lead
> Many words acquire a new meaning
> Like love and friend and God and dead
> These guys are all real as you
> And now I see that I've died too.[10]

Kays battled addiction and psychiatric problems. He lived at least several hours from the nearest VA facility and was hospitalized psychiatrically several times outside the VA system. There is little evidence that he made much contact with the VA or that the VA reached out to him, although, because he was a Medal of Honor winner, his adjustment problems were twice reported in national media. For much of the time after the war, Kays lived with his parents. After a number of years, his father, who was fighting terminal cancer, shot himself in the room next to Kenneth's. Not long after his father's death, Kenneth Kays fulfilled the last line of his poem, fashioning a wire hanger around his neck and joining the Vietnam suicide statistics.

Lewis Puller, Jr., who became apprehensive at the iciness growing in his heart while leading combat sweeps in Vietnam, was wracked by his constant responsibility for the lives of men in a world of dread, death, and killing. His father achieved an illustrious military career in wars where the enemy and objectives seemed clear. In Vietnam there was always ambiguity about the cause and who the enemy was. Lewis, Jr. resolved to leave the military when his tour was up. That decision became irrevocable when an artillery shell fashioned into a booby trap tore off both his legs and nearly destroyed one hand. He returned to his wife and child and, with her staunch support, grittily sustained himself through multiple surgeries, a protracted convalescence, arduous rehabilitation, and a severe bout with alcoholism.[11] Unlike Kays, Puller often functioned at a high level in civilian life. He fathered a second child, completed law school, ran for public office, held responsible positions, and helped found the Vietnam Children's Fund. His moving autobiography, *Fortunate Son*, won the Pulitzer Prize in 1992. Puller loathed war, but endured haunting Vietnam memories, the limits imposed on his maimed body, and the recurring pain of his mental and physical wounds. Over twenty years after his emergency evacuation from Vietnam, Puller was addicted to painkillers and had again succumbed to alcohol. The toll of Puller's torment and alcoholism finally eroded his marriage. Shortly after he and his wife separated, Lewis shot himself.[12] Both Kenneth Kays and Lewis Puller, Jr. are Vietnam casualties whose names are not inscribed on the iconic Vietnam Memorial in the nation's capital.

A Widow Confronts Her Loss

Penny Coleman initially responded to the suicide of her Vietnam veteran husband by blaming herself.[13] Following a suicide, family and friends cannot escape wondering what they might have done differently. Those closest to the person relentlessly revisit the large and small choices they made in their relationship. Conflicting emotions—grief, regret, fury, love, rejection, betrayal, and often a guilt-inducing relief—beset those who remain. They need a comforting presence and special understanding, though a newly earned wariness of close relationships may hinder access to such support. Coleman knew that her husband suffered severe PTSD[R] and was ultimately a delayed casualty of Vietnam.

Striving to make sense of what happened to her and her husband, Penny Coleman poured herself into understanding the price the Vietnam War exacted on the soldiers who waged it and on their loved ones. She sought and interviewed other women survivors of veterans' suicide—wives, mothers, daughters. She listened, researched, and wrote. She explored the history and politics of PTSD[R], the toll of PTSD[R] on veterans and their families, and the aftershocks of suicide. Coleman plumbed the gulfs between military culture, propaganda, recruitment spiels, and the realities of war. She took an unflinching look at why servicemen in Vietnam were vulnerable to trauma.

Coleman observed that most American troops, like Doc, entered Vietnam individually as soon as they finished training and then rotated out a year later. They lacked the comradeship and mutual support that exists when entire units deploy and exit a war zone together. Commissioned officers often rotated even more rapidly and were therefore inexperienced and less trusted by their men. These rotations placed greater burdens on noncommissioned officers. The goals of the war and often the tactics didn't make sense to the troops. In Vietnam, the military measured "success" brutally in "body counts" rather than in territory won. Pressed for results in an environment where one could not easily distinguish enemy and civilian, women, the elderly and even children sometimes augmented body counts. Racial tensions were often high as black troops, mobilized and emboldened by the civil rights movement at home, found themselves overrepresented among the enlisted ranks but seriously underrepresented among officers, some of whom they found overtly racist.

A number of GIs in Vietnam were men formerly considered unfit for military service—80 percent had dropped out of high school and

40 percent could not read beyond the sixth-grade level.[14] These recruits were part of Defense Secretary Robert McNamara's Project 100,000. Described as a "civil rights" or "anti-poverty" program that might "salvage" men less prepared for the civilian work force,[15] the project enlisted over 300,000 men. Many were assigned infantry duty. Critics of the program saw it as cynical recruitment for an unpopular war or even a move to deploy elements of the population viewed as expendable into combat. The men of Project 100,000 may have been more vulnerable to trauma and injury. Some vets felt that the presence of project recruits (sadly dubbed the "Moron Corps"[16]) put more capable and experienced soldiers at greater risk. Little psychological help was available for stressed GIs in Vietnam and the help often focused on returning men to duty. Finally, Vietnam was different from other wars because of the huge public protests against the war in America and the more profound and less publicized protest within America's military. The highly publicized tragedy of the killings of war protesters on the campus of Kent State University in Youngstown, Ohio, pales in comparison with the barely publicized wounding and killing that resulted as servicemen protested and retaliated against orders or officers they no longer respected. There were literal mutinies as whole units within the armed forces refused orders to advance or deploy, especially in the later stages of the conflict when men were asked to continue risking their lives while negotiations to end the conflict were under way.

Coleman collected ten stories of women who endured tortured relationships with traumatized Vietnam veterans, men who ultimately took their own lives. She relates the travail and pain of wives, daughters, and a mother. Each story is unique, but they share some striking commonalities. All the men were described as dramatically changed by the war and suffering severe PTSD[R]. Eight accounts recorded repeated nightmares and another noted serious sleep problems. Eight vets struggled with alcoholism and six (including the two for whom no alcohol problems were reported) abused medication to dull their pain, ease their depression, or calm their agitation. Some wives remained in dysfunctional marriages as hostages to their spouse's threats of suicide, but fled when such stress became intolerable. In some cases the men sought treatment in the VA or their community, often in the time before PTSD was an official diagnosis (or clinicians had a sense of how they might address it). Often they received little help beyond medication.

Coleman's book is a work of thoughtful, passionate advocacy. She speaks from her pain to prevent future pain in others. Such work moves legislators, generates funds for programs and research, and emphasizes that lives hang in the balance.

Why Do Suicides Happen?

There are a number of theories as to why people commit suicide. None of them allow clear predictions, but they guide thinking, research, and intervention. An analysis of such theories is beyond the scope of this chapter, but a theory proposed by Joiner[17] seems relevant to military suicides. Three factors are operative in Joiner's theory. The first involves meaningful connections with others. As described in this and the previous chapter, combat vets with PTSR often carry chilling memories and an altered sense of self that drives them into an isolated, private world. The second factor is a person's perception that they are a burden on others. When persons with PTSR, depression, and substance abuse suffer, so do those who love and care for them. When vets try the patience of others, cannot hold a job, or are unable to support those they love, they are in peril of seeing themselves as more burden than valued friend or family. Suicide notes often express a belief that family or friends left behind will be better off. Finally, Joiner suggests that persons contemplating suicide need to overcome a level of resistance to hurting themselves. They need a means of suicide and a readiness to use it. Veterans with exposure to combat and death and a familiarity with firearms may be quicker to act on their distress than others in comparable pain.

Prevention based on Joiner's theory would give special attention to re-connecting veterans to family and community. Veterans and family would be prepared, possibly in reverse boot camp as imagined in the previous chapter, to rejoin society. Other veterans with combat experience can be an important part of the bridge, and other military families may help families facing the homecoming of a loved one from a combat theater. The life of those on the home front may seem frivolous to returning vets. Too many questions and not enough listening may offer a vet few points of connection. Platitudes about war, patriotism, or sacrifice may ring hollow and distress a returning vet. As indicated in Kenneth Kays's poem, the meaning of ideas like love, God, friend, and death may change profoundly for combat veterans. Chad Varah, an Episcopal clergyman who pioneered volunteer-staffed suicide hotlines and crisis centers in England, warns against volunteers who are more ready to supply answers than to listen and offer practical help with concrete situations. He is especially wary of helpers who know that "God is the answer" before they've heard the question.[18] Veterans must also feel that they have something to offer those around them, a value that is readily eroded by pain, depression, substance abuse, or physical handicaps. We must help find meaningful work or volunteer opportunities where they can contribute. Finally, the availability of weapons to persons at risk for suicide greatly enhances the risk. The removal of weapons from easy access may prevent suicides frequently considered but only initiated on impulse or while high.

The two books cited in the previous chapter, *After the War Zone* and *Back from the Front*, offer thoughtful guidance for returning vets and their families when risk of suicide is an issue. The veteran who does not know where to turn when troubled by suicidal urges can call the national suicide hotline, 1-800-273-TALK. The line is always available. Vets can press 1 when connected to be routed to the hotline for veterans. This is also a critical resource for friends or family members to call when they fear for their veteran loved one and don't know what to do.

Iraq and Afghanistan

The suicide alarm for Operation Enduring Freedom (OEF) in Afghanistan and Operation Iraqi Freedom (OIF) sounded rudely in 2002 when four special forces vets recently returned from Afghanistan killed both themselves and their wives.[19] Details were not published. We don't know whether PTSR played a role, or infidelity, or the collapse of marriages that is so common during deployments. Even in cases where domestic issues are primary, one cannot discount the stress of deployment on both spouses, nor a veteran's training in the use of violence.

In a 2006 report the army's Mental Health Advisory Team reported a significant rise in suicides among active-duty soldiers.[20] Because of shortages of personnel or units to fill key military roles in Iraq and Afghanistan, the DOD had initiated procedures ("stop loss" actions) to extend the enlistments of selected servicemen and women for up to a year beyond their original contracts. Data suggests that the repeated deployments required by the smaller "all-volunteer" military add to the suicide risk engendered by combat wounds and trauma.

As reports of military suicides grew, so did concern for prevention—in the military, among military families, and in Congress. In November 2005, twenty-two-year-old Joshua Omvig returned from an eleven-month tour in Iraq. He didn't talk much about his tour of duty, but he told his parents he thought he was suffering from PTSD[R]. They urged him to seek help, but he countered that seeking psychiatric treatment might ruin his career. Less than two months after his homecoming, sitting in his pickup in his parents' driveway, Josh shot himself. It is not clear that the VA could have helped Josh if he sought help. As returning Iraq and Afghanistan veterans sought VA help, complaints about long waits for service, particularly mental health service, rose like a chorus. In this uproar, Josh Omvig's suicide and the vigorous advocacy of his parents became the focal point for the Joshua Omvig Veterans Suicide Prevention Act of 2007. The legislation requires the VA to develop and implement programs addressing the mental health needs of veterans, particularly those at risk for suicide. The bill provides increased training for VA staff, greater attention to mental health evaluation, the creation of special suicide prevention counselors, targeted research on veterans' mental health issues, and improved outreach and education for veterans and their families.[21]

While the VA received this boost in resources for veterans at risk of suicide, suicides of active military personnel continued to climb. A January 2010 article from the McClatchy newspapers described the dilemma faced by the army at Fort Campbell, Kentucky, home of the legendary and frequently deployed 101st Airborne.[22] The staff at Fort Campbell created a special mental health task force after nine soldiers committed suicide in 2007. In 2008 the number of suicides at Fort Campbell reached a dozen. In response the base hired a suicide program manager, increased mental health personnel, and even implemented a three-day educational program directed at reducing stigma and encouraging the use of mental health services while emphasizing that the use of such services would not be an impediment to a soldier's career. In 2009, the number of suicides at Fort Campbell reached fourteen. Given the stresses inherent in military service, suicide prevention is not easily achieved, and because suicide is rare, prevention efforts are difficult to research. Studies must be large and of considerable duration. A recent VA review of suicide prevention research reported promising outcomes from a multifaceted, servicewide effort initiated in 1999 by the U.S. Air Force.[23] However, many elements of the air force program were in use at Fort Campbell.

In July 2010, the army released the candid *Army Health Promotion, Risk Reduction and Suicide Prevention Report*. Based on a fifteen-month investigation into increasing suicides in the army, the report lamented the erosion of existing army standards in response to combat demands and noted a general increase in "high risk" behavior such as drug use, crimes, and suicide attempts. The report states, "In fiscal year 2009, 160 active duty Soldiers took their lives, making suicide the third leading cause of death among the Army population." The report provides a case example to illustrate the difficulties army personnel may have in suspecting suicide:

> A Staff Sergeant had a hard childhood. His father was in and out of jail and both parents used illegal drugs. When he joined the Army, he thought he had finally escaped his background. He was promoted through the ranks and was well respected by his leadership. He helped to emancipate his sister and was paying for her college.

Following a very violent improvised explosive device (IED) attack, he started having difficulty sleeping and was waking up with night-mares. Shortly after deploying, his parents stole his identity and incurred a large debt in his name. One night, after arguing with his family, he took his life. His action took his leadership by surprise. He was viewed as one of the most resilient Soldiers in his company.[24]

The report addresses such issues as the "lost art of leadership in garrison" and the role of army experiences in the adult life cycle, alerting those in leadership positions to be especially sensitive to transitions and what it terms as "stress windows." The latter part of the report details the latest army efforts to combat what it calls its suicide epidemic. In commenting on the report, army vice chief of staff General Peter Chiarelli stated, "These findings demonstrate that many of our programs are unbalanced and lack integration, while reinforcing recommendations that will help us improve the quality of our programs and services."[25]

Prevention and Clinical Intervention in Cases of Potential Suicide

The situation at Fort Campbell and the 2010 army report demonstrate that suicide prevention is a formidable task. The first chapter of a 2006 textbook on suicide published by the American Psychiatric Association is entitled "Suicide Risk: Assessing the Unpredictable." Early in the text, the author cautions that, "Suicide is a rare event. Efforts to predict who will commit suicide lead to a large number of false-positive and false-negative predictions."[26] Research has identified many risk factors for potential sui-cide, some more applicable to military situations than others. Yet, outside the direct communication of suicidal threats, few of them justify interven-tion against the will of the person at risk. The dilemma of identifying soldiers or vets with the potential for suicide is illustrated by a detailed investigation of 134 consecutive civilian suicides in St. Louis conducted by Eli Robins three decades ago.[27] Only two-thirds of the persons who killed themselves communicated the intent to do so, most within a year of their suicide. Only 41 percent of these communications were explicit and only 20 percent of them were made to persons in a professional capacity (physician, minister, etc.). The threats were most often communicated to family and secondly to friends. The persons most likely to communicate suicidal intent in the study also had a diagnosis of alcoholism, making it easier for those who received the message to pass it over as alcohol induced. Given the Fort Campbell data, it may be that GIs are even less likely than civilians to communicate suicidal intent to those most likely to respond helpfully. Too often family and friends are not sufficiently prepared, informed, or supported to take preventive steps. One implication of the St. Louis study is that fellow soldiers are more likely to see clues to suicide before officers or military mental health personnel. Even threats made while drinking heavily off base need attention. The second author recalls the story of a sailor who returned to his ship after a drinking binge. The young man climbed two ladders, tied a rope around his neck, and jumped. Knocked unconscious when he hit the main deck, he still had ten feet of slack in the rope. The watch roused him and carried him to bed. He became the butt of numerous jokes, but no one referred him for mental health help.

Most persons are not prepared to deal with such frightening information as suicidal thinking. Unable to contemplate the horror of it, they may deny it, dismiss it, or offer a reassuring comment. In some cases they may encourage the person at risk to seek help, but few are prepared to take the dramatic, possibly relationship-threatening, steps necessary (such as talking to a commanding officer or mental health personnel) if the person refuses to seek help. Today, persons may communicate suicide concerns more frequently to clinicians—over 50 percent of persons who commit suicide in the United States are in active treatment at the time.[28] Some promising reductions in suicide rates have been reported when key professional "gatekeepers"—primary care nurses and physicians, social workers, etc.—receive relevant suicide-prevention training.[29] Still, it is family and friends who may be encumbered with the most critical information, and they need education and preparation about what they must do. There is little research on the training and support of those, sometimes referred to as "emerging gatekeepers," often in the best position to initiate critical intervention.

When suicide risks are present, VA clinicians must openly abandon the usual confidentiality for the sake of the patient. Clinicians typically negotiate a signed contract that the client will not kill him or herself. Psychiatrist John Maltsberger encourages clinicians to involve family or friends who are in a position to monitor the patient and to have such monitors sign contracts when possible.[30] He warns that a suicide contract is a tenuous tool and that clients may not express an intention to violate it. Clinicians must be alert to crises or emotional shifts that make clients feel their situation is more impossible. Even clinicians are vulnerable to underestimating suicidal risks. Maltsberger cautions, "Every clinician wants to avoid signing unnecessary involuntary petitions, but when mistakes are made they are almost always in the other direction—not signing them." He stresses the wisdom of treating potential suicides within a team framework and encourages clinicians to seek regular consultation from colleagues.

Suicide potential requires concerted efforts to develop even tentative alliances, glimmers of hope, and openings in communication. The presence of a person in a clinic is evidence of his or her ambivalence about suicide and offers the opportunity to address what Eric Shneidman calls the critical "inner pain." "Where do you hurt?" and "How can I help?" are central issues for clinicians, though answers may be hard to evoke.[31]

There is a natural inertia about going the "extra mile" when clinicians treat persons at risk of suicide. In a VA clinic, extending intervention beyond the office or beyond the "identified" patient for one vet can reduce the time to see others. When there are waiting lists, administrative pressure for "productivity" may be intense. Yet there are times when home visits, extra phone calls, and the inclusion of the patient's family and supports are essential. A clinician may even need to build a support network where none is present. Mental health clinicians in the military or the VA represent their institutions in a special way to service members and vets. When they go the extra mile they may demonstrate special concern by institutions in which a distressed person has lost faith. In such cases, caring or a perceived lack of caring may have critical symbolic value.

Through different wars and different stressors, there are important common themes in veterans' suicides. Some characterize civilian suicides as well. Substance abuse, especially alcohol, is a risk factor. Many persons who commit suicide were drinking before doing so. The likelihood that comments suggesting suicide will be communicated to someone other than a professional prompts the military to stress the education of servicemen and women at all levels and to emphasize a near-combat level of vigilance for one's comrades. Many Vietnam vets were younger than current vets and were not deployed in units; Iraq and Afghanistan vets tended to be deployed repeatedly, leaving and returning as units. Their suicide risks are higher than usual while still on active duty. National Guard and reserve units serving in Iraq and Afghanistan return to local communities and disperse, thereby losing the support available to regular units. For both Vietnam and more recent vets, suicide risks are higher in the first six months after vets return than they are later. Changes on the home front that occur while soldiers are deployed may be truly confronted only on a vet's return. Still, many troops who share risk factors are not prone to suicide, and the intrusive intervention necessary for those at serious risk is difficult even for professionals. The systematic preventive effort of "reverse boot camps," suggested in the previous chapter, may promise improved prevention. The Caregivers and Veterans Omnibus Health Services Act of 2010 does increase the resources available to returning vets by authorizing readjustment counseling that includes "peer outreach and support," and provides for the VA to contract with community mental health centers and other resources in areas underserved by VA facilities. The act also provides for an extensive multiagency study of veterans' suicides.[32]

Doc's Closing Message

Doc's plan for this book did not include a chapter on suicide, nor is it likely that he set out to write this book amid thoughts of his own suicide. He wrote no suicide note, yet speculation about a suicide is inevitable. We did not violate the privacy of Doc's family with probing questions.

His friend Mike Archer suggests, "While the deleterious effects of the Vietnam War on both Doc's conscience, and consciousness, can never be overstated ... I never heard Bob fulminate about the architects of the Vietnam War as vehemently as he did about Rumsfeld, Cheney, and other architects of the Iraq War. With hindsight, I see this as what pushed him beyond his ability to cope."[33] Mike was prompted to quote from the latter part of Hamlet's famous soliloquy:

> For who would bear the whips and scorns of time,
> Th' oppressor's wrong, the proud man's contumely
> The pangs of despised love, the law's delay,
> The insolence of office, and the spurns
> That patient merit of th' unworthy takes,
> When he himself might his quietus make.[34]

Other clues about Doc's suicide lie in the content and circumstances of his manuscript for this book. Those who knew Doc remember his perfectionism, his passion, his commitment to his point of view, and his sense of humor. All but the humor are evident in the manuscript he left. Doc was writing about the betrayal of veterans and he also felt betrayed. A bit of Doc's anger remains, but those who helpfully proofread the early drafts suggested, "Let the stories speak for themselves." Doc's perfectionism and his emotions were at odds in this work. The isolation and depression that so often come with PTSR left him alone and with a narrowed, more pessimistic perspective. The manuscript he left has profited greatly from the generous assistance of his friends, fellow veterans, and professional resources. This support was all available to him, *if he had asked.* There is only one person wielding a pen or keyboard when writing takes place, but proofing, sharing, critiquing, and eliciting feedback are essential. Writing is a social enterprise. Even when the writer is alone, it makes a difference whether the imagined audiences are critical or supportive. Doc was stuck in a corner and couldn't see his way clear.

Doc's manuscript brimmed with research and valuable information, but it was the tip of the iceberg. With the manuscript discs that Terri

Topmiller gave the second author to finish this book were two cubic feet of newspaper stories, magazine articles, and studies documenting the systematic denial of veterans' claims and the tragic tales of individual veterans. The stories were a diet for despair and Doc had gorged on them in isolation. Both posttraumatic stress and depression engender social withdrawal. Because we live as social beings, the heart of suicide prevention is the mutual task of remaining open to each other. We are stymied when those who need us most place themselves out of our reach. Extending ourselves to those who close their doors is a risky venture—we can misspeak, be too intrusive, face rejection, disrupt our own lives, or precipitate a crisis. When we are worried about a person who is seriously withdrawn, our first risk must be to find and confide in someone we trust. If suicide is what we fear, we must share what seems unspeakable. We can't help the isolated by worrying in our own isolation. Realistically helping veterans at risk requires partnerships with family, friends, and professionals and maybe even voices on a hotline and help from law enforcement and institutions. When our efforts flag, we must remember what is at stake and what we've asked veterans to risk for us.

CHAPTER EIGHT

The VA Today

Humpty Dumpty sat on a wall. Humpty Dumpty had a great fall. All the king's horses and all the king's men couldn't put Humpty together again.

English Nursery Rhyme

Demands on the VA

A NURSERY RHYME INTRODUCES CHILDREN to a harsh reality—not everything can be fixed no matter what resources the king can muster. Sometimes *who* cannot be fixed is a father or mother, a brother or sister, a son or daughter. The Department of Veterans Affairs always labors under this burden. Many wounded can be patched but never put together again. Some veterans and their families will join in grateful alliance with the VA's effort to provide treatment, care, and support. The VA may become a target for the frustration of other families and their veterans when wounds persist because of poor care or in spite of the best care available.

Given the accounts of atomic veterans, Agent Orange, Gulf War illnesses, and struggles with PTSR, it is hard to believe one is not reading a cautionary tale for vets returning from Iraq and Afghanistan. Well into Operation Enduring Freedom (OEF—Afghanistan) and

Operation Iraqi Freedom (OIF), investigative reporters at the *Washington Post* disclosed serious shortcomings at the Walter Reed Army Medical Center in the nation's capital.[1] After their Walter Reed exposé, the journalists received a raft of correspondence detailing inadequate resources and poor care in other military and VA medical facilities. They reported:

> Among the most aggrieved are veterans who have lived with the open secret of substandard, underfunded care in the 154 VA hospitals and hundreds of community health centers around the country. They vented their fury in thousands of e-mails and phone calls and in chat rooms.[2]

This occurred at a time when the administration of President George W. Bush was stinting the VA's budget in spite of a flood of Iraq and Afghanistan casualties. Given the rosy scenarios for quick success in Iraq, it is not surprising that the VA was unprepared for the influx of wounded from that conflict. The foray into Afghanistan to root out Al Qaeda terrorists was also billed as a short, limited operation. Between January 2000 and September 2004, the VA strove to address growing numbers of wounded vets suffering the signature wounds of the War on Terror—PTSR, amputations, traumatic brain injury (TBI). During this period the ratio of patients to doctors at the VA grew from 335 to 1 to 531 to 1.[3] In 2006, especially for vets seeking substance abuse and mental health treatment, waiting lists were so long the VA acknowledged that treatment was "virtually inaccessible."[4]

Anthony Principi, appointed secretary of veterans affairs by President Bush in 2001, had years of experience with the VA and served as temporary secretary of the department during the presidency of Bush's father. In an effort to shore up the VA's response to the needs of returning OEF and OIF veterans, Principi sought a $1.2 billion increase in the VA's budget for 2005. His increases were rejected by the administration and the Republican Congress. Principi resigned his post in January 2005.

That same month, a DOD undersecretary suggested to the *Wall Street Journal* that the costs of veterans' care and benefits were "taking away from the nation's ability to defend itself."[5] As demands on the VA grew, George W. Bush appointed Jim Nicholson, an army veteran, attorney, and real estate developer, to succeed Principi. Nicholson, who had previously served as chairman of the Republican National Committee, faithfully hewed to the president's priorities, making no requests to increase VA funding. In 2006, veterans' groups sued for greater access to care, particularly mental health care. An editorial in early 2007 characterized the Bush administration as fighting "tooth and nail to deny VA healthcare benefits."[6] While administration officials were criticizing opponents of the Iraq War for failure to support the troops, administration attorneys were arguing that the laws providing for veterans' health care did not "entitle" the same troops, when wounded, to any particular service, alleging that such decisions must be left to the Department of Veterans Affairs and the practical issue of "available funds."

When budget relief for the VA finally came, it was initiated by Congress, including members of the president's own party, in 2007. In January 2008, as he entered his last year in office, George W. Bush signed legislation authorizing the largest increase in the VA budget ($3.7 billion) since the VA had become a cabinet-level department.

The Resurgence of Quality Care in the VA

How did veterans fare during the lean years of George W. Bush? Although a number of veterans, particularly those with PTSR, brain injury, or multiple severe injuries, found VA care wanting, many veterans received high-quality care. These veterans benefited from a revolution in the quality of VA medical care that began in the 1990s. The improvements that sprang from that revolution helped offset serious constraints imposed by lean budgets.

The Story of a Revolution

Over the years, the VA has been the target of probing congressional investigations and major exposés. News stories from 2009 and 2010 might suggest that VA care had not come very far: the VA hospital in Murfreesboro, Tennessee, notified over six thousand patients of possible complications due to poorly maintained colonoscopy equipment;[7] eighteen hundred vets risked infection from improperly sterilized equipment at the VA Medical Center in Atlanta; the Philadelphia VA was fined by the Nuclear Regulatory Commission for errors in the use of radioactive implants to combat prostate cancer.[8] In truth errors abound in the U.S. health care system. In 1999, the Institute of Medicine released *To Err Is Human,* a study that estimated that ninety-eight thousand patients die annually in the United States due to preventable medical errors.[9] Other studies suggest that almost as many die of infections acquired in hospitals.[10] There are few families in America that can't relate a story of some medical screwup or aggravation in their private-sector care. While medical errors in the VA get national coverage, recent data suggests that such screwups are much less common in the VA than in the private sector.

In 2007, under the provocative title *Best Care Anywhere: Why VA Health Care Is Better than Yours,* Phillip Longman told the story of the VA's quality revolution. He acknowledged, "By the mid 1990s, the reputation of veteran's hospitals had sunk so low that conservatives routinely used the example of the VA as a trump card in any discussion of government managed 'socialized medicine.'"[11] The conservative arguments were more than ideological. A 1977 study by the National Academy of Sciences was highly critical of VA care.[12] Market research "suggested that 3 out of 4 veterans would 'vote with their feet' and leave the VA if given a national health care card."[13] Longman reports that professionals within the VA were frustrated with the system as well. In the 1970s and 1980s, a number of VA doctors, pharmacists, and nurses began writing computer programs to make their record keeping more efficient and useful. Often encouraged by local administrators, the new records system lacked formal sanctions from the VA central office, but by the time this grassroots effort achieved official blessing, the VA was on its way to one of the most sophisticated medical records systems in the country. In today's VA, doctor's notes, x-rays, lab reports, and EKGs (no matter where performed in the VA system) lie a few computer keystrokes away at any VA medical facility. The records system helps monitor treatment to prevent errors. A nurse making a computer entry prior to giving medication or initiating a procedure can trigger a warning if the treatment is inconsistent with data in the patient's record. Accessible records in standardized formats permit the VA to conduct regular evaluation of treatment outcomes and make the Veterans Health Administration (VHA) a leader in the practice of "evidence-based" medicine. In turn, data guides VA administrators who may utilize checklists and audits to establish performance goals based on research rather than prevailing fads.[14] "Some twenty years ahead of their time," Longman reports, "VA doctors felt compelled to begin developing a new, highly effective model of care stressing prevention, primary care, and effective management of chronic disease."[15]

The VA placed strong emphasis on team-based service integration organized around primary care. Between 1993 and 1996 the number of veterans enrolled in primary care rose from around 40 percent to 90 percent; VA medical centers added new primary care training programs. The number of primary care residents increased and their rotations were lengthened. When primary care physicians were in short supply, the VA filled many openings with nurse practitioners. In 2001, when the Institute of Medicine published *Crossing the Quality Chasm,* a series of recommendations to improve medical care in the twenty-first century, the VA's bridge was well under way, led by unprecedented efforts toward quality control.[16]

The VHA's revolution sprung from the work and dedication of many staff, but credit for leading the movement goes to Dr. Kenneth Kizer. According to Longman, Dr. Kizer

liked VHA's clear mission—to keep patients healthy—and that it didn't have to maximize shareholders' profits or doctors' income. Also, because its mission centered on patients rather than profits, a core of VHA employees were highly idealistic and committed to improving quality. As Kizer saw it, the great opportunity lay in truly integrating this system and taking advantage of its potential, including investment in prevention, primary care, and highly co-ordinated, patient centered, evidence based medicine.[17]

Under Dr. Kizer, the VA adopted a policy of full disclosure of medical errors. For Dr. Kizer this was the first step in seeking "systematic solutions to safety problems, not seeking to fix blame ... except in the most egregious cases."[18] The colonoscopy and radiation mishaps cited earlier reflect VA candor in spite of resulting bad press. Less heralded are stories demonstrating the VA's steady improvement in quality care. In 2003 a study comparing VA care with fee-for-service care obtained in the private sector under Medicare found VA care to be significantly better in all eleven measures chosen.[19] A 2004 study compared diabetes care at the VA with care in a sample of seven managed care organizations—the VA outperformed the managed care programs in all seven measures.[20] Another 2004 study, by the RAND Corporation, "concluded that VA outperforms all other sectors of American health care in 294 measures of quality."[21]

A Tradition of Dedicated Staff—Two Interviews 45 Years Apart

Though administrative and political support is essential, it is interesting that much of the leadership in the VA's health care revolution occurred at the grassroots. When the second author entered graduate school in psychology after exiting the military, he trained for three years and worked an additional year in VA medical facilities. His first training site (1964–1965) was the VA hospital in Martinsburg, West Virginia. Ninety miles from Washington, D.C., Martinsburg was rural enough to be a challenge for professional recruiting. When new doctors joined the staff, one curmudgeon at the hospital would always ask, "Why would he come to Martinsburg? What's wrong with him?" Yet almost all the physicians were friendly, dedicated, and competent. The second author collaborated frequently with the physician in charge of geriatrics, a man who served many years in the private sector and enjoyed a national reputation (as president of his specialty organization). As he grew older he tired of the private-practice "rat race." He chose to finish his career delivering high-quality care without billing and insurance hassles or the pressure to move patients out of hospitals too rapidly that characterized his tenure in private practice and at large medical centers. He described the VA as the most "patient centered" system in his experience.

Forty-five years later, in preparing this book, the second author interviewed a friend and physician at the Lexington, Kentucky, VA hospital. Her reasons for working at the VA and those of the doctor in Martinsburg were strikingly similar. She also worked previously in private practice and at a major university medical center. She worked at the VA for less pay but with greater professional satisfaction—she offered quality care, enjoyed talented and supportive colleagues, and was free of the red tape ("fly paper" as she described it) of arguing insurance claims. She cited the advantages of:

- Colleagues who shared her dedication—a member of her specialty was always on call evenings and weekends, but a patient's own doctor was far more likely to come to the hospital if needed.
- User-friendly, up-to-date medical records that made for better patient care.
- Well-equipped facilities with access to treatment options and medications sometimes unavailable at other area hospitals. Vets were also eligible for referral to other hospitals if needed.
- Excellent collaboration between specialists and primary care, especially pre- and post-surgery.[22]

When Care Outside the VA Is Better

If the VA enjoys lower medical error rates than much of the private sector, VA care may not be the best for all veterans. This became dramatically evident for some veterans returning from Iraq and Afghanistan with multiple injuries, severe burns, and traumatic brain injury (TBI).

Polytrauma Centers

In 1939, Dalton Trumbo published *Johnny Got His Gun,* about the fictional Joe Bonham, who survives World War I without arms or legs.[23] Shell concussions left Joe deaf, and a cloth covers the cavity where his mouth, tongue, nose and eyes used to function. Joe is a breathing body, fed through a tube, but the reader enters Joe's thoughts, lost hopes, and fears. Joe struggles to grasp his situation. Where am I? Could I have survived all these injuries at once or did infections lead to gradual removal of my limbs and senses? Does anyone know who I am? Aware of vibrations when people enter his room, sometimes in groups, he speculates that he is no longer a man but a medical curiosity. Desperately Joe tries to communicate, faintly moving his head in a code he hopes someone will decipher.

When Trumbo wrote, Joe Bonham seemed close to science fiction. Not today. The horrible wounds sustained by some U.S. troops as a result of improvised explosive devices (IEDs) in Iraq and Afghanistan, and the rapid, expert medical care available to them brings vets to the VA who are not too far from Joe Bonham. In confronting this challenge the VA has opened a number of polytrauma centers. The most disheartening of injuries experienced by vets in these centers involve severe physical injuries coupled with traumatic brain injury (TBI). Traumatic brain injury can take many forms and calls for highly trained specialists and rehabilitation personnel. Even before the Iraq and Afghan conflicts the availability of such resources was scant in the United States. Michael Paul Mason, a case manager for civilians suffering TBI, regularly meets with distraught relatives of TBI victims from car accidents or natural disasters. Painfully he explains that the specialty hospitals and rehab facilities their loved ones need are "as accessible as the moon."[24] In the presence of such dire shortages, the VA strains to recruit or train the specialists they need.

Although the VA may be reluctant to acknowledge their limited resources, they will pay for necessary private care if veterans or their families can find it. The story of Eric Edmundson illustrates both the potential and the difficulty of looking for the "moon." Eric suffered a heart attack while undergoing surgery for injuries from an IED and was anoxic for thirty minutes before his heartbeat and breathing were restored. With severe brain trauma, Eric was sent to a VA polytrauma center. Journalist Aaron Glantz and the Public Broadcasting System program *NOW* both recount Eric's stark odyssey.[25] Eric's family rallied powerfully in his support. His parents, wife, and child moved close to the VA hospital, where they supplemented his care in what they considered an understaffed polytrauma center. Eric's father resigned his job (losing his own health insurance) to become Eric's part-time caretaker and full-time advocate. When the VA suggested custodial care in a nursing home for Eric, his father rejected such a bleak prospect. In a determined search for alternatives, he discovered the Rehabilitation Institute of Chicago, a premier center for the treatment of TBI. He arranged Eric's transfer to Chicago and worked with nonprofit veterans' organizations to find funds to live near Eric and to construct a handicapped-accessible house for the family. As his father approached exhaustion, Eric's mother gave up her job and joined the effort. They sold their home and moved in with Eric and his family. Today, Eric operates an electric wheelchair and communicates in limited but positive and caring ways with his parents, wife, and son. He can help with simple chores in the house but still requires regular care from his wife and parents, who all live together on Eric's disability income.

Conventional Care Outside the VA

Older veterans not being treated for service-related disabilities are more likely to receive private care through Medicare than through the VA. At times policy makers suggest that all veterans utilize such care. Longman quotes Dr. Kizer's declaring, "We have to ... demonstrate that we have an equal or better value than the private sector, or frankly we should not exist."[26] While the VA usually achieves high standards of care, their evidence-based approach is increasing their willingness to refer veterans to outside resources when evidence indicates that outside care is better. If a procedure is available in a VA hospital but performed more frequently in a nearby private hospital, a veteran may receive better care in the more experienced hospital. In a 2007 article in the *American Journal of Public Health*, researchers collaborating with the VA compared the outcomes of veterans receiving fourteen types of surgery in private hospitals rated as either high- or low-performance (based on surgical outcomes in the two years prior to the study). Veterans served in the high-performance hospitals had a notably lower mortality rate. The researchers suggest a role for the VA in directing veterans who receive care outside the VA to hospitals best prepared for the surgical procedures they need.[27]

Scrutiny of VA Health Care

No health care system in the world operates under closer scrutiny than the VHA. Dissatisfied veterans might address complaints to their caregivers but also their congressperson or senator. Elected representatives usually commit staff to follow up on such concerns as part of their constituent services. Congressional committees conduct hearings or commission studies of VA care, calling on resources such as the Office of Management and Budget, the Government Accountability Office, or the Institute of Medicine. Presidents may initiate studies of the VA. Most recently President George W. Bush created a commission chaired by Robert Dole, former U.S. senator and partially disabled World War II vet, and Donna Shalala, university president and former secretary of Health and Human Services, to recommend improvements in the VA.[28]

Veterans' health care facilities are reviewed and accredited by the Joint Commission (formerly the Joint Commission on Accreditation of Health Care Organizations). In the past Joint Commission evaluations relied on interviews and inspection of policies and records. Now they often establish and monitor objectives directly related to patient outcome. Major veterans' organizations also perform annual reviews of the state and needs of the VA. In 2003, the American Legion launched an annual report titled *A System Worth Saving* in which selected hospitals, clinics, and vet centers from the VA's twenty-three Veterans Integrated Service Networks are assessed based on their physical plant, staffing, budget problems, programs, and unique local challenges.[29]

Four veterans' organizations—American Veterans (AMVETS), Disabled American Veterans (DAV), Paralyzed Veterans of America (PVA), and the Veterans of Foreign Wars (VFW)—join annually to produce *The Independent Budget for the Department of Veterans Affairs* (IB).[30] The IB for 2011 lists sixty-three supporting organizations as varied as Administrators of Internal Medicine, the Lung Cancer Alliance, and the National Society of Military Widows. The IB addresses comprehensive concerns from timely provision of pensions to improved medical procedures. The IB makes recommendations to the VA, Congress, the administration, and departments intimately involved with veterans' issues such as the DOD and the Department of Labor. Veterans, their families, and groups concerned with improving the VA can find a wealth of information in the IB. Veterans and their families need to discover what veterans' organizations can offer. For example, the DAV provides service officers who assist veterans with locating important services and filing claims for benefits; the PVA publishes invaluable handbooks to assist families in home care of seriously disabled veterans.

New Challenges for the VA

Among the broad range of treatment issues addressed in the IB, two require special attention from the VA—the care of new forms of severe injury and the treatment of a growing number of women veterans. The first of these also received special attention from the Dole-Shalala Commission.

Severely Injured Veterans

While the VHA developed a number of polytrauma centers, they struggle to staff them adequately. In this effort, the VA may need to innovate and commit to training many of their own professional and rehabilitation staff. The VA has strong precedents for innovation. As noted in Chapter 2, after World War II the VA became a major source of funding and training for clinical psychologists. In the late 1990s, seeking to enhance primary care, the VA sharply increased their training of primary care physicians and made increasing use of nurse practitioners. In 2003 the VA began encouraging nursing innovation with special awards; nurses are often closer to the day-to-day needs of patients and may make creative contributions to the care of the VA's new polytrauma vets. Specialized case managers (or recovery coordinators) are of critical importance in the care of severely injured veterans. The first recommendation of the Dole-Shalala Commission called upon the VA to:

> Create a patient-centered Recovery Plan for every seriously injured service member that provides the right care and support at the right time in the right place. A corps of well-trained, highly skilled Recovery Coordinators must be swiftly developed to ensure prompt development and execution of the Recovery Plan.[31]

The commission envisioned these coordinators as helping "service members obtain services *promptly* and *in the most appropriate care facilities*— whether DOD, VA, or civilian" (emphasis in original).[32] They specified a dynamic plan, regularly revised, that identifies "patient goals for: post-acute, outpatient, and rehabilitation care; and return to military duty, home community, or into education, training, and employment programs." The Dole-Shalala Commission recognized that involvement and support of a seriously injured veteran's family is critical to the veteran's care. Their data showed that many family members relocate to where their loved one is in the hospital. Some give up jobs to become caregivers. The commission recommended "extending the Family and Medical Leave Act for up to six months for spouses and parents of seriously injured."[33] Advocacy for a strong case management system is also prominent in the IB, which notes that

> A severely injured veteran's spouse is likely to be young, have dependent children, and reside in a rural area where access to support services of any kind can be limited. Spouses must often give up their personal plans (resign from employment, withdraw from school, etc.) to care for, attend, and advocate for the veteran. They often fall victim to bureaucratic mishaps as a result of the shifting responsibility within conflicting government pay and compensation systems (military pay, military disability pay, military retirement pay, VA compensation) on which they must rely for subsistence in the absence of other personal means. For many younger, unmarried veterans who survive their injuries, the primary caregivers remain their parents, who have limited eligibility for military assistance and have virtually no current eligibility for VA benefits or services of any kind.[34]

"America's New Wounded Warriors—Why Are Their Family Caregivers Overworked and Under-Supported?" the same edition of PBS's *NOW* that told the story of Eric Edmundson, presents the story of Ryanne Noss, a young woman of twenty-six with a Ph.D. in chemical engineering.[35] Ryanne helped care for Scot, her severely brain-damaged husband, in the Tampa VA hospital for two and a half years before confronting the almost overwhelming hurdle of taking him home. Scot is a big man, only slightly responsive, and still unable to communicate even by signs. His hygiene and feeding pose challenges, and Ryanne must exercise his limbs in the hope that they may function if some neural pathways can be restored. Rehabilitation after such injuries requires persistent rep-etition of word or touch-action combinations in the search for regular responsive movements, sounds, eye-blinks—any potential channel for communication. Ryanne will need a dedicated and steady volunteer support system.

A striking element of the *NOW* documentary is the apparent failure of either of these severely wounded men to respond to therapy until their loved ones became involved. Though lacking rehab expertise, these fam-ily members offered a recognizable, caring presence that touched a spark in some deep place for men facing a life nearly as imprisoning as Joe Bonham's. At the time of the PBS program, the VA had no provision to pay family caretakers of such veterans or to pay those who can give such caretakers crucial respite. A moving scene in the documentary captured the separation of Ryanne and Ivonne Thompson. Ivonne was caring for a similarly handicapped husband and her son virtually grew up in the hospital. These women offered one another invaluable support and they clearly dreaded its loss as they returned to homes in different states.

In a number of VA hospitals staff offer counseling and support to such intrepid caretakers, because, as the IB observes, local VA officials clearly recognized "the urgency and validity of this need." Yet these officials were "concerned about the possible absence of legal authority to provide these services and that scarce resources are being diverted to these needs without recognition of their cost."[36] Caretakers of the severely disabled usually need to learn how to obtain and use specialized electronic equipment, lifts, and catheters or to hire personal assistants to help provide the care their loved one needs. As the PVA's practical guide *Managing Personal Assistants* explains, organizing, hiring, and managing personal assistants is equivalent to running a small business.[37]

Legislation to Help Severely Wounded Vets and Their Families

On May 5, 2010, President Obama signed a major piece of legislation, the Caregivers and Veterans Omnibus Health Services Act.[38] The act seeks the following:

a) To reduce the number of veterans who need institutional care and whose needs could be "substantially satisfied" at home by a family member or designated caregiver; and

b) To provide eligible veterans with choices as to the setting and personal care services that best suits their needs.

Designed for veterans with seriously disabling injuries and mental conditions incurred during their service, including TBI, the act provides for training of caretakers as needed, reimbursement of expenses incurred in training, and respite care for the veteran while a caretaker is in training. Where possible the veteran has a significant role in selecting and approving the continued service of their caretakers. The law provides for counseling and technical support for caregivers and even medical care under certain circumstances. Critically, the legislation provides a monthly stipend for approved family caretakers. This legislation offers significant relief to families with incredible burdens such as the Edmundsons or Ryanne Noss. In early versions of this act, only veterans wounded since the 2001 terrorist attacks were eligible for these benefits, but strong advocacy ensured that veterans of "all eras" are covered. Although tight budgets often deter congressional action or presidential support for expanded VA services, this helpful legislation came as America faced the deepest recession since the Great Depression and the treasury, already depleted from the Iraq and Afghanistan conflicts, confronted rising demands and sinking revenues. The legislation constitutes a major victory for veterans' advocates and a tribute to the priority given by Congress and the president to our wounded warriors.

The New Women Veterans

In Iraq and Afghanistan women are serving in unprecedented numbers and in increasingly dangerous missions. There is danger because battle lines are indistinguishable and military women are subject to mortar or rocket attacks almost anywhere in the theater. Women traveling the roads are exposed to IEDs or ambushes and must defend themselves like any infantryman. Despite public perceptions and some policies, women increasingly serve in explicit combat situations. Over two thousand women in Iraq won bronze stars and over thirteen hundred earned combat action badges.

Some women in Iraq and Afghanistan are actually chosen for dangerous missions because of their gender. Such women join all-male combat units as a "Lioness" to defuse tension with "women and children during searches of their homes and their persons" in areas where insurgents are active. Lioness teams are still deployed in Afghanistan, but such duty may not be recorded in their service record. Until the recent shift in the VA's policy for substantiating PTSD[R], such "absence of documentation" constituted a major barrier for these women to receive "care for PTSD[R] or other post-deployment mental health readjustment issues."[39]

Over 70 percent of women vets seeking counseling report being raped while in the military. According to a Pentagon report, 90 percent of rapes in the military are never reported. Journalist Helen Benedict notes that

> that same report showed that in 2008, reports of assault increased by 8 percent military-wide, and by 26 percent in the Iraq and Afghanistan wars. For many women soldiers, the result of all this persecution is that instead of finding camaraderie among their fellow soldiers, or being able to rely on comrades to watch their backs in battle, they feel dangerously alone.[40]

The number of women vets traumatized by combat, sexual harassment, and rape requires a serious shift in responses by the VA, including more female treatment staff and increased awareness of stresses encountered by women in the military. Traditionally the VA is a heavily male organization devoted to the treatment of males and employing many veterans. In serving women vets, the VA must guard against sexism, sexual innuendo, and even the sexual advances that are sadly so prominent in the military. Equal sensitivities must guide the review of women's pension and disability claims.

The Pension System

One of the most intractable problems facing the VA is the need for consistent, efficient, and timely processing of pension and disability requests. After his tenure as director of the VA, General Omar Bradley chaired the 1956 Presidents Commission on Veterans' Pensions. The commission concluded, "Our present structure of veterans' programs is not a 'system.' It is an accretion of laws based largely on precedents built up over 150 years of piecemeal development."[41] Over fifty years later the Dole-Shalala Commission repeated the lament of Bradley's group—there was still "no clear national policy of veterans' benefits." They recommended Congress "Completely restructure the disability and compensation systems" of the DOD and the VA, with a clear philosophy and guiding principles. In some cases the goal of compensation for disability seems to be income replacement. "Such a focus reduces recipients' incentives to work, to obtain education and training—in short, to get on with life," asserts the Dole-Shalala Commission.[42] In other circumstances pensions seem directed at compensation for injuries suffered. More intensive support during a period of rehabilitation followed by a reduced pension for a veteran who progresses as a wage earner has never characterized the pension system. While such individualized goals may be laudable, the VA struggles simply to process basic disability claims.

In a 2007 study, Linda Bilmes documented a backlog of 400,000 disability claims.[43] Having already noted the difficulty Iraq and Afghanistan vets faced in accessing timely mental health care, Bilmes warns, "A veteran who is discharged regularly, and has some level of disability will typically have to wait 6 months before receiving his or her disability check from the VA. This is a period during which the veterans, particularly those in a state of mental distress, are most at risk for serious problems, including suicide, falling into substance abuse, divorce, losing their job, or becoming homeless." Bilmes offers three solutions to addressing the pension system backlog:

a) A "fast track" specialty unit modeled on new technologies used by large health insurers;

b) An expanded role for vet centers to more efficiently assist veterans with more routine claims;

c) Approaching claims on the "income tax" model since close to 90 percent of claims are ultimately approved. This would approve all properly submitted claims promptly and then audit selected samples to deter fraud.

Records Problems

From the post–World War II exposure of veterans to atomic radiation forward, veterans faced problems reconciling DOD and VA records. Work on systems of compatibility allowing critical information to follow a veteran from active duty to VA care remains a high priority. Collaboration between the regular military and the VA is going forward, but much remains to be done, especially for the 40 percent of troops being deployed in Iraq and Afghanistan who come from reserve and National Guard units. Their records systems are different and, as observed in the chapter on suicide, they are at higher risk of post-deployment problems because they lack the administrative, unit, and social supports of regular service personnel.

History strongly underscores the importance of leadership in the Department of Veterans Affairs. From Harding's disastrous appointment of Charles Forbes onward it is clear that the VA fares better with competent leaders dedicated to the VA's mission. Those granted VA leadership as a political plum often fail our veterans and sometimes compound their weaknesses by filling other key posts based on political favoritism. It is notable that Dr. Kenneth Kizer, who led the VA's revolution in quality care, was a registered Republican appointed by a Democratic administration. There may also be times for even dedicated leaders to be replaced.

General Hines, who led the VA longer than any administrator, earned great respect for his personal work ethic, but did not prepare the VA for the flood of wounded from World War II. General Omar Bradley replaced Hines. In his brief stay he brought new vision and talent into the VA at a crucial time for U.S. veterans.

Congress, often a harsh critic of the VA, also bears significant responsibility for oversight of the VA and ensuring an adequate VA budget. In lauding the VA's internally generated revolution, a 1996 editorial in the *New England Journal of Medicine* described the VA as "emerging from an insular system that Congress has protected from the tumultuous forces that are reshaping other parts of American medicine."[44] The VA budget often languishes in the backwash of decisions about war—decisions that focus on the immediate military conflict but fail to reckon the long-range costs in lives, wounded, devastated families, or federal funds to care for veterans. When we place troops in harm's way we must recognize and provide for the long-term costs in care and compensation for veterans and their families. In 2007, Congress belatedly authorized funds critical to the care of vets returning from Afghanistan and Iraq.

After years of criticism and documented poor performance in the 1970s and 1980s, in the late 1990s the VHA demonstrated the capacity to leap to the forefront of American medicine when given leadership and sufficient funding. "Objectivity and openness to change" and an "investment in research on health services" to guide evidence-based innovation were critical to the VA's progress.[45] In the wake of the VA's revolution, an editorial in the *American Journal of Public Health* even suggested that the VA could serve as a domestic model for a national health care system.[46] Our political leaders owe it to our veterans to assure competent leadership at the VA and to fund, preserve, and extend the thrust of the VA's medical advances.

CHAPTER NINE

"Help Us, Doc," to Avoid
the Next War

Washington could not accept that its presence in South Vietnam sparked the instability that it decried.

Robert "Doc" Topmiller, *Lotus Unleashed*[1]

It is easy for us who are living to honor the sacrifices of those who are dead. For it helps us to assuage the guilt we should feel in their presence. Wars can be prevented as surely as they are provoked, and therefore we who fail to prevent them share in guilt for the dead.

General Omar Bradley[2]

DOC'S WISDOM ABOUT SOUTH VIETNAM persists like a refrain in our current foreign policy. We face the dilemma that our very presence in Iraq and Afghanistan spurs local insurgencies and fosters recruitment for terrorists we seek to defeat.[3] Too often we place troops in harm's way for dubious reasons, then call upon the nation to support their mission because our troops are there. The best support for our troops is to avoid war. Of all the advances in modern medicine those with the greatest impact are preventive—progress in public health such as clean water, improved hygiene, sewage systems, and vaccinations. For the VA, public health means preventing the horrors of war—*peace* is the name of public health for veterans. Doc believed in helping veterans and longed for peace. Is peace possible? In 1968, historians Will and Ariel Durant wrote, "War is one of the constants of history, and has not diminished with civilization or democracy. In the last 3,421 years of recorded history, only 268 have seen no war."[4] Yet Omar Bradley asserted, "Wars can be prevented as surely as they can be provoked." And Bradley was no disheveled sign waver at a peace rally. He was one of America's few five-star generals, the commander of the World War II landing at Normandy, and a director of the VA. Was he slipping in his old age or is his a wisdom we ignore because it calls on us to rethink our own national investment in the world's greatest war machine?

In the United States we spend close to half our national budget on current or past expenses for national security.[5] We never call it war spending; we call it defense spending. Until 1947 we had a Department of War. Now we have a Department of Defense, but a permanent war economy. Cold War military spending was provoked by real and exaggerated Soviet threats, but also by industrialists who thrived on military spending, by economists who saw continued war spending as a buffer against postwar recession, and by rampant competition between military services.[6] Early in his administration, President Dwight Eisenhower, our supreme commander in World War II, cautioned the nation:

> Every gun that is made, every warship launched, every rocket fired signifies, in the final sense, a theft from those who hunger and are not fed, those who are cold and are not clothed.... This is not a way of life at all, in any true sense. Under the cloud of threatening war, it is humanity hanging from a cross of iron.[7]

In his final presidential speech in January 1961, Eisenhower noted that America had been compelled by World War II "to create a permanent armaments industry of vast proportions," and warned that this necessary change had "grave" implications.

In the councils of government, we must guard against the acquisition of unwarranted influence, whether sought or unsought, by the military-industrial complex. The potential for the disastrous rise of misplaced power exists and will persist. We must never let the weight of this combination endanger our liberties or democratic processes.[8]

In the years since Eisenhower's presidency, the size of our military budget in relation to the U.S. gross domestic product (GDP) has decreased by close to 40 percent; yet it continues to grow in dollars. When our country faces a financial crisis, the first thing politicians place off limits for spending cuts is the military budget. When our leaders call for fiscal accountability, the department that consistently fails to contain costs or provide accounts amenable to audit is the Defense Department. The possibility of significantly reduced military spending at the end of the Cold War, symbolized by the fall of the Berlin Wall in 1989, led the country to hope for a "peace dividend." While military spending did fall relative to the overall national budget, it remained huge. The United States was an unrivaled power in the world—we "won" and were reluctant to dismantle our winning team. By the end of the Cold War, military spending was rooted in every state in the union with the tenacity of crabgrass. Members of Congress even fought for weapons programs that the military didn't need or want if the programs brought jobs to their constituents or contracts to their political donors.[9] They fought even harder if the military considered closing a military base in their district. As a consequence we continue to spend more on preparation for war than the *combined* military budgets of the next twenty largest countries—ten times more than Russia, who was our major Cold War adversary.[10]

In 1989, the movie *Field of Dreams* told the fanciful story of an Iowa farmer who heard voices telling him to build a baseball diamond in his cornfield. The voice hinted that the diamond would attract past baseball heroes. "If you build it, they will come," said the voice. The danger in having the most awesome military establishment in the world is that if we build it, we will use it.[11] Would we have considered intervention in

Vietnam or Iraq without such a huge military capability? If not, what solutions might we have sought? At the saving of how many lives? This is not to make a case for no military capacity, but for a more reasonable one and for rethinking its use—for giving serious consideration to General Bradley's assertion that wars are preventable.

Eliminating war became a driving passion for the Russian novelist Leo Tolstoy. A former soldier, Tolstoy became a radical Christian advocate for peace. He urged men to refuse induction into armies, aware that such refusal in his times could lead to execution.[12] To those who questioned the possibility of ending war, Tolstoy would counter that the abolition of legal slavery occurred in his lifetime, even though slavery had endured from the beginning of recorded history. He believed war could be the next evil to be abolished. Tolstoy was a major influence on Mahatma Gandhi, who nonviolently led India to independence from the British Empire, another campaign that seemed totally implausible.

Soldiers fight wars but think a lot about peace. Paul Chappell, a young West Point graduate and Iraq veteran, travels the country lecturing on the possibilities of ending war.[13] He often finds college military (ROTC) classes more attentive and more likely to ask relevant questions than peace classes. ROTC students envision themselves in actual combat. Peace students rarely do. Though some naive youth, imbued with machismo, posture the glories of combat, more thoughtful recruits, and combat vets, yearn for peace.

A Public Health Approach for Veterans

We may not be able to control the many forces in the world that lead to violence, but we can certainly look at forces in our own country that prompt us to put our young men and women in harm's way. Given the persistence of war, the personal, cultural, and economic transformations to end it will require a massive paradigm shift—dramatic changes in thinking, priorities, and practice. The seeds of such transformation are being sown today in ways more sophisticated than Tolstoy's moral crusade, although more religious thinkers are also rejecting war and challenging "just war" theories. In the name of preventing more horrors to our servicemen and women, we might begin by asking three questions:

- How does our present approach to national defense make it easier to go to war?
- How does our tendency to equate American business and economic interests with "national interests" encourage our misuse of military power?
- How can we conduct a foreign policy that is less reliant on military power?

Making It Easier to Go to War

Letting Others Bear the Pain and Losses

A decision to go to war depends on the anticipated costs, both human and economic. Sadly, human costs are counted differently depending on who bears them. The presence of a separate warrior class (as in Plato's Republic) relieves the rest of the community of the most serious burdens of war. In 2001, America launched a War on Terror amid tax cuts even for the wealthy. It was to be a painless war. Troops were deployed to Afghanistan and Iraq and the rest of the nation was encouraged to shop and pray[14] and to be patient in airport security lines while being fed a diet of fear. In response to a reporter's comment about America being at war, a young soldier in Iraq quipped, "No, the Army is at war; America's at the mall." The Congress that supported the U.S. invasion of Iraq included few vets and virtually no members with children in the armed services. In the absence of a draft their children could skip the conflict. Because the draft became a focus of popular resistance during Vietnam, it was put on indefinite hold in favor of an "all-volunteer military." Without new taxes, huge war costs were neatly deferred to the next generation. For the deciders, the cost of this conflict would be low.

Most Americans were not stakeholders in the Iraq War and in the absence of a draft only a predictable minority would be touched personally by the war. During the Civil War many draftees paid others (almost always poorer) to enlist in their place. Today, the all-volunteer military performs that service for the social and economic elites or anyone who doesn't want to be involved. Thousands of dollars in signing bonuses and benefit packages entice the less privileged into the service. As the Iraq War strained the military and casualties mounted, military marketing and incentives to enlist or reenlist mushroomed and lavish contracts for functions previously performed by the military enriched private corporations.[15] This war was truly outside the civic perspective of a people's defense that guided our founding fathers. In a true national defense, all but conscientious objectors would be subject to military service via a draft lottery. When the children of our elected representatives and their major contributors risk the same chance of being in harm's way as poor youth from urban ghettos or Eastern Kentucky hollows, more alternatives to war will be possible.

Switzerland, famed for its neutrality in international conflicts, requires universal military training for all males (females may volunteer). Their commitment to defense with the total Swiss populace may keep the Swiss from entering wars and aggressors from entering Switzerland. Switzerland does have a small standing army. It is most likely to deploy in support of United Nations peacekeeping missions. Of course, the Swiss model could not provide a technically sophisticated force like the American military. A military like ours is more applicable to conflicts outside one's country than to national defense. We maintain military bases across the planet and naval task forces in oceans near and far. The need for such a military posture will be addressed below as we consider our military/foreign policy.

Letting Too Few Decide Issues of War and Peace

Our vast military budget is grounded in national fear—fear that we will be subject to attack by weapons of mass destruction, fear that "American interests" abroad might not be protected, fear that we will lose a privileged way of life, fear that we might sink to "Number 2" as a national power. Fearful of losing our freedoms to enemies abroad, we give them up to our leaders at home as the role of commander in chief looms larger and larger in the American presidency. The precedent of intervening with U.S. troops far outside our hemisphere without congressional approval was set when President William McKinley dispatched troops to China during the Boxer Rebellion.[16] The era of atomic weapons institutionalized the McKinley precedent. When mass destruction could be rapidly delivered by aircraft, missiles, or submarines, momentous decisions of war and peace might be required in hours or even minutes. In the United States those decisions lie squarely in presidential hands, the hands that can pick up the "hotline" or press the panic button. The doctrine of preemptive war outlined in the "National Security Strategy" issued by the White House in September 2002 suggests that even decisions about "conventional war" now gravitate to the Oval Office:

> A preemptive attack widely known and discussed ... would risk being preempted by a preemptive attack on the other side. The idea of a government acting alone in preemptive war is inherently undemocratic, for it does not require or even permit the president to obtain the consent of the governed. As a policy, this new strategy depends on the acquiescence of a public kept fearful and ignorant.[17]

In matters of war, we forgo serious national deliberation by going to war indirectly. We subvert a Constitution framed in vigorous debate, risk, and courage by eschewing those traits and resorting to imprecise resolutions that cede crucial powers to the executive branch—powers the framers envisioned as requiring formal declarations of war. The United States has not been in a declared war since World War II. Executive actions supported by congressional resolutions carried us into Vietnam, Afghanistan, and Iraq. Resolutions may be obtained with considerable misrepresentation, as in the case of the Gulf of Tonkin "attacks" on U.S.

ships in Vietnam or the pre-invasion claims that Iraq possessed weapons of mass destruction. "Authorizations" to conduct armed conflicts can also be interpreted with incredible latitude, as evidenced by President Richard Nixon's incursion into Cambodia during the Vietnam War (after consulting only a handful of sympathetic congressmen).[18]

Letting the Pentagon Dominate Foreign Policy

For the past six decades it is appropriate to refer to America's foreign/ military policy. The Cold War shifted much of the focus of American power and policy from the Department of State to the Department of Defense, or, as James Carroll observed, using the former names of the neighborhoods where the State Department Headquarters and the Pentagon now stand—from Foggy Bottom to Hell's Bottom.[19] Throughout the Cold War the dominance of military thinking in the United States was reflected in the term *national security state*. This referred to our national preoccupation with threat and security and proportional increases in influence for government organizations concerned with intelligence and defense. The end of the Cold War did not shift the balance back. In fact, the United States, unlike other countries, has a military presence throughout the world (conservatively 250,000 troops in over 700 overseas bases),[20] but also engages in clandestine military-to-military activities outside most national supervision. This occurs when we train military officers in the School of the Americas in Fort Benning, Georgia (an appalling number of these trainees have been implicated in atrocities against their own people), or when we conduct military operations in other countries under the auspices of the often-secret Special Operations Command.[21] Military Special Forces sometimes participate in clandestine operations outside of congressional oversight.[22]

As we entered the twenty-first century, the Defense Department was in the hands of men who urged an invasion of Iraq even prior to the terrorist attacks on the World Trade Center,[23] and the State Department was under the direction of a former chairman of the military Joint Chiefs of Staff. The drive and planning (or lack of planning) that led to the fiasco in Iraq came from the Pentagon and a vice president who was a former secretary of defense. The State Department played a cameo role, futilely urging United Nations support for the venture.

America's recent foreign/military policy includes a military capacity sufficient to engage in two significant conflicts anywhere in the world. Unlike other nations, military power undergirds much of our diplomacy. In spite of many examples to the contrary, most Americans presume that we intervene on the behalf of peace and justice. While we can cite examples of "noble" intervention, our own interests were usually clearly on the line as well.

Letting Violence Trump Nonviolent Alternatives

The Prussian war theorist Carl von Clausewitz described war as a political tool on a continuum with diplomacy. When a nation resorts to war, casualties are part of a political calculus and costs are balanced against the value of the objective. Clausewitz had no notion of modern techniques of nonviolence, but may well have embraced them. He suggests that if "the political object itself is not suitable for the aim of military action; then such a one must be chosen as will be an equivalent for it, and stand in its place as regards the conclusion of peace."[24] A strong case can be made in today's world that nonviolent civil resistance is more rational and applicable to national defense than are armies. Conventional thinking may recoil at such ideas, but conventional thinking is almost totally unschooled in nonviolence. In America we study war. We seem addicted to weapons and violent solutions in our national policies, our entertainment, and even our play. We know far too little of the methods of Gandhi and Martin Luther King, Jr., or the strategies for noncooperation in the work of Gene Sharp's *Civilian-Based Defense: A Post-Military Weapons System*.[25] There may be casualties in nonviolent struggles (Gandhi and Martin Luther King, Jr. were both casualties), but they are far fewer than when violence confronts violence. Estonia, Latvia, and Lithuania, small countries that broke away from the former Soviet Union, have adopted Sharp's ideas to thwart their reoccupation by Russia. Unlike these vulnerable little republics, the United States enjoys the protection of oceans to the east and west and a fierce sense of independence. As our powerful military discovered in Vietnam and Iraq, dominating another people depends on their cooperation. A country such as the United States with a united and resistant populace is unconquerable. We are more vulnerable to our own mistakes than we are to outside forces.

Misusing Our Military Power in Our "Economic Interests"

Many U.S. interventions in the world are done in the name of our "national interests," when they actually represent the "interests" of narrow sectors of American business. General Smedley Butler, who served over thirty-three years in the U.S. Marines, starting in 1889, won two Congressional Medals of Honor for bravery. He also wrote a four-chapter pamphlet titled *War is a Racket* that is highly critical of American military operations in which he served in Latin America and occasionally in Asia. Between 1890 and the early third of the twentieth century, U.S. Marines regularly deployed to various countries in support of U.S. business "interests" that were exploitative of local resources and people. Our intervention often left in place dictators amenable to U.S. businesses. These military adventures attracted little national attention, were easily portrayed by their advocates in a favorable light, and were rarely labeled for what they often were—economic colonialism. In 1937, Anastasio Somoza Garcia rose to dictatorial power in Nicaragua. He was corrupt and brutal but wise enough to favor American business interests, prompting President Franklin Roosevelt's cynical comment, "Somoza may be a son of a bitch, but he's our son of a bitch." Such crass willingness to favor repressive regimes in exchange for favorable treatment of "U.S. interests" became a dominant U.S. policy. The United States facilitated the overthrow of Guatemala's fledgling democracy in 1954 at the behest of the United Fruit Company.[26] In 1973, during the Nixon administration, Secretary

of State Henry Kissinger provided resources to help install the mur-
derous dictatorship of Augusto Pinochet in Chile even though Viron
Vaky, his primary advisor on Latin America, argued that Chile posed
no plausible threat to the United States.[27]

In the thrall of anticommunism and in support of narrow business
elites, President Ronald Reagan supported the grisly repression of popular
movements in Central America—championing General Rios Montt in
Guatemala while Montt perpetrated genocide against Guatemala's indig-
enous Mayans. The Reagan administration also violated congressional
restrictions on efforts to overthrow the leftist successor to the Somoza
dynasty in Nicaragua. After a virtual century of Latin American policy
dictated by U.S. business interests, most Latin American countries are
particularly wary of the United States. Brazil is not alone in making a
concerted effort to create an economy with limited dependency on U.S.
patronage.

American projection of power-for-business is hardly confined to
Latin America. We assisted in the overthrow of Iran's new democracy
in 1953, and for twenty-six years we supported the repressive shah, who
granted U.S. corporations access to Iranian oil. We still face the defi-
ance of the Iranian revolutionaries who replaced the shah in 1979. The
2003 invasion of Iraq hardly played out as predicted. Though the Bush
administration emphasized Iraq's military threats to the United States
and the need to liberate the Iraqi people from a terrible dictator, no
weapons of mass destruction were found, resistance to U.S. occupation
grew deadly, sectarian violence grew out of control, and most educated
and professionally trained Iraqis ended up as refugees outside the country.
Iraq remains a troubled country with little to entice its professional class
to return. Prior to the invasion, many in the United States and most in
the rest of the world saw the United States as concerned for Iraq's oil
reserves rather than Iraq's people. A persuasive 2007 piece in the *London
Times Book Review* moves beyond pre-conflict conjecture and takes a
hard look at post-invasion U.S. recommendations to the fledgling Iraqi
government regarding the management of Iraqi oil. The writer concludes,
four years post-invasion, "It's the oil!"[28] In the late 1990s the United

States was spending $11 billion on the purchase of oil from the Persian Gulf States, but spending over several times that amount to maintain a carrier task force protecting the sea-lanes in the Gulf.[29]

When we use our armed forces to truly preserve peace or in peaceful response to major disasters across the world we put the best face on our foreign policy and win broad international praise. A foreign policy dominated by U.S. economic interests will not foster a more peaceful world. The United States often resists stronger multilateral international partnerships and greater support and reliance on the United Nations as encroachments on our national sovereignty, but such partnerships are crucial to the greater rule of international law and improving chances for peace.[30]

Rethinking Our Foreign/Military Policy

Learning About the Wider World

In our current struggles in Iraq and Afghanistan the U.S. military frequently defines its primary mission as winning the hearts and minds of the people, not something readily accomplished at the point of a gun. Between 2002 and 2005 the Pew Global Attitudes Project collected public opinion information about the United States in both the United States and over fifty other countries, primarily in Europe, the Middle East, and Asia. In the report of that data, *America Against the World*, Pew's Andrew Kohut cites the sharp decline in America's image across the world, especially in Muslim countries, after the U.S. invasion of Iraq. Public opinion can be fickle, but Kohut worried that negative views were growing, not just for the American government but for the American people, whose image often remains positive even when other peoples disagree with our government's policies. Moreover, Kohut reported that "this new found anti-Americanism was proving itself to be quite robust and long-lived."[31] As former U.S. secretary of state Madeleine Albright warns in her foreword to Kohut's book:

The gap between how we see ourselves and how others see us has become a chasm. Dangerously so. U.S. military and economic power notwithstanding, we cannot be secure without the respect, support, and yes, the affection, of people in other lands.[32]

America's policies suffer from American ethnocentrism, although this is changing as we become more diverse. Still we know far too little of other countries, other languages, and other cultures. Critics of our limited vision joke, "If you speak three languages, you are trilingual; if you speak two, you are bilingual; if you speak one, you're American." We carry the seeds of misunderstanding in our national character and pay a high price for that misunderstanding. If we are to have a more informed and robust foreign policy, one that makes us safer by winning minds and hearts, we must begin with greater understanding of other nations and cultures, with more Americans mastering the world's languages, living in other cultures, and attending to news beyond our borders. The generally positive experiences of many foreign students who study in the United States is another unheralded aspect of a more constructive U.S. foreign policy.

As became obvious over most of our twentieth-century Latin American policy, even many members of our foreign service interacted too often with local elites and failed to grasp the pulse of largely impoverished nations. When resistance to dictators or oligarchies arose, the United States was too quick to focus on potential communist tendencies of the resistance and too slow to recognize the nationalism, cries for justice, and desire for American-style freedoms that underlay such movements. Our understanding of other nations must run deeper than our interactions with governing elites.

When our politicians misinform us, they undermine the essence of democracy, which depends on an informed electorate. When U.S. politicians explain terrorists' aggression by declaring that the attackers "hate our freedom," it may succeed as domestic propaganda. To the wider world, we are more likely to appear foolish or untrustworthy. If the terrorists behind the 9/11 attack "hated our freedom," it was their perception of our freedom to station U.S. troops on Saudi soil, or to support Israel more strongly than Palestine, or to export cultural mores abhorrent to fundamentalist Islam. These reasons don't justify terrorism, but misrepresenting the reasons fails to help us understand terrorism. It is hard to defeat what you don't understand.

Foreign/Military Policy and Economics

Critically, our foreign policies are strongly dictated by economics, and prevailing economic practice will not lead to peace. When our leaders claim that terrorists are a threat to our "way of life," they are much closer to the mark. We need to understand the relationship between our foreign policy and defending our way of life. With less than 5 percent of the world's population, we consume far more than our share of the world's resources, nearly 25 percent of the world's fossil fuels, for example. Our national policies work to preserve that imbalance. This is understandable, but also untenable. The changes we must make for a more equitable world are enormous. If one were to list the things we might do without if we didn't project our economic and military power, few Americans would fail to choose a strong military posture over such sacrifice. However, families that lose a spouse, a son, or a daughter in the military would almost certainly make even greater sacrifices to have their loved one back. We are careful never to put the choice in such clear material terms. We offer families the illusion that their loved one died in glorious defense of their nation. Many families, desperate for purpose in such a profound loss, accept that rationale. In his essay on the failure of war, Wendell Berry observes that in our recent conflicts, the killed and the crippled "are so widely distributed among our population as hardly to be noticed."[33] Huge sacrifices are made, but few feel the pain.

If pain is not evenly distributed, either within our nations or in a globalized world, information is. We live in a world of instant mass communication. Impoverished families in squatter communities in New Delhi, or Cairo, or Mexico City peer at televisions powered by electricity pirated from local wires. As Richard Barnet of the Institute for Policy Studies writes, "For poor people around the world television and movies offer a window into a life of affluence beyond their wildest dreams, but no door."[34] The international soccer star Pele emerged from such squalid slums, but demoralized, unskilled, and unemployed youth among the mass of urban poor are far more likely candidates for radical ideologies. As Cortright and Lopez emphasize, a key element of any major terrorism strategy includes "persuasive policies that seek to win the hearts and minds of the many young citizens across an array of nations who have yet to decide whether their political participation will take the form of violence or not."[35]

Aid to poor countries often has too little impact after being filtered through corrupt bureaucracies. Local elites often work to maintain the status quo. Peruvian economist Hernando de Soto identifies significant wealth in poor countries that is unavailable as capital even though these resources are in the hands of the poor. The land where the poor live is untitled. Their shanties have no value as collateral, though their monetary potential may exceed the microfinance loans that launch successful small businesses in many areas of profound poverty. Entrepreneurship thrives in third world barrios, but these businesses never become legitimized. Governments in these poorer countries must get in touch with the mass of their people and accept the political challenge of implementing a legal and property system that gives legitimacy to what de Soto calls their "dead capital."[36]

More than anything we need economic models that are not grounded in greed and maximizing profit to the exclusion of other values. Michael Edwards, formerly of the World Bank, describes the attitude we need in facing the future as the "cooperative imperative,"[37] and Riane Eisler makes an urgent case for "creating a caring economics" that moves from hypermasculine models of domination to models of partnership.[38] Eisler emphasizes that

> neither capitalist nor communist systems have been able to solve chronic problems such as environmental degradation, poverty, and

the violence of war and terrorism that diverts and destroys economic resources and blights so many lives.

While observing that "even putting economics and caring in the same sentence is alien to conventional thought," Eisler demonstrates that only a caring economics is realistic. Economic activity is a human enterprise and must support rather than undermine human welfare and the natural world upon which human welfare depends. Wendell Berry states in his gifted simplicity:

> Rats and roaches live by competition under the laws of supply and demand; it is the privilege of human beings to live under the laws of justice and mercy.[39]

The world our children and grandchildren face will include almost unimaginable competition for resources. Climate change is already altering growing seasons and agricultural production in many parts of the world. Disasters driven by storms and flooding are increasing. The world population is growing and fossil fuels and other critical natural resources are shrinking. At its present rate of growth, in less than twenty-five years China alone will require more oil daily than the world's current total daily oil production. Prior to the middle of the twenty-first century, India's population is expected to exceed China's. There will be great pressure in the United States to maintain our own unsustainable use of oil. Then there is the rest of the world. Writer James Howard Kunstler laments that we are "sleepwalking" into what he calls "the long emergency," and asks how "we become a reality based nation."[40] International competition for resources will be pitted against an unparalleled need for international cooperation. If the pace of success on climate change is any predictor, the chances of needed cooperation are bleak. What struggles will grow out of this persisting crisis and how many will involve war? The incisive futurist Jacques Attali (a French historian, economist, and banker) suggests that we will begin to experience the early stages of planetary hyperconflict within the lifetime of today's teens.[41]

Building a Capacity for Peacemaking

In the United States we devote miniscule resources to studying peace, but this is changing. Much of conflict resolution theory first developed in the realm of business and business-labor negotiations, but the study and practice of negotiation, mediation, and arbitration continue to grow dramatically. Academic programs in conflict resolution thrive in many undergraduate and graduate programs and are a staple in advanced programs in peace, diplomacy, and international relations. Principles of conflict resolution guide the healing of marital disputes, the exercise of international diplomacy, and the planning of post-conflict reconciliation.[42] Creative approaches to conflict resolution now exist in preschools and high schools. Montessori education is grounded in principles of peacefulness.[43] Formal peace programs, pioneered in colleges affiliated with the traditional peace churches (Mennonites and Quakers), now flourish in private and state universities. Joan Kroc, heir to the McDonald's hamburger fortune, endowed major graduate peace programs at the Universities of Notre Dame and San Diego. A quick search on the Internet reveals a wealth of institutes and organizations devoted to peace.

A movement to develop a national peace academy in the model of the nation's military academies developed and grew in the 1970s. President Jimmy Carter established a commission chaired by Senator Spark Matsunaga (D-HI) to explore plans and possibilities for such an academy. The most immediate result of these efforts was the federally funded United States Institute of Peace, created by legislation signed by President Reagan in 1984. Though short of a peace academy, the institute encourages peace studies; publishes significant works on peacemaking, conflict resolution, and diplomacy; and organizes conferences and workshops on peacemaking. Legislation to develop a U.S. Department of Peace, which would include a peace academy, is regularly introduced in Congress[44] but has made limited progress. The parallel between a peacemaking academy and the military academies is apt. Like military campaigns, peacemaking requires discipline, courage, teamwork, bonding, careful planning, tactics, and creative strategies. (A small National Peace Academy finally developed, like most other organizations supportive of peace, as a private initiative, and incorporated in 2010; it develops workshops and curricula but still lacks a geographical campus.)[45] Of course, in that growing convergence between modern military thinking and the peace movement, peacemaking requires one to win hearts and minds.

To the critic who asks what kind of job you can get by studying peace there are compelling answers from the personal to the global. Perspectives and skills that enhance peacemaking also enhance marital relationships, parenting, and friendships. Peacemaking builds caring communities. We urgently need skilled peacemakers and negotiators in our polarized legislatures and government service. We may need them even more in global corporations. As the chairman of a large profit-focused corporation once said, global companies "can't be emotionally bound to any particular asset," be those assets workers, communities, or nations.[46] Peacemaking requires very different thinking and, as Eisler makes clear, a sharply different economic calculus, one based on caring and partnerships.

More than finding employment through peace, peacemaking needs to become as basic as the teaching of civics. We require civics and understanding the basic workings of American democracy of all our high school graduates. We test immigrants seeking U.S. citizenship for a similar understanding. A grasp of peacemaking and peacemaking skills are serious requisites for today's changing world and our inescapable roles as global citizens.

For centuries we have tried war to make peace. At best it has given a respite between wars. While peacemaking requires creativity and a deep curiosity that carries understanding beyond the superficial, most of all it requires profound commitment. The committed may be charismatic leaders or the nameless crowd in a grassroots movement. Those who are unaware of the possibilities can begin their orientation by securing and watching the powerful documentary *A Force More Powerful*.[47] The film is a fine primer for nonviolent thinking and understanding the sacrifices that produce peace. Wars give us thousands or millions of dead and shattered veterans and grieving families. Modern wars give us unspeakable civilian casualties from infants to grandparents. Because the stakes are so high, we may live in both the most auspicious and most dangerous period of history to work for peace. The long emergency of climate change, rising population, and shrinking resources will produce seismic economic and lifestyle changes throughout the world. Increased sharing, tempered demands, and true partnerships are essential. Working for peace is the only alternative. Countless lives are in the balance. Peace is public health for veterans and for us all.

Notes

Chapter One

1. There are conflicting death counts for Khe Sanh; this one is based on the detailed account of Ray Stubbe, U.S. Navy chaplain at Khe Sanh: Stubbe, Ray W. 2005. *Battalion of Kings: A Tribute to Our Fallen Brothers Who Died Because of the Battlefield of Khe Sanh, Vietnam*. Milwaukee, WI: Khe Sanh Veterans, Inc.

2. Noyes, Rick, telephone interview.

3. Tom Topmiller found the reel-to-reel tapes among his father's effects. They were transferred to a CD.

4. Topmiller, Robert J. 2007. *Red Clay on My Boots: Encounters with Khe Sanh 1968 to 2005*. Minneapolis, MN: Kirk House, p. 35.

5. Archer, Michael. 2004. *A Patch of Ground: Khe Sanh Remembered*. Central Point, OR: Hellgate Press, p. 117.

6. Examples are many—World War II Congressional Medal of Honor winner Audey Murphy experienced post-combat PTSD. The WWI war novel *All Quiet on the Western Front* describes the hero as alternately daring and paralyzed with fear.

7. Topmiller, *Red Clay*, p. 37.

8. Noyes, Rick.

9. Ibid.; Bob makes a very similar observation in *Red Clay*.

10. Topmiller, *Red Clay*, p. 73.

11. Summers, Jr., Harry G. 1981. *On Strategy: The Vietnam War in Context*. Carlisle Barracks, PA: U.S. Army War College, p. 69.

12. Summers, *On Strategy*, p. 83.

13. Topmiller, *Red Clay*, p. 38.

14. Ibid., p. 23.

15. The names of all but Doc have been changed from the story as Mike Archer told it.

16. From the eulogy for Bob by his daughter, Jamie Topmiller Sadler.

17. Herring, George C. 2002. *America's Longest War: The United States and Vietnam, 1950–1975* (4th ed.). Boston: McGraw-Hill, p. xiii.

18. Herring, George, interview with the author.

19. Topmiller, Robert J. 2002. *The Lotus Unleashed: The Buddhist Peace Movement in South Vietnam 1964–1966.* Lexington: University of Kentucky Press, p. 143.

20. Recording from 2008 Khe Sanh Veterans Reunion, http://mikefishbaugh .homestead.com/doctopmiller.html.

21. From the eulogy for Bob by his daughter, Jamie Topmiller Sadler.

22. Personal communication from Bob's former student Jared Kelley.

23. Topmiller, *Red Clay,* pp. 17–18.

24. American Psychiatric Association. 1994. *Diagnostic and Statistical Manual of Mental Disorders* (4th ed.). Washington, DC: APA, p. 428.

25. Topmiller, *Red Clay,* p. 84.

26. From Bob Topmiller's draft introductory notes for this book.

27. Health Care Eligibility Reform Act of 1996.

28. In January 2003, the Bush administration raised the bar for priority-8 vets, proposed increased copays for many vets, and asked for an annual fee. Between January 2000 and September 2004 the ratio of doctors to patients in the VA declined by 58 percent. See Glantz, Aaron (2009). *The War Comes Home: Washington's Battle Against America's Veterans.* Berkeley: University of California Press, pp. 119–120.

29. Topmiller, *Red Clay,* p. 12.

30. See note 20.

31. American Psychiatric Association, *Diagnostic and Statistical,* p. 428.

32. Glantz, *The War Comes Home,* p. xiii.

Chapter Two

1. Kang, Sung W., and Hugh Rockoff. 2007. "After Johnny Came Marching Home: The Political Economy of Veterans' Benefits in the Nineteenth Century." Cambridge, MA: National Bureau of Economic Research, NBER Working Paper 13223. Kang and Rockoff tracked benefits and budgets through the nineteenth century and make a case that budgets were the strongest factor in the limitation or expansion of veterans' benefits.

2. Topperwein, Bruce. 1999. "History of Veterans' Disability Pension Systems." *Sabretache,* December 1.

3. Today states offer a number of benefits to veterans. The nature of these benefits and the conditions of eligibility vary from state to state.

4. Bonds or securities issued by the Continental Congress were considered so unlikely to be redeemable that most were sold to states to reduce debts or to speculators for a pittance. Once the new federal government was in a position to honor them, very few veterans had them. Kang, "After Johnny," p. 13.

5. Resch, John. 1999. *Suffering Soldiers: Revolutionary War Veterans, Moral Sentiment, and Political Culture in the Early Republic.* Amherst: University of Massachusetts Press, p. 3.

6. Ibid., p. 65.

7. MacGregor, Morris, Jr. "The Formative Years, 1783–1812," in *American Military History*, Army Historical Series, 102, http://www.history.army.mil/books/amh/AMH-05.htm.

8. Kang, "After Johnny," p. 22.

9. Ibid., p. 27.

10. Taylor, Richard H., and Sandra Wright Taylor. 2007. *Homeward Bound: American Veterans Return from War*. Westport, CT: Praeger Security International, p. 27.

11. Singletary, Otis A. 1960. *The Mexican War*. Chicago: University of Chicago Press, p. 5.

12. Taylor and Taylor, *Homeward Bound*, p. 43.

13. Sons of Union Veterans of the Civil War, http://www.suvcw.org/gar.htm.

14. History of the Department of Veterans Affairs—Part 1, http://www1.va.gov/opa/feature/history/history1.asp.

15. Dickson, Paul, and Thomas B. Allen. 2004. *The Bonus Army: An American Epic*. New York: Walker & Company, p. 22.

16. Taylor and Taylor, *Homeward Bound*, p. 63.

17. Ibid., p. 65.

18. Ibid., p. 63.

19. Kinzer, Stephen. 2006. *Overthrow: America's Century of Regime Change from Hawaii to Iraq*. New York: Henry Holt, p. 47.

20. Taylor and Taylor, *Homeward Bound*, p. 69.

21. Dickson and Allen, *The Bonus Army*, p. 4.

22. Ibid.

23. Ibid., p. 31.

24. Mitchell, Wesley, ed. 1922. *Income in the United States: Its Amount and Distribution 1909–1919* (Vol. II). New York: National Bureau of Economic Research, Inc., p. 270.

25. Butler, Smedly. 1995. *War Is a Racket*. Gainesville, FL: Crisis Press.

26. Dickson and Allen, *The Bonus Army*, p. 21.

27. Ibid., p. 24.

28. Parascandola, John L. 1998. "Public Health Service." In *A Historical Guide to the U.S. Government*, ed. George Thomas Kurian. New York: Oxford University Press, pp. 487–493.

29. The lower estimate is from Wikipedia's account of Charles Forbes; the larger is from Dickson and Allen, *The Bonus Army*, p. 27.

30. Ibid., p. 28.

31. Ibid., p. 29.

32. Ibid., p. 48.

33. Dickson and Allen, *The Bonus Army*; see estimates on p. 317, note 33.

34. Ibid., pp. 127–130.

35. Ibid.

36. Ibid., pp. 136–137.

37. Ibid., p. 158.

38. Ibid., p. 180.

39. Ibid., pp. 181–182.

40. Ibid., p. 200.

41. Ibid., pp. 241–246.

42. Ibid., p. 8.

43. Ibid., p. 274.

44. Taylor and Taylor, *Homeward Bound*, p. 31.

45. Wings Across America, http://www.wingsacrossamerica.us/wasp/38/38 .html. The Women's Army Corps (WACS) and their navy counterpoint the WAVES were considered regular military and eligible for benefits.

46. Ross, Davis R. B. 1969. *Preparing for Ulysses: Politics and Veterans During WW II*. New York: Columbia University Press; quote, p. 139; account of the move from Hines to Bradley, pp. 133–140.

47. History of the Department of Veterans Affairs—Part 5, http://www1.va.gov/opa/feature/history/history5.asp.

48. See Baker, Rodney, and Wade E. Pickren. 2007. *Psychology and the Department of Veterans Affairs: A Historical Analysis of Training, Research, Practice, and Advocacy*. Washington, DC: American Psychological Association.

49. Ross, *Preparing for Ulysses*, p. 273.

50. Kolb, Richard K. 1997. "Korea's 'Invisible Veterans' Return to an Ambivalent America." *VFW Magazine*, November.

51. Taylor and Taylor, *Homeward Bound*, p. 118.

52. Ibid., p. 119.

53. Puller, Lewis B., Jr. received the Silver Star after losing both legs and several fingers in Vietnam. Surviving his injuries against most odds, Puller went on to become a lawyer with the VA, but cited his frustration with the negative attitudes toward Vietnam vets of VA administrators from World War II and Korea when he decided to leave the VA. Puller, Lewis B., Jr. 1991. *Fortunate Son: The Autobiography of Lewis B. Puller, Jr.* New York: Grove Weidenfeld, p. 291.

54. From interview with Douglas Vollmer, associate executive director, Paralyzed Veterans of America, October 15, 2009.

55. *Life* magazine, May 22, 1970, pp. 24, 26.

56. Ibid., p. 26.

57. Nicosia, Gerald. 2001. *Home to War: A History of the Vietnam Veteran's Movement*. New York: Three Rivers Press, p. 326.

58. Ibid., p. 331.

59. Ibid., pp. 332–334.

60. Ibid., p. 351.

61. Ibid., p. 353.

62. Ibid., p. 375.

63. See Cortright, David. 2005. *Soldiers in Revolt: GI Resistance During the Vietnam War*. Chicago: Haymarket Books.

64. See information on Project 100,000 in Chapter 7.

65. MacGregor, Jr., Morris J. 1985. *Integration of the Armed Forces 1940–1965*. Washington, DC: Center of Military History, United States Army.

66. Gardner, Michael. 2003. "Harry Truman and Civil Rights: Moral Courage and Political Risks," http://www.virginia.edu/uvanewsmakers/newsmakers/gardner .html.

67. Jerome, Fred. 2004. "Einstein, Race, and the Myth of Cultural Icon." *ISIS* 95, pp. 627–639.

68. Truman, Harry. 1948. Executive Order 9881, July 26.

69. Latty, Yvonne. 2004. *We Were There: Voices of African American Veterans from WWII to the War in Iraq*. New York: Amistad, pp. 67–75.

70. Although the navy was early among the armed forces to develop positive policies for integration, it was very slow to act on them and major progress in many discriminatory navy practices was not seriously addressed until Admiral Elmo Zumwalt, Jr. became chief of naval operations in 1970.

71. VA Health Services Research & Development Service. 2007. *Racial and Ethnic Disparities in the VA Healthcare System: A Systematic Review*. Washington, DC: Department of Veterans' Affairs.

72. Mehta, J. L., Z. Bursac, P. Mehta, et al. 2010. "Racial Disparities in Prescriptions for Cardioprotective Drugs and Cardiac Outcomes in Veterans Affairs Hospitals." *The American Journal of Cardiology* 105 (7), pp. 1019–1023.

73. Jackson, Kenneth. 1985. *Crabgrass Frontier: The Suburbanization of the United States*. New York: Oxford University Press.

74. Schram, Martin. 2008. *Vets Under Siege: How America Dishonors and Deceives Those Who Fight Our Battles*. New York: St. Martins Press, pp. 211–221.

75. CBS/Associated Press. "Mission Accomplished Five Years Later," http://www. cbsnews.com/stories/2008/05/01/iraq/main4060963.shtml.

76. Stiglitz, Joseph E., and Linda J. Blimes. 2008. *The Three Trillion Dollar War: The True Cost of the Iraq Conflict*. New York: W. W. Norton.

77. Adelman, Ken. 2002. "Cakewalk in Iraq." *Washington Post*, February 13, p. A27.

78. McGrory, Mary, quoted in Nicosia, *Home to War*, p. 307.

Chapter Three

1. The basis and need for President Truman's decision is the subject of much historical debate, which is not within the scope of this book.

2. Moreno, J. D., and P. R. Josephson. 2000. *Undue Risk: Secret State Experiments on Humans*. New York: W. H. Freeman, pp. 172–174.

3. Advisory Committee on Human Radiation Experiments (ACHRE). 1996. *The Final Report of the Advisory Committee on Human Radiation Experiments*. New York: Oxford University Press, p. 317.

4. Former German scientist and later British citizen Klaus Fuchs worked in Los

Alamos on the development of America's atomic bomb. In 1950 he confessed to British intelligence that he had been conveying information on the Manhattan Project to a Soviet operative.

5. This competition is detailed in Carroll, James. 2006. *House of War: The Pentagon and the Disastrous Rise of American Power*. Boston: Houghton Mifflin.

6. ACHRE, *Final Report*, p. 284.

7. Welsome, Eileen. 1999. *The Plutonium Files: America's Secret Medical Experiments in the Cold War*. New York: Dial Press, pp. 99–104.

8. Welsome, *Plutonium Files*, p. 179.

9. Miller, R. L. 1986. *Under the Cloud: The Decades of Nuclear Testing*. The Woodlands, TX: Two Sixty Press, p. 48.

10. Ibid., p. 61.

11. Ibid., pp. 60–61.

12. Welsome, *Plutonium Files*, pp. 115–117.

13. Ibid., pp. 118–119.

14. Miller, *Under the Cloud*, p. 79.

15. Ibid., p. 78.

16. Welsome, *Plutonium Files*, p. 171.

17. Miller, *Under the Cloud*, p. 78.

18. Welsome, *Plutonium Files*, pp. 172–175.

19. ACHRE, *Final Report*, p. 299.

20. Miller, *Under the Cloud*, p. 101–102.

21. ACHRE, *Final Report*, p. 291.

22. Welsome, *Plutonium Files*, pp. 265–266.

23. Ibid., pp. 258–260.

24. Ibid., pp. 261–262.

25. Caldwell, Clark, Atomic Veterans' History Project (AVHP), September 19, 2003, http://web.archive.org/web/20060129130400/www.aracnet.com/~pdxavets/caldwec.htm.

26. Cook, Stanley, AVHP, May 27, 2003, http://web.archive.org/web/20060207224806/www.aracnet.com/~pdxavets/cooks.htm.

27. Bair, Tom, AVHP, March 26, 2002, http://web.archive.org/web/20030426093024/www.aracnet.com/~pdxavets/bair.htm.

28. Harmon, James, AVHP, April 14, 2004, http://web.archive.org/web/20060210062744/www.aracnet.com/~pdxavets/harmon.htm.

29. Cited by Keith Whittle, AVHP, August 19, 1997, http://web.archive.org/web/20030413062210/www.aracnet.com/~pdxavets/byers.htm.

30. AVHP, Folder C2D91, TR338, 19 Radiation Injuries, Operation Sandstone, Los Alamos National Laboratory Records Center, http://web.archive.org/web/20071115171126/www.aracnet.com/~pdxavets/radburn2.htm.

31. Cited by Keith Whittle, AVHP, August 19, 1997, http://web.archive.org/web/19991012185438/www.aracnet.com/~pdxavets/coker.htm.

32. Cushing, Edward, AVHP, December 10, 2002, http://web.archive.org/web/20030413064040/www.aracnet.com/~pdxavets/cushing2.htm.

33. Bentley, Dennis, AVHP, December 24, 2000, http://web.archive.org/web/20030413054935/www.aracnet.com/~pdxavets/bentley.htm.

34. Halsey, Ashley. 1983. "Navy Ignored Atom Test Risks." *Detroit Free Press,* May 25, p. 1A.

35. Associated Press. 1985. "New Study Disputes Pentagon's Radiation Claims." *San Jose Mercury News,* December 4, pp. 16 and 16A.

36. Pimentel, Ricardo. 1985. "GAO Report Confirms Nuclear Test Illnesses." *Sacramento Bee,* December 5, p. A13.

37. ACHRE, *Final Report,* p. 301.

38. Broussard, John. 2007. *Newsletter for America's Atomic Veterans,* April.

39. ACHRE, *Final Report,* p. 285.

40. Ibid., p. 286. "There was a consensus that America's war fighting capability would be crippled unless servicemen were cured of the 'mystical' fear of radiation." ACHRE, *Final Report,* pp. 293–300.

41. Welsome, *Plutonium Files,* pp. 252–254; and Miller, *Under the Cloud,* pp. 126–156.

42. ACHRE, *Final Report,* pp. 59–60, 290.

43. Ibid., p. 305.

44. Ibid., p. 285.

45. Miller, *Under the Cloud,* 122; also Judy Foremen. 1981. "Nuclear Safety/Veterans Claim Delayed Reaction to Decades-Old Weapons Tests. National Association of Atomic Veterans Bands Together." *Boston Globe,* March 8.

46. ACHRE, *Final Report,* p. 293.

47. Ibid., p. 298.

48. Bennett, Susan. 1983. "Study GIs Contaminated in A-Blasts." *Philadelphia Daily News,* May 24, p. 3; and Ashley Halsey. 1983. "Files: Navy Ignored Nuclear Risk." *Philadelphia Inquirer,* May 24, p. A1.

49. Welsome, *Plutonium Files* (a point made throughout her work), esp. pp. 481–489.

50. Ray, Roddy. 1984. "'We Were Guinea Pigs': Ailing A-Test Veterans Blame Superiors." *Detroit Free Press,* May 18, p. 1A.

51. Stroup, Robert, AVHP, October 23, 2000, http://web.archive.org/web/20030228132239/www.aracnet.com/~pdxavets/stroup.htm.

52. Lewis, Diane. 1981. "Atom Test Witnesses Organize to Warn of Radiation Effects." *Boston Globe,* August 23.

53. Braucher, Bill. 1983. "Atomic Vets Zeroing in on US Assistance." *Miami Herald,* March 6, p. 1 BR.

54. Cushing, Edward, AVHP, December 10, 2002, http://web.archive.org/web/20030413064040/www.aracnet.com/~pdxavets/cushing2.htm. Records indicate the sinking of the USS *Barton* in 1969 was unrelated to any radiation from Operation Crossroads.

55. Schultz, Tim, AVHP.

56. Kelsch, Al, AVHP, September 21, 1998, http://web.archive.org/web/20060210033915/www.arcanet.com/~pdxavets/kelsch.htm.

57. Jacek, Marty D., AVHP, August 31, 1998, http://web.archive.org/web/20060210033650/www.aracnet.com/~pdxavets/jacek.htm.

58. Christian, Charles, AVHP, May 21, 2005, http://web.archive.org/web/20060203033830/www.aracnet.com/~pdxavets/christia.htm.

59. Halsey, Ashley. 1983. "A Sailor's Health Problems Began Soon After Bomb Tests." *Philadelphia Inquirer*, May 24, p. A1.

60. Halsey, Ashley. 1983. "Atomic Veteran's Latest Blow: Cancer." *Philadelphia Inquirer*, June 11, p. A1.

61. Eberspecher, Tom R., AVHP, December 28, 2001, http://web.archive.org/web/20030413064814/www.aracnet.com/~pdxavets/eberspec.htm.

62. Early, Pete. 1983. "The VA." *Washington Post*, November 11, p. A15.

63. Eberspecher, AVHP.

64. Lewis. "Atom Test Witnesses."

65. McGrory, Mary. 1983. "Atomic Veterans." *Washington Post*, May 29, p. C1.

66. ACHRE, *Final Report*, p. 300.

67. Ibid.

68. Department of Veterans Affairs. 2006. "Facts About the 1973 St. Louis Fire and Lost Records." *Fact Sheet*, October, pp. 1–3.

69. Owens, Patrick. 1985. "Fallout from Ground Zero." *Newsday*, November 15, p. 2.

70. Testimony of Dr. Rosalie Bertell before U.S. Senate Committee on Veterans' Affairs, 10 a.m., April 21, 1998.

71. Loeb, Vernon. 1983. "US: Exposure from A-Tests Was Low." *Philadelphia Inquirer*, May 25, p. A07.

72. McGrory, "Atomic Veterans," p. C1.

73. Early, Pete. 1983. "The VA." *Washington Post*, November 11, p. A15.

74. Ball, Joanne. 1984. "Atomic Test Victims Gather, Express Anger." *Boston Globe*, May 16.

75. McGrory, Mary. 1985. "Help Our First Atomic Victims." *Washington Post*, July 18, p. A2.

76. Humes, Edward. 1987. "Atomic Veterans." *Orange County Register*, November 22, p. M01.

77. *Feres v. United States*, 340 U.S. 135 (1950). In the course of their suit, the veterans discovered a statute dating back to the Civil War that denied vets the ability to hire private counsel to support their claims by limiting the amount that could be paid to a lawyer to $10. Whether this law would still be applied became moot in light of *Feres*.

78. Prochnau, Bill. 1982. "From Gadget to Doomsday Capability." *Washington Post*, April 25, p. A1.

79. In later years, Warner attempted to have his amendment repealed, claiming that he was assured by government officials at the time he introduced the measure that the VA would care for the atomic vets.

80. Thaul, S., W. F. Page, H. Crawford, and H. O'Maonaigh. 2000. *The Five Series Study: Mortality of Military Participants in U.S. Nuclear Weapons Tests*. Washington, DC: National Academy Press, p. 4.

81. Braucher, Bill. 1983. "Atomic Vets Zeroing In on US Assistance." *Miami Herald*, March 6, p. 1 BR.

82. Editorial. 1983. "Atomic Veterans." *Washington Post*, April 9, p. A18.

83. Ruane, Michael. 1983. "Atomic Veterans Mark Official Day." *Philadelphia Inquirer*, July 17, p. B07.

84. Associated Press (AP). 1983. "Scientists Discount Vets' Cancer Claims." *Miami Herald*, July 16, p. 2A.

85. Feinsilber, Mike (AP). 1983. "Finding of Radiation-Cancer Study Challenged." *Detroit Free Press*, August 25, p. 19A.

86. Feinsilber, Mike (AP). 1983. "N-Study of Veterans is Criticized." *Boston Globe*, December 18.

87. Rothstein, L. 1992. "No Matter What, Says NAS, Atomic Vets Are O.K." *The Bulletin of Atomic Scientists*, December, pp. 3–4.

88. ACHRE, *Final Report*, p. 284.

89. Ibid., p. 304.

90. Ibid., p. 305.

91. Ibid., p. 303.

92. Welsome, *Plutonium Files*, pp. 459–461.

93. ACHRE, *Final Report*, p. xix.

94. Thaul et al., *The Five Series Study*, p. 4.

95. Ibid.

96. ACHRE, *Final Report*, p. 303.

Chapter Four

1. Topmiller, Robert. 2007. *Red Clay on My Boots: Encounters with Khe Sanh 1968 to 2005*. Minneapolis, MN: Kirkhouse, p. 184.

2. Ibid., p. 183.

3. Ibid., p. 187.

4. Ibid., p. 182.

5. Ibid., p. 179.

6. There are many deformed and handicapped children in the United States but the most seriously damaged are often in institutions where they are rarely seen. Most American visitors to third world countries are taken aback at the handicapped children they encounter. Nutritional shortages and other factors also increase the risks of deformities in these countries. Though Vietnam may not have produced the controlled studies that meet U.S. expectancies and there are fears that Vietnam uses these children for propaganda purposes, few serious observers doubt that there have been huge increases in severe birth defects in South Vietnam since the war.

7. Grotto, James, and Tim Jones. 2009. "Agent Orange's Lethal Legacy," five-part series. *Chicago Tribune*, December 4–17.

8. Bouny, André. 2007. From "The Effects of Agent Orange and Its

Consequences." Testimony before the Human Rights Council of United Nations (UN) in Geneva, http://www.globalresearch.ca/index.php?context=va&aid=4490.

9. Technically 2,4,5-T is 2,4,5-trichlorophenoxyacetic acid and TCDD is 2,3,7,8-tetrachlorodibenzo-p-dioxin.

10. Stellman, Jeanne M., Steven D. Stellman, Richard Christian, Tracy Weber, and Carrie Tomasallo. 2003. "The Extent and Patterns of Usage of Agent Orange and Other Herbicides in Vietnam." *Nature* 422, 17 April, pp. 681–687.

11. *U.S. Veteran Dispatch Staff Report.* 2009. "The Story of Agent Orange." November, http://www.usvetdsp.com/agentorange.htm.

12. Interview by Peter Berres of his father, General John P. Berres.

13. Bouny, "The Effects of Agent Orange."

14. Grotto and Jones, "Agent Orange's Lethal Legacy," part 4.

15. Ibid.

16. Topmiller, *Red Clay.* Doc discusses racist attitudes and disrespect of Vietnamese amply in his book.

17. *U.S. Veteran Dispatch Staff Report.*

18. Ibid.

19. Schuck, Peter H. 1987. *Agent Orange on Trial: Mass Toxic Disasters in the Courts* (enlarged ed.). Cambridge, MA: Belknap Press, p. 23.

20. Schuck, *Agent Orange on Trial,* p. 24.

21. Ibid., pp. 77–78.

22. Ibid., pp. 37–42.

23. *U.S. Veteran Dispatch Staff Report.*

24. Shuck, *Agent Orange on Trial,* pp. 42–43.

25. *U.S. Veteran Dispatch Staff Report.*

26. Wilcox, Fred A. 1983. *Waiting for an Army to Die: The Tragedy of Agent Orange.* New York: Vintage Books.

27. Grotto and Jones, "Agent Orange's Lethal Legacy," part 5.

28. Schuck, *Agent Orange on Trial,* gives a detailed account of the evolution and complex legal issues in the case.

29. Smoger, Gerson H. "Agent Orange Lawsuit," http://www.agentorangelaw.net/agent_orange_lawsuit.htm.

30. *U.S. Veteran Dispatch Staff Report.*

31. Philpot, Tom. 2010. "Shinseki Stopped Hearing on Agent Orange Decision." June 10, http://www.military.com/features/0.15240.216032.00.html.

32. Stellman, Jeanne Mager, Steven D. Stellman, Tracy Weber, Carrie Tomasallo, Andrew B. Stellman, and Richard Christian, Jr. 2003. "A Geographic Information System for Characterizing Exposure to Agent Orange and Other Herbicides in Vietnam." *Environmental Health Perspectives* 111 (3), pp. 321–328.

33. Stellman, Jeanne M., and Steven D. Stellman. 2010. Book Review of "The History, Use, Disposition, and Environmental Fate of Agent Orange" in *Environmental Health Perspectives* 118 (6), p. A266.

34. Grotto and Jones, "Agent Orange's Lethal Legacy," part 2.

35. *U.S. Veteran Dispatch Staff Report.*

36. *U.S. Veteran Dispatch Staff Report.*

37. Young, A. L., J. P. Giesy, P. Jones, M. Newton, et al. 2004. "Assessment of Potential Exposure to Agent Orange and Its Associated TCDD." *Environmental Science and Pollution Research* 11 (6), pp. 347–348.

38. Young et al., "Assessment."

39. The researchers may have had their article "in press" prior to the publication of Stellman's work, but the publication by Young of a subsequent book reiterating many of his arguments suggest that he was unfazed by contradictory findings. Endnote 33 cites the Stellmans' review of Young's book.

40. Research reviews are posted at http://www.vva.org/veteran/1207/agent_orange_feature.html.

41. Stancliff, Dave. 2010. "Suffer the Children: The Lethal Legacy of Agent Orange." For the *Times-Standard*, posted 02/21, htpp://www.times-standard.com/davestancliff/ci_14444017.

42. Grotto and Jones, "Agent Orange's Lethal Legacy," part 4.

43. Ibid.

44. Ibid., part 5.

45. Topmiller, *Red Clay*, p. 185.

Chapter Five

1. Research Advisory Committee on Gulf War Veteran's Illnesses (RAC). 2008. *Gulf War Illnesses and the Health of Gulf War Veterans.* Washington, DC: U.S. Government Printing Office, pp. 106–114, 130.

2. Congressional Research Service. 2009. *America's War and Military Operations Casualties: Lists and Statistics,* www.crs.gov, RL32492.

3. RAC, *Gulf War Illnesses,* p. 1.

4. Johnson, Alison. 2001. *Gulf War Syndrome: Legacy of a Perfect War.* Brunswick, ME: MCS Information Exchange, pp. 22–23.

5. Ibid., p. 23.

6. Ibid., pp. 23–24.

7. Ibid., pp. 24–25.

8. Ibid., pp. 27–28.

9. Ibid., pp. 28–29.

10. RAC, *Gulf War Illnesses,* p. 75.

11. Johnson, *Gulf War Syndrome,* p. 187.

12. RAC, *Gulf War Illnesses,* p. 133.

13. Johnson, *Gulf War Syndrome,* p. 74.

14. RAC, *Gulf War Illnesses,* pp. 208–210.

15. Johnson, *Gulf War Syndrome,* pp. 101–102.

16. Ibid., pp. 41–42.

17. Schram, Martin. 2008. *Veterans Under Siege: How America Deceives and Dishonors Those Who Fight Our Battles.* New York: St. Martin's Press.

18. Schram, *Veterans Under Siege*, p. 12.

19. Ibid., pp. 33–39.

20. Johnson, *Gulf War Syndrome*, p. 19.

21. RAC, *Gulf War Illnesses*, p. 313; Johnson, *Gulf War Syndrome*, pp. 135–140.

22. Ibid., p. 103.

23. Ibid., p. 130. Although a case was made for the use of a toxic PB because of its many years of use in the treatment of myasthenia gravis, in that situation PB restores the body chemistry to a normal level. When used with healthy troops it moves it away from a normal level (Johnson, *Gulf War Syndrome*, p. 56).

24. Johnson, *Gulf War Syndrome*, p. 38.

25. Ibid., p. 17.

26. Ibid., p. 93.

27. Ibid., p. 92.

28. Defense Science Board. 1994. *Report of the Defense Science Board Task Force on Persian Gulf War Health Effects*. Conclusion 1, www.gulflink.osd.mil/dsbrpt.

29. Documents declassified in 1997 indicated that the CIA knew of chemical weapons at Khamisiyah as early as 1984. UN inspectors discovered unexploded chemical weapons shells still at the Khamisiyah depot in October 1991.

30. NIH Technology Assessment Workshop Panel. 1994. *The Persian Gulf Experience and Health*. Recommendations 5, 6, 7.

31. Committee to Review the Health Consequences of Service During the Persian Gulf War, Medical Follow-up Agency, Institute of Medicine (IOM). 1995. *Health Consequences of Service During the Persian Gulf War: Initial Findings and Recommendations for Immediate Action*. Washington, DC: National Academy Press, p. 15.

32. Committee to Review the Health Consequences of Service During the Persian Gulf War, Medical Follow-up Agency, Institute of Medicine (IOM). 1996. *Health Consequences of Service During the Persian Gulf War: Recommendations for Research and Information Systems*. Washington, DC: National Academy Press, p. 4.

33. IOM, *Recommendations for Research*, p. 8 (note also the First Recommendation to the IOM report, p. 10).

34. IOM, *Recommendations for Research*, p. 7.

35. Ibid., p. 16.

36. Ibid., p. 5.

37. American Psychiatric Association. 1994. *Diagnostic and Statistical Manual of Mental Disorders* (4th ed.) (DSM-IV). Washington, DC: APA. This includes diagnostic criteria for PTSD (pp. 428–429) and somatization disorder (pp. 448–450). These disorders were also included in the DSM-III, which was the guide for psychiatric diagnoses from 1980 until 1994.

38. Fullerton, Carol S., George Brandt, and Robert Ursano. 1996. "Chemical and Biological Weapons: Silent Agents of Terror." In *Emotional Aftermath of the Persian Gulf War: Veterans, Families, Communities, and Nations*, ed. R. J. Ursano and A. E. Norwood. Washington, DC: American Psychiatric Press, pp. 127–129.

39. RAC, *Gulf War Illnesses*, pp. 61–72.

40. Johnson, *Gulf War Syndrome*, p. 5.

41. Committee on Government Reform and Oversight. 1997. *Gulf War Veterans' Illnesses: VA, DOD Continue to Resist Strong Evidence Linking Toxic Causes to Chronic Health Effects*, p. 63, http://www.gulfweb.org/bigdoc/hsr105-388.cfm.

42. RAC, *Gulf War Illnesses*, p. 61.

43. Johnson, *Gulf War Syndrome*, p. 20, cites seventeen metric tons of sarin gas in targets destroyed in the initial U.S. air assaults.

44. Ibid., pp. 12, 17.

45. Ibid., p. 45.

46. Ibid., p. 37.

47. U.S. Chemical and Biological Warfare-Related Dual-Use Exports to Iraq and the Possible Impact on the Health Consequences of the Gulf War, Committee Staff Report (No. 3). October 7, 1994. Opening section on Background.

48. Haley, R. W., J. Horn, P. S. Roland, W. W. Bryan, P. C. Van Ness, F. J. Bonte, M. D. Devous, Sr., D. Matthews, J. L. Fleckenstein, F. H. Wians, Jr., G. I. Wolfe, and T. L. Kurt. 1997. "Evaluation of Neurologic Function in Gulf War Veterans: A Blinded Case-Control Study." *Journal of the American Medical Association (JAMA)*. 277 (3), pp. 223–230.

49. Haley, R. W., and T. L. Kurt. 1997. "Self-Reported Exposure to Neurotoxic Chemical Combinations in the Gulf War: A Cross-Sectional Epidemiologic Study." *JAMA* 277 (3), pp. 231–237.

50. Iowa Persian Gulf Study Group. 1997. "Self-Reported Illness and Health Status Among Gulf War Veterans: A Population Based Study." *JAMA* 277 (3), pp. 238–245.

51. "Gulf War Syndrome Research Contract Cancelled." 2009. *Dallas Morning News*, August 27.

52. Ibid.

53. Veterans Health Care Act of 1992, PL 102-585.

54. Committee on Banking, Housing, and Urban Affairs with Respect to Export Administration. 1994. *U.S. Chemical and Biological Warfare-Related Dual Use Exports to Iraq and their Possible Impact on the Health Consequences of the Gulf War*. Introduction, May 25, www1.va.gov/RAC-GWVI/page.cfm?pg=14.

55. Committee on Banking, *U.S. Chemical*, Introduction.

56. Committee on Banking, *U.S. Chemical*, Conclusions, Chapter 3.

57. Committee on Government Reform and Oversight, *Gulf War Veterans' Illnesses*, p. 1.

58. Ibid., pp. 3–4.

59. Ibid., p. 4.

60. Research Advisory Committee on Gulf War Veterans' Illnesses. 2005. Committee Meeting Minutes, December 12–13, pp. 70–73.

61. RAC, *Gulf War Illnesses*, p. 66.

62. Lee, H., and E. Jones, eds. 2007. *War and Health: Lesson from the Gulf War*. Chichester, UK: John Wiley & Sons.

63. RAC, *Gulf War Illnesses*, p. 83.

64. Ibid., p. 99.

65. Committee on Government Reform and Oversight, *Gulf War Veterans' Illnesses*, p. 29.

66. RAC, *Gulf War Illnesses*, p. 103.

67. Ibid., pp. 106–114; Rempfer, T. L., and R. E. Dingle. "Anthrax Vaccine Immunization Program Project Analysis," http://www.airpower.maxwell.af.mil/airchronicles/cc/rempfer.html.

68. Ibid., p. 128.

69. Ibid., p. 129.

70. Ibid., p. 133.

71. Ibid., pp. 140–142.

72. Ibid., pp. 184–185.

73. Ibid., p. 185.

74. Ibid., p. 199.

75. Stiglitz, J. E., and L. J. Bilmes. 2008. *The Three Trillion Dollar War: The True Cost of the Iraq Conflict.* New York: W. W. Norton, p. 71.

76. RAC, *Gulf War Illnesses*, p. 311.

77. Ibid., p. 128.

Chapter Six

1. Remarque, Erich Maria. 1975. *All Quiet on the Western Front.* New York: Fawcett, p. 140.

2. Topmiller, Robert J. 2007. *Red Clay on My Boots: Encounters with Khe Sanh 1968 to 2005.* Minneapolis, MN: Kirk House, pp. 7–8.

3. Ford, Julian. 2009. *Post Traumatic Stress Disorder: Scientific and Professional Dimensions.* Burlington, MA: Academic Press, p. 25.

4. Nicosia, Gerald. 2001. *Home to War: A History of the Vietnam Veterans Movement.* New York: Three Rivers Press, p. 350.

5. American Psychiatric Association. 1980. *Diagnostic and Statistical Manual of Mental Disorders* (4th ed.). Washington, DC: APA.

6. The term *complex* is used by some clinicians to describe trauma that adversely impacts the development of a child: Ford, *Post Traumatic Stress Disorder*, p. 86. Judith Herman (1992) has also proposed a complex PTSD category for prolonged trauma, particularly when the person is a prisoner of the stress situation: *Journal of Traumatic Stress* 5 (3), pp. 377–391.

7. Shay, Jonathan. 2003. *Odysseus in America: Combat Trauma and the Trials of Homecoming.* New York: Scribner, p. 150.

8. Ford, *Post Traumatic Stress Disorder*, p. 35.

9. Ibid., pp. 107–108.

10. Nash, W. P., C. Silva, and B. Litz. 2009. "The Historic Origins of Military and Veteran Mental Health Stigma and the Stress Injury Model as a Means to Reduce It." *Psychiatric Annals* 39 (8), pp. 789–794.

11. Marx, Brian. 2009. "Posttraumatic Stress Disorder and Operations Enduring

Freedom and Iraqi Freedom: Progress in a Time of Controversy." *Clinical Psychology Review* 29 (8), pp. 671–673.

12. Shay, Jonathan. 1994. *Achilles in Vietnam: Combat Trauma and the Undoing of Character*. New York: Touchstone, p. 167.

13. American Psychiatric Association. 2000. *Diagnostic and Statistical Manual of Mental Disorders* (4th ed.). Washington, DC: APA.

14. Shay, *Achilles in Vietnam*, p. 169.

15. Tick, Edward. 2005. *War and the Soul: Healing Our Nation's Veterans from Post-Traumatic Stress Disorder*. Wheaton, IL: Quest Books, p. 16.

16. Ibid., p. 6.

17. Litz, B. T., N. Stein, E. Delaney, L. Lebowitz, W. P. Nash, C. Silva, and S. Maguen. 2009. "Moral Injury and Moral Repair in War Veterans: A Preliminary Model and Intervention Strategy." *Clinical Psychology Review* 29 (8), pp. 695–706. Also Fontana, A., and R. A. Rosenheck. 2004. "Trauma, Change in Strength of Religious Faith, and Mental Health Service Use Among Veterans Treated for PTSD." *Journal of Nervous and Mental Disease* 192, pp. 579–584; and 2005. "The Role of Loss of Meaning in the Pursuit of Treatment for Posttraumatic Stress Disorder." *Journal of Traumatic Stress* 18, pp. 133–136.

18. Puller, Jr., Lewis B. 1991. *Fortunate Son: The Autobiography of Lewis B. Puller, Jr.* New York: Grove Weidenfeld, p. 137.

19. Ibid., p. 145.

20. Nash et al., "Historic Origins," p. 791.

21. Wolfe, J., T. M. Keane, and B. L. Young. 1996. "From Soldier to Civilian: Acute Adjustment Patterns of Returned Persian Gulf Veterans." In *Emotional Aftermath of the Persian Gulf War: Veterans, Families, Communities, and Nations*, ed. R. J. Ursano and A. E. Norwood. Washington, DC: American Psychiatric Press, pp. 477–499.

22. Shay, *Achilles in Vietnam*, p. 125.

23. Sheehan, Neil. 1969. "Letters from Hamburger Hill." *Harper's Magazine*, November, pp. 40–52.

24. Cortright, D. 2005. *Soldiers in Revolt: GI Resistance During the Vietnam War*. Chicago: Haymarket Books, p. 125.

25. Kurlansky, Mark. 2006. *Nonviolence: 25 Lessons from the History of a Dangerous Idea*. New York: Modern Library, p. 128.

26. Karlin, Wayne. 2009. *Wandering Souls: Journeys with the Dead and Living in Vietnam*. New York: Nation Books.

27. Grossman, D. 2009. On Killing: The Psychological Cost of Learning to Kill in War and Society (revised ed.). New York: Back Bay Books.

28. Mills, Randy K.. 2006. *Troubled Hero: A Medal of Honor, Vietnam, and the War at Home*. Bloomington: University of Indiana Press.

29. Nash et al., "Historic Origins," p. 789.

30. Dingfelder, S. F. 2009. "The Military's War on Stigma." *Monitor on Psychology* 40 (6), pp. 53–55.

31. Army Behavioral Health Website. 2010. FAQs, 1/26/10, http://www.behavioralhealth.army.mil/tools/faqscomb.html.

32. Testimony of Mike Bowman. Hearing before the Committee on Veterans' Affairs of the House of Representatives, December 12, 2007. Serial No. 110-61, 8.

33. Coleman, Penny. 2006. *Flashback: Posttraumatic Stress Disorder, Suicide and the Lessons of War.* Boston: Beacon Press.

34. Testimony of Penny Coleman. Hearing before the Committee on Veterans' Affairs of the House of Representatives, December 12, 2007. Serial No. 110-61, 33.

35. Cleland, Max (with Ben Raines). 2009. *Heart of a Patriot: How I Found the Courage to Survive Vietnam, Walter Reed, and Karl Rove.* New York: Simon and Shuster.

36. Nash et al., "Historic Origins," pp. 789–794. Shay, in *Odysseus in America,* also states, "An injury is not a disorder," p. 149.

37. O'Beirne, Kate. 2004. "One Vet's Valor: B. G. Burkett is a Myth-Buster, a Truth-Teller, and a Hero." National Review, October 11, http://www.nationalreview.com/articles/212354/one-vets-valor/kate-obeirne.

38. Kulka, R. A., W. E. Schlenger, J. A. Fairbank, R. L. Hough, B. K. Jordan, C. R. Marmar, D. S. Weiss, and D. A. Grady. 1990. *Trauma and the Vietnam War Generation: Report of Findings from the National Vietnam Veterans Readjustment Study.* New York: Brunner/Mazel.

39. Chatterjee, S., A. Spiro, L. King, D. King, and E. Davison. 2009. "Research on Aging Military Veterans Lifespan Implications of Military Service." *PTSD Research Quarterly* 20 (3), p. 2.

40. Stiglitz, J. E., and L. J. Bilmes. 2008. *The Three Trillion Dollar War: The True Cost of the Iraq Conflict.* New York: W. W. Norton, p. 83.

41. Stiglitz and Bilmes, *Three Trillion Dollar War,* p. 41.

42. Peace Corps website and conversation with Kat Edwards of the Peace Corps National Office.

43. Slone, L. B., and M. J. Friedman. 2008. *After the War Zone: A Practical Guide for Returning Troops and Their Families.* Philadelphia, PA: Da Capo Press, pp. 50–51.

44. Slone and Friedman, *After the War Zone,* pp. 56–64.

45. Matsakis, Aphrodite. 2007. *Back from the Front: Combat, Love and the Family.* Baltimore, MD: Sidran Institute.

46. Nash et al., "Historic Origins," p. 792. These authors state, "Military resilience training based on the current 'BATTLEMIND' program teaches that the 'inner strength' that enables soldiers to courageously face adversity in combat will also empower them to overcome the readjustment difficulties and stress symptoms they experience after deployment. Implied in this otherwise encouraging and normalizing training is the pernicious message that a failure either to withstand adversity in a war zone or to recover quickly and completely from postdeployment PTSD[R] symptoms may be due to a deficit in 'inner strength' or willpower."

47. Glantz, Aaron. 2009. *The War Comes Home: Washington's Battle Against America's Veterans.* Berkley: University of California Press, p. xiii.

48. Remarque, *All Quiet,* pp. 160–165.

49. Slone and Friedman, *After the War Zone.*

50. "Reintegration: The Role of Spouse Telephone BATTLEMIND." Study under way at VA Medical Center, Memphis, TN. From VA brochure.

51. Kantor, Martin. 2008. *Uncle Sam's Shame: Inside Our Broken Veteran's Administration*. Westport, CT: Praeger Security International, p. 3.

52. Ibid., p. 182, emphasis in original.

53. See Kantor, *Uncle Sam's Shame*, Chapter 2, "Psychological Reasons for Staff Mistreating Veterans."

54. Norwood, A. E., and R. J. Ursano. 1996. "The Gulf War." In *Emotional Aftermath of the Persian Gulf War: Veterans, Families, Communities, and Nations*, ed. R. J. Ursano and A. E. Norwood. Washington, DC: American Psychiatric Press, p. 17.

55. Rosenheck, R. A., and A. Fontana. 1996. "Treatment of Veterans Severely Impaired by Posttraumatic Stress Disorder." In *Emotional Aftermath of the Persian Gulf War: Veterans, Families, Communities, and Nations*, ed. R. J. Ursano and A. E. Norwood. Washington, DC: American Psychiatric Press, p. 528.

56. Roberts, N. P., N. J. Kitchiner, J. A. Kenardy, and J. Bisson. 2009. "Systematic Review and Meta-Analysis of Multiple-Session Early Interventions Following Traumatic Events." *American Journal of Psychiatry* 166 (3), pp. 293–301.

57. Hamblen, J. L., P. P. Schnurr, A. Rosenberg, and A. Eftekhari. 2009. "A Guide to the Literature on Psychotherapy for PTSD." *Psychiatric Annals* 39 (6), pp. 348–353.

58. Ozer, E. J., S. R. Best, T. L. Lipsey, and D. S. Weiss. 2003. "Predictors of Posttraumatic Stress Disorder and Symptoms in Adults: A Meta-analysis." *Psychological Bulletin* 129 (1), pp. 52–73.

59. Halpern, Sue. 2008. "Virtual Iraq: Using Simulation to Treat a New Generation of Traumatized Veterans." *The New Yorker*, May 19, pp. 32–37.

60. Grossman, *On Killing*, Section VIII.

61. Department of Veterans Affairs. 2010. Fact Sheet, "New Regulations on PTSD Claims." July 12.

62. Stiglitz and Bilmes, *Three Trillion Dollar War*, p. 83.

Chapter Seven

1. Coleman, Penny. 2006. *Flashback: Posttraumatic Stress Disorder, Suicide and the Lessons of War*. Boston: Beacon Press, p. 2.

2. Anderson, R. 1981. "Vietnam Legacy: Veteran's Suicide Toll May Top War Casualties." *Seattle Times*, March 18.

3. Coleman, *Flashback*, pp. 7, 176.

4. Pollack, D.A., P. Rhodes, M. S. C. A. Boyle, P. Decoufle, and D. L. McGee. 1990. "Estimating the Number of Suicides Among Vietnam Veterans." *American Journal of Psychiatry* 147 (6), pp. 772–777.

5. Bullman, T. A., and H. K. Kang. 1996. "The Risk of Suicide Among Wounded Vietnam Veterans." *American Journal of Public Health* 86 (5), pp. 662–668.

6. Shneidman, E. S. 2001. *Comprehending Suicide: Landmarks in 20th Century Suicidology*. Washington, DC: American Psychological Association, pp. 55–56.

7. Bullman, T. A., and H. K. Kang. 1994. "Posttraumatic Stress Disorder and the Risk of Traumatic Deaths Among Vietnam Veterans." *Journal of Nervous and Mental Disease* 182 (11), pp. 604–611.

8. Bullman and Kang, "Risk of Suicide."

9. Zivin, K., H. M. Kim, J. F. McCarthy, K. L. Austin, K. S, Hoggatt, H. Walters, and M. Valenstein. 2007. "Suicide Mortality Among Individuals Receiving Treatment for Depression in the Veterans Affairs Health System: Associations with Patient and Treatment Setting Characteristics." *American Journal of Public Health* 97 (12), pp. 2193–2198. (In this study younger vets who were depressed and suffered from PTSD[R] were at higher risk than older vets with the same diagnoses.) Also see Sher, Leo. 2009. "Suicide in War Veterans: The Role of Comorbidity of PTSD and Depression." *Expert Review of Neurotherapeutics* 9 (7) pp. 921–923.

10. Mills, R. K. 2006. *A Troubled Hero: A Medal of Honor, Vietnam, and the War at Home.* Bloomington: University of Indiana Press, pp. 116–117.

11. Puller, Jr., Lewis B. 1991. *Fortunate Son: The Autobiography of Lewis B. Puller, Jr.* New York: Grove Weidenfeld.

12. Witteman, P., and S. Levy. 1994. "Lewis B. Puller, Jr.: The Wound That Would Not Heal." *Time,* May 23.

13. Coleman, *Flashback,* pp. 4–5.

14. Ibid., pp. 66–77.

15. Stern, Sol. 1968. "When the Black GI Comes Back for Vietnam." *New York Times Magazine,* March 24.

16. MacPherson, Myra. 2002. "McNamara's 'Moron Corps.'" May 29, http://dir.salon.com/story/news/feature/2002/05/29/mcnamara.

17. Anestis, M. D., C. J. Bryan, M. M. Cornette, and T. E. Joiner. 2009. "Understanding Suicidal Behavior in the Military: An Evaluation of Joiner's Interpersonal-Psychological Theory of Suicidal Behavior in Two Case Studies of Active Duty Post-Deployers." *Journal of Mental Health Counseling* 31 (1), pp. 60–75.

18. Varah, Chad. 1985. *The Samaritans: Befriending the Suicidal.* London: Constable, p. 36.

19. Cvetanovich, B., and L. Reynolds. 2008. "Recent Development: Joshua Omvig Veterans Suicide Prevention Act of 2007." *Harvard Journal on Legislation* 45 (2), pp. 619–640.

20. Mental Health Advisory Team (MHAT-III). 2006. "Operation Iraqi Freedom 04-06, Report," May 29.

21. Cvetanovich and Reynolds, "Recent Development," pp. 623–628.

22. Abdullah, H. 2010. "Military Losing Ground in Fight Against Suicides." *Lexington Herald Leader,* January 25.

23. Shekelle, P., S. Bagley, and B. Munjas. 2009. *Strategies for Suicide Prevention in Veterans.* Washington, DC: Department of Veterans Affairs Health Services Research & Development Service; Knox, K. L., D. A. Litts, G. W. Talcott, J. C. Feig, and E. D. Caine. 2003. "Risk of Suicide and Related Adverse Outcomes After Exposure to a Suicide Prevention Program in the US Air Force: Cohort Study." *British Medical Journal* 327, p. 1376.

24. *Army Health Promotion, Risk Reduction and Suicide Prevention Report 2010,* http://usarmy.vo.llnwd.net/e1/HPRRSP/HP-RR-SPReport2010_v00.pdf, p. 11.

25. "Army Health Promotion Risk Reduction Suicide Prevention Report, Office of the Chief of Public Affairs Press Release." July 28, 2010, http://www.army .mil/-news/2010/07/28/42934-army-health-promotion-risk-reduction-and-suicide -prevention-report/.

26. Simon, R. I. 2006. "Suicide Risk: Assessing the Unpredictable." In *Textbook of Suicide Assessment and Management,* ed. R. I. Simon and R. E. Hales. Washington, DC: American Psychiatric Publishing, p. 1.

27. Robins, Eli. 1981. *The Final Months: A Study of the Lives of 134 Persons Who Committed Suicide.* New York: Oxford University.

28. Fawcett, J. 2001. "Treating Impulsivity and Anxiety in the Suicidal Patient." In *The Clinical Science of Suicide Prevention,* ed. H. Henden and J. J. Mann. New York: New York Academy of Sciences, pp. 94–105.

29. Isaac, M., B. Elias, L. Y. Katz, S. Belik, F. P. Deane, M. W. Enns, and J. Sareen. 2009. "Gatekeeper Training as a Preventive Intervention for Suicide: A Systematic Review." *Canadian Journal of Psychiatry* 54 (4), pp. 260–268.

30. Maltsberger, J. 2006. "Outpatient Treatment." In *Textbook of Suicide Assessment and Management,* ed. R. I. Simon and R. E. Hales. Washington, DC: American Psychiatric Publishing, pp. 367–379.

31. Shneidman, *Comprehending Suicide,* p. 203.

32. Caregivers and Veterans Omnibus Health Services Act of 2010, PL 111-163, http://veterans.house.gov/legislation/111th/S1963summaryforfloor.pdf.

33. Archer, Mike, personal communication.

34. Shakespeare, *Hamlet,* act III, scene 1, lines 70–75.

Chapter Eight

1. Priest, Dana, and Anne Hull. 2007. "Soldiers Face Neglect, Frustration at Army's Top Medical Facility." *Washington Post,* February 18.

2. Hull, Anne, and Dana Priest. 2007. "'It Is Just Not Walter Reed': Soldiers Share Troubling Stories of Military Health Care Across U.S." *Washington Post,* March 5.

3. Glantz, A. 2009. *The War Comes Home: Washington's Battle Against America's Veterans.* Berkeley: University of California Press, p. 120.

4. Bilmes, Linda. 2007. "Soldiers Returning from Iraq and Afghanistan: The Long-Term Costs of Providing Veterans Medical Care and Disability Benefits." Cambridge, MA: Harvard University.

5. Glantz, *The War Comes Home,* p. 52.

6. King, T. 2008. "Bush Lawyers Fight Tooth and Nail to Deny VA Healthcare Benefits." *Salem News,* February 7.

7. "VA Clinic Patients Who Received a Colonoscopy Warned of Infection Risk."

2009. Accessed at http://www.aboutlawsuits.com/va-clinic-colonoscopy-infection -risk-2786/.

8. Goldstein, Josh. 2010. "NRC Levies $227,500 Fine Against Philly VA Medical Center." *Philadelphia Inquirer*, March 17.

9. Committee on Quality of Health Care in America. 2000. *To Err Is Human: Building a Safer Health System*. Washington, DC: Institute of Medicine.

10. Longman, Phillip. 2007. *Best Care Anywhere: Why VA Healthcare is Better than Yours*. Sausalito, CA: PoliPointPress, p. 56.

11. Ibid., p. 1.

12. National Academy of Sciences NRC. 1977. *Study of Health Care for American Veterans*. Washington, DC.

13. Yano, E. M., B. F. Simon, A. B. Lanto, and L. V. Rubenstein. 2007. "The Evolution of Changes in Primary Care Delivery Underlying the Veterans Health Administration's Quality Transformation." *American Journal of Public Health* 97 (12), pp. 2151–2159.

14. Fihn, S. D. 2000. "Does VA Health Care Measure Up?" *New England Journal of Medicine* 343, pp. 1962–1965.

15. Longman, *Best Care*, p. 10.

16. Yano et al., "Evolution of Changes."

17. Longman, *Best Care*, p. 47.

18. Ibid., p. 61.

19. Jha, A. K., J. B. Perlin, K. W. Kizer, and R. A. Dudley. 2003. "Effect of the Transformation of the Veterans Affairs Health Care System on the Quality of Care." *New England Journal of Medicine* 348, pp. 2218–2227.

20. Kerr, E., R. Gerzoff, S. Krein, J. Selby, J. Piette, J. Curb, W. Herman, D. Marrero, K. Narayan, M. Safford, T. Thompson, and C. Mangione. 2004. "A Comparison of Diabetes Care Quality in the Veterans Health Care System and Commercial Managed Care." *Annals of Internal Medicine* 141 (12), pp. 272–281.

21. Asch, S. M., E. A. McGlynn, M. M. Hogan, R. A. Hayward, P. Shekelle, L. Rubenstein, J. Keesey, J. Adams, and E. A. Kerr. 2004. Comparison of Quality of Care for Patients in the Veterans Health Administration and Patients in a National Sample." *Annals of Internal Medicine* 141 (12), pp. 938–945.

22. Interview with Dr. Nadia Rasheed, Lexington, KY, VA Medical Center.

23. Trumbo, Dalton. 1939. *Johnny Got His Gun*. Secaucus, NJ: Lyle Stuart.

24. Mason, Michael Paul. 2008. *Head Cases*. New York: Farrar, Straus and Giroux, p. 3.

25. Glantz, *The War Comes Home*, beginning p. 62; Broncachio, David. 2009. "America's New Wounded Warriors—Why Are Their Family Caregivers Overworked and Under-Supported?" *NOW*, PBS.

26. Longman, *Best Care*, p. 49.

27. Weeks, William B., Alan N. West, Amy E. Wallace, R. E. Lee, D. C. Goodman, J. B. Dmick, and J. P. Bagian. 2007. "Reducing Avoidable Deaths Among Veterans: Directing Private-Sector Surgical Care to High-Performance Hospitals." *American Journal of Public Health* 97 (12), pp. 2186–2192.

28. *Serve, Support, Simplify: Report of the President's Commission on Care for America's Returning Wounded Warriors.* 2007. Washington, DC: U.S. Government Printing Office (Dole-Shalala Commission).

29. Rehbein, David K. 2009. *A System Worth Saving: The Condition of VA Health Care in America.* Indianapolis, IN: The American Legion.

30. AMVETS, DAV, PVA, and VFW. 2009. *The Independent Budget for the Department of Veterans Affairs Budget—Fiscal Year 2011.* Washington, DC.

31. *Serve, Support,* p. 5.

32. Ibid.

33. Ibid., p. 9.

34. AMVETS et al., *Independent Budget,* p. 74.

35. Broncachio, "America's New Wounded."

36. AMVETS et al., *Independent Budget,* pp. 9–10.

37. Casebolt, Gordon, and Stephen F. Gilson. 2000. *Managing Personal Assistants: A Consumers Guide.* Washington, DC: Paralyzed Veterans of America.

38. Caregivers and Veterans Omnibus Health Services Act (S. 1963), http://frwebgate.access.gpo.gov/cgi-bin/getdoc.cgi?dbname=111_cong_bills& docid=f:s1963enr.txt.pdf.

39. AMVETS et al., *Independent Budget,* pp. 75–76.

40. Benedict, Helen. 2009. "The Plight of Women Soldiers." *The Nation,* May 5.

41. Presidents Commission on Veterans' Pensions. 1956, https://www. 1888932 -2946.ws/vetscommission/e-documentmanager/gallery/Documents/Reference_ Materials/ApprovedResearchQuestions_10-14-05.pdf.

42. *Serve, Support,* p. 6.

43. Bilmes, "Soldiers Returning."

44. Iglehart, John K. 1996. "Reform of the Veterans Affairs Health Care System." *New England Journal of Medicine* 335 (18), pp. 1407–1412.

45. Fihn, "Does VA."

46. Ibrahim, Said A. 2007. "The Veterans Health Administration: A Domestic Model for a National Health Care System?" *American Journal of Public Health* 97 (12), pp. 2124–2126.

Chapter Nine

1. Topmiller, Robert J. 2002. *The Lotus Unleashed: The Buddhist Peace Movement in South Vietnam 1964–1966.* Lexington: University of Kentucky Press, p. 31.

2. Bradley, Omar. 1948. *That We Might Learn to Live as Bravely as They Died—Memorial Day Address.* Longmeadow, MA: Albert T. Wood Post 175, The American Legion.

3. Cortright, David, and George Lopez. 2007. "Strategic Counter-Terrorism." In *Uniting Against Terror: Cooperative Nonmilitary Responses to the Global Terrorist Threat,* ed. David Cortright and George Lopez. Cambridge: Massachusetts Institute of Technology.

4. Durant, Will, and Ariel Durant. 1968. *The Lessons of History*. New York: Simon and Schuster, p. 81.

5. War Resisters League. http://www.warresisters.org/militaryspending.

6. Carroll, James. 2006. *House of War: The Pentagon and the Disastrous Rise of American Power*. New York: Houghton-Mifflin.

7. Eisenhower, Dwight. 1953. *Cross of Iron*, http://www.informationclearinghouse .info/article9743.htm.

8. Eisenhower, Dwight. 1961. *Farewell Address*, http://www.ourdocuments.gov/ doc.php?flash=true&doc=90.

9. In 1998 Newt Gingrich, then speaker of the House, added $2.5 billion to the defense budget for aircraft and Senate majority leader Trent Lott added a helicopter aircraft carrier. The armed services needed neither, but much of the construction would occur in the politicians' home states. See endnote 20: Johnson, *Nemesis*, p. 91.

10. Several sources give different numbers for the combined national defense budgets the United States exceeds. I have selected a conservative number based on the Stockholm International Peace Research Institute (SIPRI)'s 2009 Year Book. The Center for Arms Control estimates that U.S. defense spending exceeds that of the next forty-five largest nations. http://www.armscontrolcenter.org/policy/securityspending/ articles/fy09_dod_request_global.

11. Preble, Christopher. 2009. *The Power Problem: How American Military Dominance Makes Us Less Safe, Less Prosperous, and Less Free*. Ithaca, NY: Cornell University Press.

12. Tolstoy, Leo. 1967. *Tolstoy's Writings on Civil Disobedience and Non-Violence*. New York: Bergman.

13. Paul Chappell has written two brief and engaging books, *Will War Ever End?* (Ashoka Books, 2009) and *The End of War: How Waging Peace Can Save Humanity, Our Planet, and Our Future* (Easton Studio, 2010).

14. George W. Bush's address to Congress. September 20, 2001, http://www .time.com/time/nation/article/0,8599,175757,00.html.

15. Commission on Wartime Contracting in Iraq and Afghanistan. 2009. *At What Costs? Contingency Contracting in Iraq and Afghanistan*. Arlington, VA: CWC.

16. Herring, George. 2008. *From Colony to Super Power: U.S. Foreign Relations since 1776*. New York: Oxford University Press, p. 332.

17. Berry, Wendell. 2003. *Citizenship Papers*. Washington, DC: Shoemaker and Hoard, p. 2.

18. Herring, George. 2002. *America's Longest War* (4th ed.). New York: McGraw-Hill, p. 293.

19. Carroll, *House of War*, p. 130.

20. Estimates lowered from those in Johnson, Chalmers. 2006. *Nemesis: The Last Days of the American Republic*. New York: Metropolitan Books.

21. Johnson, Chalmers. 2000. *Blowback: The Costs and Consequences of American Empire*. New York: Owl Books, pp. 71–74.

22. Most famously with CIA and other colluders in the Iran-Contra operations during the Reagan administration.

23. Letter to President Clinton on Iraq, www.newamericancentury.org/iraqclintonletter.htm.

24. Clausewitz, Carl von. 1968. *On War* (trans. J. J. Graham). London: Penguin, p. 18.

25. Sharp, Gene. 1990. *Civilian-Based Defense: A Post-Military Weapons System.* Princeton, NJ. Princeton University.

26. Schlesinger, Stephen, and Stephen Kinzer. 2005. *Bitter Fruit: The Story of the American Coup in Guatemala* (rev. ed.). Cambridge, MA: Harvard University, David Rockefeller Center for Latin American Studies.

27. Kinzer, Stephen. 2006. *Overthrow: America's Century of Regime Change from Hawaii to Iraq.* New York: Times Books, p. 180.

28. Holt, Jim. 2007. "It's the Oil." *London Review of Books* 29 (20), October 18, pp. 3–4.

29. Johnson, *Blowback,* p. 81.

30. Coicaud, Jean-Marc. 2007. *Beyond the National Interest: The Future of UN Peacekeeping and Multilateralism in an Era of US Primacy.* Washington, DC: United States Institute of Peace.

31. Kohut, Andrew. 2006. *America Against the World: How We Are Different and Why We are Disliked.* New York: Times Books. p. xviii–xix.

32. In Kohut, *America Against the World,* p. ix.

33. Berry, Wendell. 2003. *Citizenship Papers: Essays,* Berkeley, CA: Shoemaker & Hoard, p. 26.

34. Barnet, Richard J. Undated. *The Global War Against the Poor.* Washington, DC: Servant Leadership Press, p. 31.

35. Cortright and Lopez, "Strategic Counter-Terrorism," p. 11.

36. de Soto, Hernando. 2000. *The Mystery of Capital: Why Capitalism Triumphs in the West and Fails Everywhere Else.* New York: Basic Books.

37. Edwards, Michael. 1999. *Future Positive: International Cooperation in the 21st Century.* London: Earthscan.

38. Eisler, Riane. 2007. *The Real Wealth of Nations: Creating a Caring Economics.* San Francisco: Berrett-Koehler.

39. Berry, Wendell. 1990. "Economy and Pleasure." In *What are People For?* New York: North Point Press, p. 135.

40. Kunstler, James H. 2005. *The Long Emergency: Surviving the End of Oil, Climate Change, and Other Converging Catastrophes of the Twenty-first Century.* New York: Grove Press.

41. Attali, Jacques. 2009. *A Brief History of the Future: A Brave and Controversial Look at the Twenty-first Century* (English translation with update). New York: Arcade Publishing.

42. Kriesberg, Louis. 2002. "The Conflict Resolution Field: Origins, Growth, and Differentiation." In *Peacemaking in International Conflict: Methods and Techniques,* ed. William Zartman. Washington, DC: United States Institute of Peace.

43. Montessori, Maria. 1965. *The Absorbent Mind.* New York: Holt Rinehart and Winston.

44. Originally introduced by Dennis Kucinich (D-OH) in 2001, the current bill (HB 808) has over sixty cosponsors.

45. A chronology of the movement for a national peace academy can be found online at http://www.nationalpeaceacademy.us/files/resources/chronologyofnpa.pdf.

46. Barnet, *The Global War*, p. 11.

47. Available through the Public Broadcasting System, from many film rental resources, or through the website http://www.yorkzim.com.

Index

About the Authors

Robert J. Topmiller joined the navy at seventeen and served as a hospitalman with the marines at Khe Sanh, Vietnam. Later a businessman and professor of history at Eastern Kentucky University, "Doc" Topmiller wrote two books on Vietnam: *The Lotus Unleashed: The Buddhist Peace Movement in South Vietnam 1964–1966* (2002) and *Red Clay on My Boots: Encounters with Khe Sanh 1968 to 2005* (2007). He was working on *Binding Their Wounds* when he died. He left a wife, four children, and three grandchildren.

T. Kerby Neill is a navy veteran and clinical psychologist. Dr. Neill worked in the VA and later spent most of his career as a child psychologist. He is the editor of *Helping Others Help Children: Clinical Supervision of Child Psychotherapy* (2006) and author of a number of articles and chapters in psychological journals and books. Retired from psychology in 2004, he devotes much of his time to peace education. He is married, a father, and a grandfather.